Sunset Travel Guide to
MEXICO

By the Editors of Sunset Books and Sunset Magazine

LANE PUBLISHING CO. • MENLO PARK, CALIFORNIA

Hours, admission fees, prices, telephone
numbers, and highway designations in
this book are accurate as of May 1977.
    Maps have been provided in each chapter for the
special purpose of highlighting significant regions,
routes, or attractions in the area. Check automobile
clubs, insurance agencies, government tourist
offices, or travel agents as possible sources for
detailed road maps of Mexico.

Mariachis, *Mexico's wandering minstrels,*
serenade everywhere south of the border.

Our thanks . . .

to the many people and organizations who assisted
in the preparation of this travel guide. Special
appreciation goes to Editorial Minutiae Mexicana,
Dan Sanborn, Ellen Kadelburg, Patti Senterfitt, and
Jose Sales, who gave invaluable help in compiling
and verifying information.

Edited by Barbara J. Braasch

Design: Steve Reinisch

Cartography: Roberta Edwards

Cover: Beach at Akumal on the Caribbean
        Photographed by Barbara J. Braasch

Editor, Sunset Books: David E. Clark

First Printing May 1977

Contents

Bienvenidos! 6
Baja California 10
Mexico's West Coast: Resort Land 22
Guadalajara & the Colonial Circle 46
Mexico City...Road's End 66
North & East to the Gulf 98
Southern Mexico 110
Yucatan--Ruins of a Civilization 126
Know Before You Go 136
Index 143

Special Features

Tips for the Baja driver 20

Into Copper Canyon by rail 28

Tequila--the spirit of Mexico 37

Condominium vacations...the total experience 44

Craft towns around Guadalajara 53

Easter in San Miguel 60

Days of the Dead: cause for celebration? 77

Always on Sunday 83

The Olmec, Mexico's mother culture 85

Cave exploring at Cacahuamilpa 93

Oaxaca's festive December fiestas 117

The colorful Chiapas 124

The green gold of Yucatan 133

Signs for good driving 137

Bienvenidos!

You'll feel welcome in Mexico from your first *bienvenidos* (greetings) to your last *hasta luego* (until you return). And return you will, to experience more of this colorful country.

Pick your pleasure

Fun in the sun? Mexico offers countless resorts along its 6,000 miles of coastline. Peek into the past? View ancient ruins hacked from the clinging jungle. Nose for nostalgia? Revel in cities impressed with a Spanish stamp; follow the route of this country's struggle for independence. Seeking shopping? This is a land of handcrafts; try village markets for browsing and buying.

From spectacular game fishing, skin diving, and just plain loafing in the sun to boating on high plateau lakes to tackling the jungle on horseback —the range of activities is wide. You won't have to travel far to find the contrasts of this land.

In short treks from Mexico City, the country's cosmopolitan capital, you can visit tranquilizing mountain spas, sparkling seacoast resorts, quaint and historically interesting towns, picturesque artists' colonies, and awe-inspiring archaeological wonders.

Meet the people

To understand Mexico it's necessary to understand its people. Fairly early in your visit, you're apt to realize that they are one of the country's greatest attractions.

Friendly, happy, gracious, and expressive, these people are both quick and gentle in personal interchanges. Spontaneity and sensitivity are reflected in their faces, especially those faces representative of the various Indian cultures. In music and arts the Mexicans are more liberated and exuberant than the North Americans. Bold colors and powerful forms are characteristic of both ancient and modern artists and architects.

Folk art is special

For the U.S. shopper, accustomed to his machine-made world, part of the appeal of Mexican folk art lies in its handcrafted quality. Perhaps more important, it represents a way of life that is still in touch with nature. Many of these objects could not emerge from our culture—Tarascan altar offerings of wheat, for example; Huichol altar depictions of animals in yarn; or Metepec visions of paradise in ceramic. Nor are we accustomed to everyday kitchen bowls, baskets, or bird cages individually designed and made by hand.

The Mexican techniques vary from primitive pottery making to refined lacquerwork, from weaving of rough-textured fabrics to intricate embroidery. Designs are nearly always geometric, often with a childlike simplicity that is deceptive because it is anything but naive. And they are generally traditional, for the motifs may have been in use for generations, if not for centuries.

Whole villages in Mexico do one kind of work. But from village to village and from region to region, you'll find astonishing diversity because Mexico's mountains have provided the long isolation that is a prime ingredient in the development of distinctive local cultures.

Your introduction to Mexico

Mexico appeals to almost everyone. We hope this book will lead you to happy discoveries in this land of variety. Consider it an introduction to the country, its people, its customs, and its atmosphere.

You won't find an itemized directory of places to stay or foods to eat, although the "Details at a glance" feature in each chapter offers a general idea of what to expect. Your best bet before setting out on a trip to Mexico is to check with a travel agent for current information. Use the maps within these chapters as general area guides; they won't replace an up-to-date road map from an automobile club.

Maya temple at Palenque

Mexico-where yesterday, today, and mañana merge...

Leisure, West
Coast style

Chiapas Indians

Acapulco's native dancers

...this welcoming land offers color, spirit, creative flair

Classic encounter at Mexico City bullring

Sea of Cortez prize

Braided tassel brooms

Colorful fiesta balloons

Multicolored plates and pots

Rock outcropping *becomes craggy island when tide comes in along wide beach at Baja's tip.*

Baja California

hangeable Baja presents two faces to visitors. One is the stark beauty of a rugged terrain with arroyos and barrancas crowned by cactus forests and brilliant desert flowers and punctuated by towering peaks mantled in pines. The other face is a vast winter playground for vacationers who appreciate miles of isolated beaches, fish-rich seas, and palm-shaded resorts that dot the peninsula's eastern side and southern tip.

The big news from Baja California has been the opening of the 1,061-mile Transpeninsular Highway (Mexico 1) extending from the U.S. border to the southern tip at Cabo San Lucas (poetically named "Land's End"). Noting that they act as filters, Joseph Wood Krutch once wrote, "Baja California is a wonderful example of how much bad roads can do for a country." While it is true that most of Baja was once the preserve of private pilots and auto adventurers with all-terrain vehicles, the paved highway has made the whole peninsula a motor route complete with a string of government-financed hotels, and with campgrounds in such startling locations as the Vizcaino Desert.

Baja offers no ancient cathedrals, large marketplaces, or brassy night life beyond the border. Tijuana and Mexicali—both border towns—are its largest cities. Only Ensenada and La Paz qualify as small towns; other spots are little more than villages.

But beyond the main highway lies a land of antiquity, of pastel deserts and startling green oases, of deep blue waters and crashing surf, and of supreme peace and quiet.

A peek into the past

Conquerors, colonizers, and developers have found Baja California's rugged terrain inhospitable in the extreme. Even today, a good portion of the peninsula remains uncultivated, unmined, virtually uninhabited, and almost unexplored.

Since its discovery (when it was thought to be an island), Baja has changed little. Most of Mexican territory was rapidly explored, subjugated, and mapped by the Spaniards, but the peninsula continued to be an enigma until the end of the 17th century.

Hernando Cortez sent the first exploratory expedition to Baja in 1532, and he stayed there himself in 1535 after hearing tales about great pearl-fishing grounds. No permanent settlement resulted from his efforts, though in 1539 his last envoy, Captain Francisco de Ulloa, was the first to sail along both the Pacific Coast and the body of water he named after his benefactor—the Sea of Cortez.

Pirates and buccaneers—Sir Francis Drake among them—made it necessary for the Spanish to occupy Baja, establish defenses, and locate a safe port for galleons en route from the Philippines. It was then that the Bay of La Paz (Peace) received its name.

In 1697 a Jesuit missionary, Padre Juan Maria Salvatierra, landed on the coast of Baja to establish a chain of 17 missions. Along with his followers he brought fruit trees, dates, and vegetables that remain today as reminders of the settlers' perseverance and toil. Dominicans and Franciscans helped in the actual construction of the stone edifices (San Ignacio, rebuilt in 1786; Santa Gertrudis, built in 1796; and San Borja, built in 1801).

After 400 years of exploration and settlement, these fortresslike stone missions are the only marks of civilization that look at all permanent. Probably nowhere else in the habitable world is there so much land without roads and railroads, or so much shoreline without ports and power lines.

Throughout its history, Baja has been shunned by civilization. Baja's Indians were the poorest and most despised, and its deserts the most feared of all in Mexico. In 1847 the United States forces that conquered Alta California had an equally secure grip on Baja California, but they let it go; nobody considered Baja worth keeping.

La Frontera

For most residents of the southwestern United States, Mexico is just a few hours or, at most, a day's journey away. It is not at all unusual for a

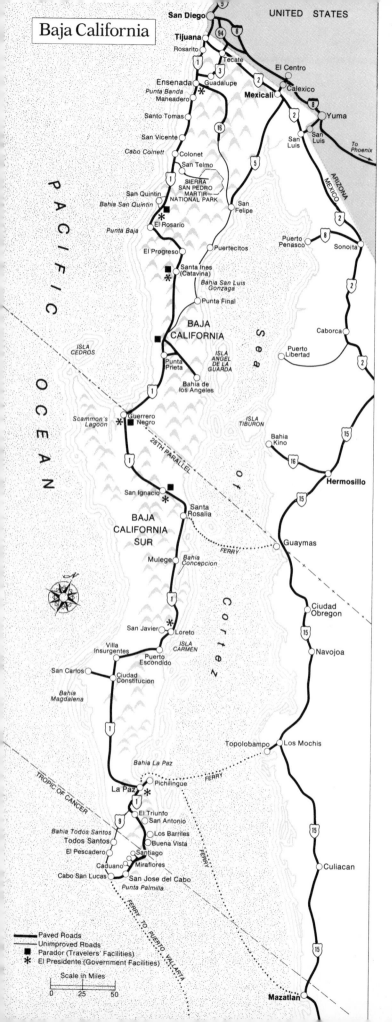

Baja California

Details at a glance

How to get there. Millions of people cross the border into Baja for a day or so of shopping or sports. Until recently only the most adventurous attempted to trek down the wild peninsula—Now you can do it in your car.

Many travelers don't realize there are alternate ways to visit Baja that let you enjoy the peninsula without the time and energy commitment of driving your own car or camper.

By air. Scheduled airlines serve major Gulf Coast settlements as far south as La Paz, and commuter airlines cover the resorts of the Cape country. Almost every resort has its own landing strip for private planes.

By boat. Good harbors are open for private boats, and modern car-ferries crisscross the Gulf between Santa Rosalia and Guaymas, between La Paz and the mainland ports of Mazatlan and Topolobampo, and between Cabo San Lucas and Puerto Vallarta. You can make reservations with your travel agent in advance or book passage yourself by writing to Caminos y Puentes Federales, Independencia #107-A, La Paz, B. C., Mexico. Confirm reservations as soon as you arrive in town (the La Paz office is closed Sunday and Monday). You'll need a car permit from customs to take your vehicle to the mainland, so get it first. Arrive at the ferry terminal early on the morning of your departure date to make arrangements.

By tour. Most bus or jeep trips cover only northern Baja. Baja Adventures, Los Angeles, has a combination air and bus tour of the entire peninsula.

Getting around. If you fly in to a large town or resort strip you can expect to be picked up by hotel vehicle or taxi. Car rentals are available in most border towns, La Paz, and Cabo San Lucas. There's also bus service from La Paz to the Cape.

Accommodations. Attractive government-owned El Presidente hotels and paradores (deluxe facilities for highway travelers including super-Pemex gas, cafes, and campgrounds) stretch up and down the highway. For complete information and reservations write to El Presidente Hotels, 8721 Beverly Blvd., Los Angeles, CA 90048.

A comprehensive travel service started to provide Baja pilots with air charts and resort reservations has recently added services for other travelers, too. For information write to Patti Senterfitt, Baja Reservation Service, P.O. Box 80324, San Diego, CA 92138, or call (714) 291-3491.

Climate and dress. Visiting Baja's high northern mountains is best in late spring, summer, and early fall. From La Paz to the tip of the peninsula it is always warm and sunny—hot during the summer. Winter and spring are ideal for traveling; fall is pleasant but sometimes subject to *chubascos* (rain-wind storms).

Casual attire is the note. At plush resorts you'll see women in cocktail gowns and men in jackets (never ties) for evening.

family to run down from San Diego to Baja for a spur-of-the-moment shopping spree.

La Frontera (Mexico's border) is often the first and only impression many *Norteamericanos* have of Mexico. Because of the concentration of visitors along the border, many Mexican border areas are a strange mixture of elements. Unique and atypical of the rest of Mexico, the towns and villages near the border provide a gradual transition to the Mexico that awaits those smitten with greater curiosity.

To Tijuana for shopping or sports

Each year Americans from the north make literally millions of border crossings into Tijuana, making it "the most visited city in the world." From here they can catch planes or buses or join adventurous expeditions to the interior of Baja. Most visitors come to shop and play.

At first glance the town doesn't present a very attractive appearance, though it is gradually being upgraded; the most visible change is the vast central redevelopment district. But there are also excellent new hotels and restaurants, and a racetrack rebuilt after a fire a few years ago. A few good parking lots and stop lights make Tijuana's traffic less terrifying to the tourist.

Shopping here can be fun and truly rewarding if you know what to look for. The traditional shopping section on Avenida Revolucion (from the border, follow signs to downtown Tijuana) has pretty well shed its unsavory reputation. Finds can range from the best in Mexican folk art to the gaudiest of tourist horrors—all displayed in a profusion rivaling that of Hong Kong. Because Tijuana enjoys free port status, some of the best buys are imports—fabrics, perfumes, and cameras.

Following Revolucion south, then east after it becomes Boulevard Agua Caliente, and continuing all the way to the new racetrack (Hipodromo de Aguacaliente), you'll discover some surprisingly good Mexican folk art—tree-of-life candelabras, yarn paintings, Huichol costumes, Paracho guitars, copper ware, fabrics, tiles, and more. One hint: On any shopping trip take along Roberta Ridgely's *The Tijuana, Mexicali, Ensenada Shopping, Restaurant & Entertainment Guide, Ole!* (J. P. Tarcher, Inc., 9110 Sunset Blvd., Los Angeles, CA 90069, 1975; $3.95).

Sporting events draw sizable crowds: year-round horse racing and greyhound racing at Agua Caliente Racetrack; Sunday afternoon bullfights from May through September at Plaza de Toros or the bullring-by-the-sea, Plaza Monumental; jai alai at Fronton Palacio Friday through Tuesday evenings; and *charreadas* (Mexican-style rodeos) at any of five *charro* rings. Check the glass information tepee on Revolucion for schedules.

Other attractions in Tijuana include a verdant city park that few north-of-the-border people visit. On a Sunday afternoon it teems with life and a carnival atmosphere prevails. In summer you'll hear band concerts in the tall central pavilion donated by Tijuana's sizable Chinese colony. Six blocks west of Revolucion, between Third and Fourth streets, is the hulking Church of San Francisco, with lofty Gothic windows and unfinished towers.

One of Baja's two cathedrals (Nuestra Senora de Guadalupe) is downtown at Second and Ninos Heroes—on Sunday mornings the city's busiest intersection.

Ensenada—bargains on a beautiful bay

The 65-mile drive to Ensenada takes you along a scenic coast reminiscent in part of California's cliffside stretch around Big Sur. From Tijuana, follow the signs for "Ensenada Cuota" (a toll road with a small charge for autos, slightly more for trailers and motor homes). You'll pass by Rosarito Beach, once the site of a famous gambling casino and now noted for its extensive Sunday market-on-wheels, where you can buy goods from food and clothing to curios; Halfway House, where surfers search for the perfect wave; and Cantamar, where Southern California's hang gliders gather on cliffs that beetlebrow the beaches.

You can follow the old road from Tijuana (Ensenada Libre) past farms and dairies in the La Joya valley, reaching the coast north of Rosarito Beach. The road is slow, narrow, and curving; most motorists prefer the highway.

Ensenada differs widely from Tijuana, partly because of its setting on lovely Bahia de Todos Santos. A busy seaport and commercial hub, Ensenada also attracts tourists. You'll find a wide choice of many charming small hotels and restaurants; rates are pretty much in line with what you would pay on the U.S. side of the border.

Getting around town is easy. Shops, hotels, restaurants, and sport-fishing boat rental offices line the main street—Lopez Mateos—which becomes the highway leading south to the airport (at the edge of town), Estero Beach (6 miles, resort and shops), and La Bufadora, the famed blowhole on the coast at Punta Banda (20 miles). Seaward of Lopez Mateos, the new waterfront esplanade with its small park provides access to horse rentals on the beach, an open-air fish market, and some sport-fish boat landings.

Shopping is attractive for imports as well as for Mexican goods, since Ensenada, like Tijuana, is a free port. To do some comparison pricing for Mexican handcrafts, stop first at the government-owned Centro Artesanal de Ensenada, also home for the tourism office.

Fishing is big—mostly for yellowtail, barracuda, albacore, white sea bass, bonita, and halibut—especially from April to November. Bring your own boat or rent one of the many available. Check established catch limits, closed seasons, and license requirements. You'll find places to have your fish cleaned, filleted, iced, packed, smoked, or stored.

Other attractions include visits to the Santo Tomas Winery, Hussong's Cantina (a turn-of-the-century landmark), and any of the hot springs in the mountains behind town. Todos Santos Island, just opposite the shores of Ensenada, is open to adventurous visitors for hiking, fishing, and swimming.

Ensenada celebrates an annual Mardi Gras (the 4 days preceding Ash Wednesday) and Cinco de Mayo, a holiday commemorating the Battle of Puebla in 1863 when Mexico defeated the French on May 5—also the day of completion of the annual Newport-Ensenada International Yacht Race.

An upper Baja loop

With the recent completion of the paved road between Ensenada and San Felipe, motorists get an unusual opportunity to cover a wide area of Baja Norte (including its three largest cities). The drive embraces many scenic surprises and several types of climate, and includes a variety of affordable attractions.

San Felipe, on the east coast of Baja, nestles between the Sea of Cortez and the foothills of the Sierra San Pedro Martir. It is a popular place for fishermen and well known to the camper set.

There's good fishing year-round for such bottom fish as sea trout, corbina, and baya. Punta San Felipe (north of town) is a good spot to try your luck ashore, or you can rent a boat and equipment in town. If you take your own boat, you can launch it at the village or at the cove of Punta Ensenada Blanca. Large boats take passengers for a day of fishing around Gonzaga Island, 18 miles out, as well as to Punta Estrella or Punta Ensenada Blanca. Fishing boats can be chartered for trips to Bahia de los Angeles.

If you'll be fishing from a small boat, do it in the morning; the breeze that comes up around noon makes offshore boating dangerous. Also watch for the freak tides that leave shore boats high and dry—a good time to try clamming.

Plans are afoot to pave the highway south of town past the rather aloof little American fishing resort of Puertecitos to Bahia Gonzaga and Bahia de los Angeles.

Mexicali, 125 miles north of San Felipe on paved Highway 5, is Baja California's largest city and the state capital—but little known as border towns go. Though Mexicali has had a reputation for vice since U.S. prohibition days, its bawdy past is little evident today.

Agriculture is the backbone of Mexicali's economy, though tourism is on the rise. As part of a Mexican large-scale experimental renewal project, Mexicali is literally on the move. They're relocating the shopping center from its present downtown location farther east along Boulevard Justo Sierra. Already you'll discover a Holiday Inn, a new bullring, new shops and dining spots. Construction also progresses on a new Governor's Palace and several new theaters. Avenida Madero takes you to both "old town" and new. Two restaurants you might want to try: La Casa Grande (Spanish elegance with French overtones) and El Meson Vegetariano (disguised vegetarian lunches). Beer buffs will enjoy the tasting room at the fortresslike Mexicali brewery—Baja's first.

Tecate is small, simple, and clean. Located on Highway 2 (the scenic border-hugging route between Mexicali and Tijuana), Tecate is a pleasant place to stop. This is the home of Tecate and Carta Blanca beers; both breweries are good spots to tour and offer tasting rooms. Around town you'll notice piles of Tecate's famous bricks and kilns where the bricks are fired; if you want to buy, make your deal directly with the owner. Also look for stacks of colorful ceramic tiles (made-to-order for about 50 cents a square foot) and the local glass blower's shop.

For a change of pace, try a complete physical renovation at Rancho La Puerta, a famed health spa. Here guests enjoy organic repasts, swimming classes, early morning jogging, yoga, jazz calisthenics, massage, facials, herbal wraps, and much more.

In the mountains a few miles southeast of Tecate lies Rancho Santa Veronica, a 6,000-acre ranch where Senor Bustamente raises bulls. He also puts on weekend exhibitions in a tiny bullring, and sells land. Adjoining Santa Veronica is La Juntas, the ranch where many of Mexico's movies are filmed.

A paved 2-mile road connects Tecate with California State Highway 94 across the border. South of Tecate, Highway 3 leads up and over the mountains, joining Highway 1 about 15 miles north of Ensenada. A Russian religious sect settled the village of Guadalupe along the way.

Northern Baja highlights

If you plan to drive down the peninsula, use Ensenada as a springboard. From here it is 357 miles to Guerrero Negro at the boundary of the state of Baja California, an easy 2-day (or grueling 1-day) drive. You'll probably be tempted by several attractive detours along the way. Twelve miles below Ensenada is the check point of Maneadero for validation of tourist cards—the first place you'll use them in northern Baja.

Scenery along this stretch of Baja varies widely: Pacific coastal views, green farming valleys, and towering peaks. The high desert is alive with tall tapering *cirio*, grooved *cardons*, graceful *ocotillo*, and tortured elephant trees.

From the sea to the mountains

Long visualized by most travelers as a vast, cactus-studded wasteland between border towns and distant fishing resorts, Baja contains some startling surprises for travelers. It is only a few hours drive from the border to some virtually unexplored vacation retreats in the Sierra San Pedro Martir where peaks rise to their highest on the peninsula in Baja's first national park.

The easiest way to reach these mountains is via Highway 1, turning off at San Telmo (84 miles south of Ensenada). From here a graded road—passable to standard cars in good weather—leads into the foothills to two ranches offering guest facilities. Beyond, you'll need a four-wheel-drive vehicle for the steep, ever-climbing road that terminates deep in the mountains at the Mexican observatory. From this spot you are rewarded with spectacular views of the Pacific Ocean to the west and the gulf to the east. Directly below are the barren plains of the San Felipe Desert; looking southeast, you'll see the precipitous, double-peaked El Picacho del Diablo (10,156 feet)—highest point in Baja.

Though the pinon and ponderosa country is ideal for camping, you must take your own food, water, and supplies; the park has no developed areas. For this reason you may prefer to make one of the following foothill ranches your home base for exploration. Reservations are advisable; both have dirt landing strips for pilots flying their own private planes.

Meling Ranch, one of Baja's oldest cattle ranches, still looks much as it might have at the turn of the century with the exception of modern guest accommodations that include a family-style dining room and stream-fed swimming pool. Horses and guides are available for pack trips.

Mike's Sky Ranch (also accessible from the road between Ensenada and San Felipe) is a more sophisticated resort, offering four-wheel-drive vehicles instead of horses for high-country trips. Campers will find developed sites along the San Rafael River below the ranch.

Flopping fish *fill net hauled in by energetic scoopers at San Felipe. Fishing is good the year around from shore or boat.*

San Quintín—beach of 11,000 virgins

Cabrillo named this bay in 1542. History doesn't add much about his obviously warm reception, but the name lends a colorful note to the area. A popular tourist destination despite the frequent coastal fogs, San Quintín attracts visitors who come to fish, observe waterfowl, or enjoy the wide sweep of sandy beaches and rocky tidepools. Bird watchers stop here because the marshes are a major resting area along the Pacific Flyway. You'll see reminders near the Old Mill Motel and in the weathered cemetery of an English attempt at colonization in the late 1800s.

The high desert

Before the new highway was built, El Rosario (south of San Quintín) was the jumping-off spot into the rugged heart of Baja. Now the paved road cuts sharply east into the southern edge of the Sierra San Miguel where you'll catch your first glimpse of cirios and cardon cactus.

Turn off to El Progreso to view the impressive ruins of Mission San Fernando, the only mission in Baja founded by Father Serra. Hike a little farther up the canyon to see a grove of native Mexican blue palms.

For desert lovers, the following 104 miles can be the most fascinating part of their trip. The high desert is best glimpsed after winter rains when the desolate land blooms with kaleidoscopic color. Santa Ines (Cataviña) is right in the midst of the most spectacular part of the desert. There you'll find an El Presidente and a parador. Or stay at rustic Rancho Santa Ines—once a pit stop for the Baja Mil Road Race—which offers food and dormitory-style accommodations.

Bahia de los Angeles—on the Sea of Cortez

From the parador at Punta Prieta, a 42-mile paved road leads across the narrowest part of the peninsula to Bahia de los Angeles on the Gulf of California.

This incredibly beautiful bay is usually the first goal of people who pilot their own boats and aircraft down the gulf side of the peninsula or across the gulf by way of the stepping-stone islands of "The Midriff." Some visitors make the bay their objective by car or camper, either by choice or from lack of time to venture farther. Traffic on the road is light at present, but growing steadily, causing a littering problem at this once pristine spot.

The channel is protected by the mountainous 45-mile length of Guardian Angel Island only a quarter of the way across the bay, and is filled with fish. There are yellowtail, cabrilla, and grouper year-round, with billfish and dorado as well during the summer and early fall. Large schools of porpoise and whales move through the channel within sight of land. Once a productive turtle fishing region, the channel has been badly depleted due to overharvesting. Shrimp boats spend some nights here anchored only 100 yards from the soft, sandy beach.

Campers have a wide choice of sites, but there's only one lodge at present. To inquire in advance about fishing conditions, boat rentals or charters, or to make reservations, write to Casa Diaz, Bahia de los Angeles, Apartado Postal 579, Ensenada, B.C., Mexico.

Inlets and coves *of Bahia Concepcion offer secluded camping, good boating and swimming.*

Guerrero Negro—salt and whales

On the 28th Parallel (dividing the old state of Baja California from the new state of Baja California Sur) sits Guerrero Negro, a rather bleak spot on the Pacific mainly concerned with salt production in the ponds bordering Scammon's Lagoon. You can't miss it because as you approach from the north you'll see two massive fins sticking up into the sky—*Monumento Azteca*, a seven-story-high abstract study in steel that is the focal point of the stadium where President Echeverria dedicated the highway. Across the street are an El Presidente and a parador.

From November through February hundreds of California gray whales head for Scammon's Lagoon to breed and train their young. Right after them come the tourists. For whale-watching, follow signs that take you to the best viewing spots; carry binoculars, and go early in the morning.

Central Baja highlights

An increasing number of vacationers and sportsmen lured by good weather, water, scenery, and comparatively low-priced resorts, are arriving at Loreto and Mulege (moo-la-hay) by plane and road. There you're on the Sea of Cortez with some of the best fishing in the world. In the summer you can have your pick of marlin, sailfish, and grouper—smaller fish are available all year.

Mellow dates in San Ignacio

Southbound drivers come to the first interruption in desert harshness along the road south of the in-

Palm-studded *San Ignacio softens harsh desert landscape.*

land turn at El Rosario. Date palms introduced by Jesuit colonists spread a shadowy green roof up and down the valley. In town you can explore the well-stocked store in the plaza and the massive stone church built by the Dominicans in 1786 and still in use today. In the fall you'll find racks of drying dates in the narrow streets up behind the plaza.

No airline touches down here, but light planes can land at the short, rough, rocky strip bulldozed out of the cactus-covered lava east of town (buzz town for a taxi).

Santa Rosalia—northern port for Cortez ferries

Curiosity is the best reason for visiting bustling Santa Rosalia, long famous but no longer functioning as a French-owned, French-operated, French-speaking copper mining town. The town is Mexican now, though some French names and customs persist. View the prefabricated metal church designed by Alexandre Gustave Eiffel (of tower fame) for a Paris exposition; it ended up here around the turn of the century.

A ferry accommodating up to 500 passengers and 120 cars operates between Santa Rosalia and Guaymas on the mainland. Private planes and a "commuter" plane service from the mainland come and go on an airstrip 1 mile south of town.

Palms, papayas, and mangroves in Mulege

As far inland as you can see, the valley of the Mulege River is a forest of majestic date palms where you can hear the rustling of breeze-stirred fronds, the trickling of water, and the calls of tropical birds. Just upstream from the sheltered village, the water is dammed and partly diverted to irrigate citrus, mangoes, papayas, bananas, and palms. Downstream it is a brackish tidal estuary

where—if you can resist the lure of the Sea of Cortez beyond—you can try for the big snook that lurk there.

Mulege is a sleepy, palm oasis located 420 miles south of the border along the Mulege River. The village is small enough so that even at a stroller's pace you can visit all the shops and displays. Highlights include the mission church, built in 1766 on a high point upstream from the rest of town, and the imposing state prison, on a hillside north of the plaza. Prisoners who may have jobs and families on the outside are paroled during the day, but must return to the prison at sunset.

Everyone who visits Mulege should spend at least 1 day on an excursion (preferably by water, though you can get there by road) to Concepcion Bay, deservedly famous for its fine white beaches, sheltered inlets, warm water, and good fishing. This is the place for the get-away-from-it-all beachcomber. Here you can dive for scallops and lobsters, scoop up clams and oysters by the bucketful, and, if you wish, sleep out overnight on a beach of your own discovery.

You'll find Posada Concepcion trailer park just 13 miles south of Mulege, and two and three-bedroom cottages fronting part of the beach at Coyote Bay. Primitive beach campsites reached by detours off the highway can be found at Santispac Lagoon, Coyote Bay, and El Requeson. Water is sometimes a problem; you might want to bring your own.

A large fly-in resort and several smaller hotels in Mulege provide the visitor with a choice of adequate overnight accommodations.

Loreto—the original heart of Baja

Leaving Concepcion Bay, the highway snakes up into spectacularly rugged mountains before dropping down to Loreto on the gulf. Loreto, Baja's

Swimmers stroll *away from pool at plush Cape resort to view Cabo San Lucas bay beyond.*

first city and capital for 132 years (founded by Salvatierra in 1697) still enjoys its one-time prominence and is rapidly gaining a new reputation as a fisherman's haunt. Located here is the Mother of Missions—Baja's first—rebuilt again and again, and most recently restored in 1941. It was from Loreto in 1769 that Junipero Serra began his northward march.

A canopy of date palms covers parts of town and extends right down to the beach; the trees lean out over the sand very much as coconut palms do in the South Seas. Resorts front this beach and a seaside walkway makes a good spot for watching the spectacular sunrises and sunsets.

Fly-in guests at the Flying Sportsman Lodge use a private landing strip, and facilities there now include camper sites. The large main airstrip where commercial airliners land discharges visitors to waiting taxis for the trip to the verdant Oasis or the new El Presidente (formerly Playa Loreto).

Fishing is great. In proportions that vary somewhat with the seasons, all the valiant game species are ready to do battle—yellowtail, marlin, sailfish, roosterfish, tuna, bass, sierra mackerel, bonito, cabrilla, pompano, and others. For shellfishing and shore casting, you can go south of town a few miles to where the hills come right down to the water, forming headlands and sheltered coves.

You're not a fisherman? Visit the mission museum to see the artifacts collected from all over Baja; stroll along the side streets until you discover the outdoor mud-and-brick oven of Loreto's bakery; visit the few shops for souvenirs; sit in the plaza and people-watch; or lie in a hammock and look out to sea. Most hotels have pools and tennis courts. The large island in the channel is Isla Carmen, noted for its spectacular grottos and good skin diving.

A visit to San Javier, a hidden little community back in a spiny mountain gorge, takes almost all day. Ask your hotel to pack a lunch; then hire a truck and driver and allow 3½ hours for the 22 miles each way on very primitive road. The goal of this rough but beautiful trip is to see the finest example of mission architecture in Baja—the only original mission church remaining intact. It was finished in 1758, 10 years before the arrival of the Franciscans.

South of Loreto, it is a long 225-mile drive through desert and agricultural communities to reach La Paz. For 23 miles below Loreto the road hooks in and out along the gulf. Notable stops are Nopolo, where pelicans go berserk in winter months when currents and winds combine to pile up schools of small fish; Notri, with limited camping under palm trees; and Puerto Escondido, a natural harbor where you can rent a boat or fish off the dock. Watch for changes in Puerto Escondido as plans proceed for ferry service to the mainland.

Villa Insurgentes and Ciudad Constitucion, the two principal inland towns, offer a minimum of appeal for tourists but are centers for the farming communities surrounding them. At Ciudad Constitucion a paved road cuts across to Mag Bay on the Pacific. Fishing, clamming, and even swimming are great, but don't expect any facilities.

La Paz to the Cape

From La Paz to the tip of Baja you're in resort land where campers are outnumbered. Almost everyone arrives here by air or by water, exactly as if this area were an island—an island about 100 miles long and 50 miles wide, with sea and land mixed in most agreeable proportions. It is also a desert island, though, and that is one of its special qualities. Cactus comes right down to the beach, even in the lower half of the peninsula which lies south of the Tropic of Cancer. Many of the beaches are as empty as Robinson Crusoe's. It is impossible to get more than about 20 miles from water on either one side or the other. Going inland usually means going up a little (peaks are over 6,000 feet), so you're always looking out toward sea.

Private pilots make Baja's tip a favorite target. Surprisingly luxurious resorts south of La Paz have their own airstrips that are also used by the air taxi service from La Paz.

You can drive through this region in a loop trip from La Paz (rental cars available) down the gulf side of the peninsula to Cabo San Lucas, and then up the Pacific side by way of Todos Santos. Roads are paved except for a stretch on the Pacific side. You'll see campgrounds and new hotels under construction; this is the area of Baja's greatest new development.

A friendly welcome in La Paz

La Paz, capital of Baja California Sur, lost part of its drowsy charm when it geared up for the tourists who arrive by ferry from Topolobampo and Mazatlan and by jet from the U.S. No longer a backwater town, La Paz is still an intriguing city of 50,000 that is fondly remembered by most visitors. Attractions are within 2 or 3 blocks of the coconut palm-lined waterfront drive—a circumstance encouraging strolling, even though cabs hover about.

The life of the city centers around the water. Even the bandstand — traditional center of the Mexican town plaza—adjoins the *malecon*, the beach walk alongside the sea wall in La Paz. You'll see two piers: one serving sport-fishing boats, the other serving commercial shipping. Farther west is the Topolobampo ferry terminal; the ferry to Mazatlan is 12 miles north of the city at Pichilingue.

La Paz seems quite different from cities of mainland Mexico, and many find it more friendly. More than a few of the buildings are quaint and almost Victorian in appearance. The most conspicuous landmark is the mission, a large rose pink church facing the plaza. On the opposite side, a theater and museum have replaced the old Government Palace. A new impressive state capitol has been built in the south part of town.

Accommodations. Several hotels face the malecon (only La Posada is on the beach); four others including a new El Presidente are at the northwest corner of town. Here too you'll find four recreational vehicle facilities.

Water sports. Superb angling brings most people to La Paz. You can rent fishing equipment, boats, and guides, or take a several-day cruise on the gulf. Baja's fishing bible is *The Sea of Cortez* by Ray Cannon and the *Sunset* editors. You'll encounter this book—and references to it—in every hotel and resort where fishermen stay.

Snorkelers and scuba divers-for-sport will enjoy bay waters that are warm and wonderfully clear, teeming with brilliantly colored fish not at all frightened by a human presence. Around the rocks near the beaches you'll find legions of hermit crabs or enormous chitons, and starfish with 20 or more feathery rays.

You can rent a small boat to reach the sandspit across the estuary—a fine place for beachcombing. The swimming beaches of Coromuel and La Ramada, 2 miles from shore hotels, are best reached by round-trip taxi excursions.

Shopping. La Paz is a free port so you'll find a few stores offering bargains. The best shopping is around Hotel La Perla, but remember that stores close in the afternoon for siesta. Some shops carry native crafts brought in from surrounding villages and from the mainland. The gulf waters' spiny, puffy blowfish are caught, cured, and sold by small Mexican boys; price depends on your bargaining ability.

Countryside villages and remote resorts

From La Paz the highway through El Triunfo and San Antonio—towns that whisper of a mining past —climbs gradually into foothills pocked with prospectors' holes and draped with yellow flowering

Tips for the Baja driver

How's the highway? It can be an enjoyable experience to drive the length of the peninsula. What was formerly accomplished only by jeep or pickup is now easily managed by an ordinary passenger car. The key to a pleasant trip is to be well informed and well prepared.

• Arm yourself with a good road map and a mile-by-mile guidebook. Wheelock and Gulick's *Baja California Guidebook*, with good maps and listings of beaches and campsites, is a long-time favorite. Other suggestions might include the AAA publications on Baja, Dan Sanborn's *Mexico Travelog* (available from his insurance office in San Ysidro), or *The Baja Book* by Tom Miller. Recreational vehicle owners will enjoy Paul Fischer's *Adventure to Land's End.*

• The Transpeninsular Highway is slightly narrow; there are no shoulders; curves may be poorly banked; and *vados* (creek beds that cross the road) may hide not only water but cattle. Don't drive at night!

• Fill up with gasoline wherever you find it— the next service station may be "just out." Carry Mexican pesos or only small U.S. bills. Brush up on your Spanish and bring along a good translating dictionary because Baja's rural folk know little English. Also, don't expect accurate road directions from a man on a burro who has never been 10 miles from home.

• Carry a complete set of tools and such replacement parts as a fan belt, spark plugs, points, condenser, and extra motor oil and radiator coolant in your car.

• Travelers staying in motels should carry a minimum of camping gear just in case—sleeping bags, a heavy ground cloth (to double as an emergency sun shade), a day's supply of food, and at least a gallon of water per person.

• If you plan to travel anywhere off the main highway, you'll be on gravel or dirt roads. It is a good idea to carry a shovel and tire chains, and to put inner tubes in your tires (cactus spines can puncture a steel-belted radial tire and you may have to drive a ways to find someone to repair it). Unless you have an all-terrain vehicle and know where you're headed, stay on the main road. Remember—no road holds any terror for the Mexicans who shake cars and trucks to pieces with utter nonchalance.

• Keep a lookout for green utility trucks with *Departmento de Turismo* printed in orange on the side. These are the "green angels"—the travelers' friend. A fleet of seven of these trucks is supposed to cruise all sections of the highway at least twice a day to help motorists. Service is free; you pay for parts or gas. In a true emergency, they will relay messages by radio to your family at home.

palo de arco shrubs. A tall smokestack, landmark of El Triunfo, towers black against the distant sky. Two yellow church towers rise between the smokestack and mine buildings on the hill where once $50,000 worth of gold and silver were produced monthly. San Antonio, now a cattle ranching center, possesses a church of rare simplicity—one of the most handsome in this region. From San Antonio come the baskets, hats, and ornaments sold in the shops of La Paz.

A short drive takes you easily to Los Barriles and the gulf. Here several fishing resorts (Palmas de Cortez, Rancho Buena Vista, Punta Pescadero, Punta Colorada, and Las Lagunas) provide comfortable accommodations.

Inland past the high peaks of the cape region's jagged blue ranges, you'll come to Miraflores, well-known for its leather work. Craftsmen here make fine saddles, belts, shoes, and holsters; practically all the *cueras* (leather gun belts worn by cowboys throughout Baja) are made in Miraflores. Leather goods bought here cost slightly less than they do in La Paz. Caduano, also off the main highway, turns out leather work. Whether or not you're shopping, take time to stop and watch these craftsmen at work.

Land's End: Cabo San Lucas

The end of the great Baja peninsula comes into sight at last. Gradually the desert shore curves westward toward the green splash of San Jose del Cabo, then on and on to the final tall rocks that stand apart and unapproachable—The Friars.

Here Baja California reaches a climax of sorts, not only in geography but also in the beguiling settings, extravagant spaciousness, and elaborate embellishments of its hotels. Prices don't really soar until you get past San Jose del Cabo, a neat, sunny little town that invites exploring.

Between San Jose del Cabo and the end of the Cape you'll pass many protected coves with small white beaches that, unfortunately, are often fenced off and inaccessible to the visitor. Pirates lay in wait in bygone years planning to loot the richly laden Manila galleon, a trading ship on its annual voyage to Acapulco with stores of Oriental finery and spices and sometimes a fortune in gold. After the long voyage of 6 months or more, the ship headed in toward shore to stop at San Jose del Cabo for fresh water and supplies. Frequently, bold sea dogs—Thomas Cavendish among them—made off with the rich booty. That wreck on the beach just east of the Cape is the Japanese longliner *Inari Maru No. 10* that ran aground in 1966, lured ashore by local fishermen using a transmitter placed in the hills above the rocks. Old traditions die hard.

Miles and miles of spectacular shores are unbelievably deserted. At Punta Palmilla you'll find an exception—Hotel Palmilla, a luxurious resort standing above the red rocks and white sands of the headland. So opulent is the resort's appearance that for a moment you may think it is a Moorish mirage. Hotel guests fly in on the hotel's private landing strip for fishing that ranks with the best.

Ten miles beyond Palmilla—and an additional step up in price and lavishness—is Hotel Cabo San Lucas, spreading grandly and improbably on a desert shore where a few years ago only an obscure rancho stood.

The very tip of the peninsula has several modest hotels and three luxury hotels (Hacienda Cabo San Lucas, Hotel Solmar, Hotel Finisterra) set beside the fine skin diving bay formed in the shelter of the southernmost headland. Here is Cabo San Lucas, a small village where Roberto, one of Mexico's top ready-to-wear designers, works. The village is also a terminal point for the Puerto Vallarta ferry, and a shore port for Mexico coastal cruises.

A loop trip through Todos Santos

For the next 50 miles northward the road parallels the Pacific, sometimes within view of the water, sometimes well inland. This section of the road is about the worst you'll encounter on this trip.

At El Pescadero the worst of the road is behind you. From here it is about 8 miles to Todos Santos, a village surrounded by a verdant valley close to the sea. Tall mango trees, light green and shiny-leafed, line the roadway. Sugar fields and towering palm trees mark fertile lands.

The primitive sugar cane mill attracts visitors. The cane, delivered by donkey cart, is crushed to produce a liquid. This liquid simmers and later thickens in a great wooden vat; then it hardens in hollowed-out forms. The blow of a mallet knocks the cone-shaped pieces of candylike *panocha* (raw sugar) from the forms, ready to be packed in shipping cases woven of palo de arco branches.

The mission (founded in 1732, rebuilt in 1840, and remodeled in 1941) retains evidences of age in its hand-carved doors and hand-hewn benches; a bell-ringing rope hangs down from the high tower to within reach of your hand.

Todos Santos is about 50 miles from La Paz or a 1½ to 2-hour drive over paved road. It is a pretty route in spring and after the summer rains. The desert glows with yellow clouds of *palo verde* flowers, pink blossoms come out on the cholla, and the wands of the *palo adan*, relative of the ocotillo, are tipped with red flowers.

A few miles from Todos Santos on the Pacific side of Baja is San Pedrito, a languorous beach with dangerous waves—swim here with caution.

Mexico's West Coast: Resort Land

The Golden Coast or Mexico's Riviera—these are two of the names bestowed on the western side of the Mexican mainland. Mexico's west coast offers the nearest tropical destination for motorists from the western United States. It is also the closest by sea, and regularly visited by cruise ships mainly from Los Angeles but also from San Francisco and occasionally from San Diego. By air, cost of the trip is comparable to or slightly less than the other nearest tropical destination—Hawaii. Ferry service to and from Baja make it an increasingly popular "leg" on a triangle trip from California or Arizona.

Natural attractions include great mountain ranges and grand canyons, or lush jungles and sparse deserts. Its bay-indented coasts are ringed with superb swimming beaches, and the many rocky points are favored by anglers. Mixed emotions greet the increased accessibility of formerly remote spots now easily reached via the "sunshine route" (Highways 15 and 200), lacking only a few miles of a coastal connection between the U.S. and Guatemala borders.

Luxurious hotels cover spaces where fishing huts used to stand. Today's bare feet on once-secret ribbons of sand belong to the tourists.

Weather is better during winter and early spring; the "in" season is from November to May. Hotel prices drop sharply during the rest of the year and many a canny traveler braves the warmer temperatures and summer rains to sun at half the price. One interesting exception is Guaymas. You pay more in the summer for rooms there because of the necessary additional air conditioning.

From the border to Guaymas

One of the most accessible portions of Mexico is the northwest corner of the state of Sonora, which includes the 253-mile stretch of Highway 15 from Nogales to Guaymas.

The desert in this area is spacious and unscarred. Flying over the desert or driving through it, you see how light civilization's touch has been—out toward the coast, vast areas never have been inhabited; in many regions, European culture and industry gained footholds three centuries or so ago, but now are memorialized only by ruins.

The people who still live in the desert have attempted to transform their environment, though they and their goats and cattle are scattered too thinly to change the look of the land very much. The brown adobe houses, barns, and corral walls blend easily into the desert setting.

Nogales—border town in a new style

Nogales, Arizona, and its Mexican counterpart, Nogales, Sonora, are primary entry gateways for Mexico's west coast beaches. From one year to the next you can never expect to find Mexican Nogales as you left it. It is a border town of constant change; of rebuilding, tearing down, and restoring.

Nogales—agricultural and commercial center of the state of Sonora—gets an added boost from tourism. The income from bullfights, parades with floats, and fiestas adds to the town's economy.

The customs offices at the border are open 24 hours a day; here you can acquire tourist permits, if you haven't already. The sheer joy of shopping brings weekend visitors to Nogales and attracts tourists on their way to other points within Mexico. Handicraft shops and markets, a shopping center called Casa Margot, and artisans' galleries are scattered throughout the town. For those interested in sightseeing, La Caverna restaurant (where Apache chief Geronimo was briefly imprisoned when the restaurant was a jail), Sacred Heart Church, and the old Customs House provide historical interest.

For trailer facilities, motels, and hotels, the U.S. side of the border provides more selection with higher standards.

The Gran Desierto: population zero—almost

Mexico's Highway 2 follows the border on the Mexican side from Tijuana through Mexicali and San Luis Rio Colorado to Sonoita, and then turns southeast to meet Highway 15 at Santa Ana.

Colorful sail boards *punctuate beaches at many resorts along Mexico's western side.*

For approximately 126 miles along the Arizona-Sonora line, the thin track of the old Camino del Diablo once wandered uncertainly among the rocks, cactus, and soft sand between San Luis Rio Colorado and Sonoita; it was no place for the casual traveler. Today there is still a 92-mile gap between gas stations, but the smooth pavement of Highway 2 invites—and gets—speeds of 60 to 70 miles per hour. The nearest thing to the old "Devil's Highway" is the sandy trail on the U.S. side used by our Border Patrol.

From San Luis Rio Colorado, Highway 2 heads east into the flat, silty, creosote-dotted desert. The road reaches out for the nearly featureless horizon ahead; on your left you can see the Gila Mountains of Arizona, and far off to the right is the faint blue line of Baja California's 10,000-foot-high backbone.

South of the road, the Gran Desierto—all sand and even less hospitable than the Sahara—broadens and spreads all the way to the Sea of Cortez. Here the population per square mile gets down to zero. But all the way along the route you'll meet cars and trucks, and a helping hand will always be extended in case you have trouble.

El Golfo de Santa Clara, 70 miles south of San Luis Rio Colorado on a paved road, sounds more impressive than it is—a remote fishing village in an unspoiled, natural setting on the Sea of Cortez. Wide white beaches stretch for about 35 miles with soft, clean, inviting sand. Tides are among the highest in the world, rising as much as 25 feet. Fishing is the prime attraction. You can also explore the beaches in a dune buggy, or swim and sun. Facilities include gas stations, drug store, grocery store, restaurants, and trailer parks (no hookups).

About halfway to Sonoita, the highway forsakes the straight-arrow course out of San Luis Rio Colorado to wind easily among some of the fringing cones and basalt mesas of Cerro Pinacate. It is hard to find a greater single volcano than this anywhere in the world. The volcano's broad, symmetrical, black lava mass studded with hundreds of cinder cones and pocked with explosion pits and calderas, lies south of the highway, which cuts across some of the lava flows. U.S. astronauts practiced here before their first moon mission.

The final approach to Sonoita is through a natural conservatory of desert vegetation. If you drive this route in the spring, you may see the spectacular golden blooms of the palo verde. Other perennial plants that blossom in the spring are the cholla, giant saguaro, ocotillo, creosote, and organ pipe cactus. You may also see such annuals as poppies, mallows, and mariposa lilies.

Sonoita, though on the border, would be a typical Mexican country town except for its modern gas stations. An air-conditioned motel is also available. The scenery becomes slightly more attractive south of Sonoita.

Puerto Penasco, or Rocky Harbor

The 62-mile paved highway to Puerto Penasco (also called "Rocky Harbor") starts at Sonoita. This Mexican shrimping port is fast becoming a tourist town, but the beach-camping settlements of Choya Bay and Sandy Beach nearby are more primitive than Sonoita. The sun, clamming, and tidepool exploring, as well as the long empty beaches and good shell-hunting appeal to beachcombers. The Sea of Cortez is renowned for its abundance of fish. Ho-

Sun, sand, and water *wash away worries along Mexican Riviera.*

tels, motels, and restaurants are more available in Puerto Penasco than in Choya Bay. You'll find boats for hire in both areas; launching is better at Choya (launch permits are required for Mexican waters).

If you want to camp, check the trailer parks in Puerto Penasco, or head toward Sandy Beach and Choya Bay beach. There you can park recreational vehicles for a small fee, but you'll find no facilities, wood, or running water. (You can buy water and some staple foods at the grocery store.)

What to do? The "night life" is usually on the beach. Special events include the Marine Carnival on June 1 and the Choya Bay Fishing Derby on Father's Day weekend in mid-June.

About the only sightseeing attractions in this area are the desalting plant and hothouse experimental station, the new seaside community of Las Conchas with its Moorish architecture, and the marina on the bay where ferries will dock when service is established across the Sea of Cortez to Baja.

A chain of missions in Kino country

An Italian Jesuit priest, the incredibly tough and daring Father Eusebio Kino, settled in the vast Sonoran desert and endured thirst, hunger, and hostile Indians while exploring (often alone) great stretches of northwestern Mexico, including parts of what are now Arizona and California. When he died in 1711, he had founded 25 missions.

The only traces left of these original structures are the crumbling, weathered remains of the mission at Magdalena. The increase of curious visitors to this town can be attributed to the 1966 discovery of Father Kino's remains, now on display in the carefully tended town plaza.

In addition to establishing missions, Father Kino is remembered for Christianizing seven Indian tribes and teaching them how to farm, discovering the Gila River, and mapping much of the surrounding desert area. He also became the first person to learn that Baja California was a peninsula, not an island.

Crumbling Cocospera, *original 18th century Kino mission, stands mutely in Sonora desert.*

On green *at Ixtapa, golfer pars hole with short putt.*

Fishing boats *form holding pattern to await next day's venture.*

Details at a glance

How to get there

Westerners often drive to northern resorts.
Highway 2 from Tijuana and Mexicali joins
Highway 15 from Nogales. Follow this route to
reach Kino Bay, Guaymas, Mazatlan, and San
Blas. At Tepic, take Highway 200 to Puerto
Vallarta, Manzanillo, Ixtapa, Zihuatanejo, and
Acapulco. Along the way, campers find miles of
seductive shoreline for overnight stops.

Most travelers pick a resort and find the
fastest way to get there, allowing themselves
maximum time on sunny beaches.

By air. Aeromexico and Mexicana reach some
resorts directly from the U.S.; they also supply
connecting service from major Mexican cities.
Hughes Airwest and Western Airlines, along with
some international carriers, offer direct flights
to major tourist areas. Check with a travel agent
for schedules.

Private pilots may obtain a copy of *Airports
of Mexico* from Pilots Reservation Service,
P.O. Box 80324, San Diego, CA 92138.

Once on the ground you can rent cars in most
larger resorts or use local transportation for
sightseeing.

By boat. Ferry service connects Baja California
and the West Coast between Santa Rosalia and
Guaymas, La Paz and Topolobampo/Los Mochis
and Mazatlan, and Cabo San Lucas and Puerto
Vallarta.

Cruise ships often stop at Mazatlan, Puerto
Vallarta, Manzanillo, and Acapulco, allowing
on-shore excursions.

Private boats with experienced captains sail
the protected Sea of Cortez. Harbors are plentiful, especially in major fishing areas.

By tour. Scheduled airline and hotel packages
offer savings. Check with a travel agent for
current information.

From Mexico City, you can make arrangements
for a 3 or 4-day coastal tour at any Mexican
travel agency. Typical Acapulco trips are
combination bus-plane service.

Accommodations. "Varied" best describes hotels,
motels, and recreational vehicle parks along the
coast. Finding suitable accommodations is
limited only by season and your budget. Most
hotels offer air conditioning, dining facilities,
and swimming pool. Beachfront hotels are
usually more expensive. Villa, condominium, or
apartment rentals are popular for long stays.

Climate and clothes. The farther south you
travel, the warmer it becomes. The "in" season
is winter and spring. Summer, a rainy time,
brings a decrease in room price (Guaymas is an
exception) to compensate for heat.

In northerly areas you may need a jacket
during windy weather; otherwise, bring cool,
casual clothing for beach or street. Good buys
in local attire make it wise to wait to add to
your wardrobe.

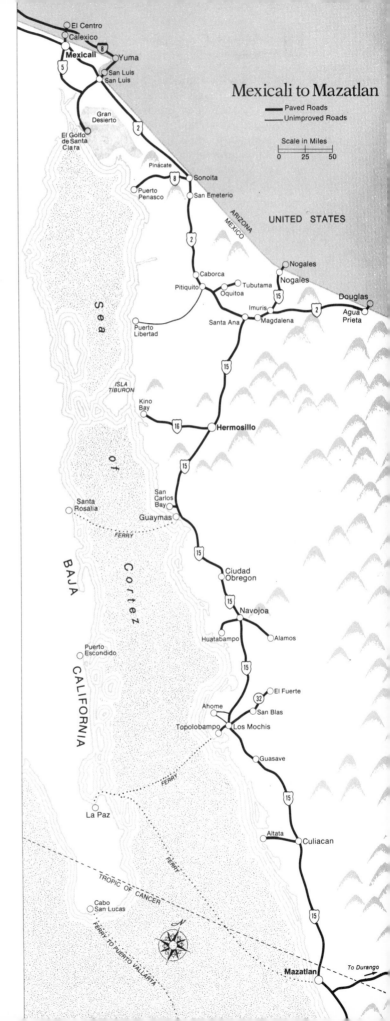

Mexicali to Mazatlan

— Paved Roads
— Unimproved Roads

Scale in Miles
0   25   50

Other than its significance as Father Kino's final resting place, Magdalena offers very little in the way of sightseeing except for the attractive plaza surrounded by arched, missionlike building housing restaurants and shops that sell religious articles. Magdalena is a mining and agricultural center, and serves as a departure point for trips to Mission San Ignacio de Caborica, one of five original Kino missions in the area. The other mission locations are at Pitiquito, Oquitoa, Tubutama, and Caborca. Motels at Caborca and Magdalena offer overnight accommodations.

Hermosillo—clean capital of Sonora

Well worth a stopover, Hermosillo is a lovely clean city with wide tree-lined boulevards and tiled walks. The town offers a variety of places to stay and things to do. Much of the original ornate colonial architecture still lines the plaza, but old adobes are being replaced with brick and many modern public buildings have sprouted up. Despite the smartness of Hermosillo's modern appearance, the "old" Mexico is still there—in the evening promenade in the plaza, and in the shops where you'll find a wide selection of Mexican crafts and imported goods from Portugal, Italy, England, and Scotland. Markets are clean, and the seafood from Guaymas is plentiful and inexpensive.

The University of Sonora is located on the highway in the northcentral part of the city. Other points of interest in Hermosillo include the cathedral, the handsome museum, and the attractively planted Parque Madero. Several motels offer golfing privileges. Or, you may enjoy the excellent hunting and fishing available in nearby areas.

Kino Bay: land of the Seri Indians

Beautiful Kino Bay is one of the few accessible spots for the motorist on the long undeveloped coastline stretching from the northern end of the Sea of Cortez down to the resort center of Guaymas. Kino Bay and the little town of "Old" Kino are 66 miles from Hermosillo by good paved road. A long landing strip is a convenience for private pilots.

Into Copper Canyon by rail

Most scenic of all Mexico rail trips is the Copper Canyon run along the Chihuahua-Pacific Railway. Originating at Ojinaga, a border town opposite Presidio, Texas, the trip takes you south to Chihuahua, then southwest to Los Mochis. Once past Chihuahua you're swept deep into spectacular Sierra Madre country where your adventure begins.

Rumbling across bridges, the train snakes through tunnels and passes by deep ravines. Waterfalls slip over rims of red rock where palms and ferns grow in the shade and bush poppies tumble over the sunlit slopes.

Yet all is not wild in the Sierra Madre. Juxtaposed against the forested ridges and simple huts of the Tarahumara Indians are busy towns and small adobe villages. Perhaps you'll decide to stop at Divisadero, Cerocahui, or Creel, welcome breaks in the 14-hour ride from Chihuahua to Los Mochis. All offer hotels and exciting side trips into once inaccessible canyon territory. Explore the Urique and Copper canyons by horseback. Hike along canyon rims, or go shopping in town for crafts made by the Tarahumaras.

Pullman trains make two round trips weekly between Ojinaga and Los Mochis via Chihuahua. For information or reservations you can write directly to the Chihuahua-Pacific Railway, Apartado Postal 46, Chihuahua, Chih., Mexico. Or, you can arrange for a package tour from Sanborn's, McAllen, Texas 78501, or from Big

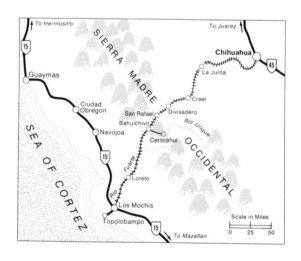

Bend Travel Service, Alpine, Texas 79830. Wampler Tours (Box 45, Berkeley, CA 94701) conducts tours each year.

In addition to the above service, the line also operates streamlined vistadome Italian Fiat coaches between Ojinaga and Los Mochis by daylight only. You stop over in Chihuahua, where you'll find several good hotels, and resume the trip early the next morning.

The residents of the tiny village, with its simple chapel and single cantina, make their living chiefly by fishing from small boats or dugout canoes.

South of the village are some luxury condominiums, but most of the new development is north of town in the newer, more urban shoreline community of "New" Kino, a modern development with paved streets, sidewalks, and sewers. A progressive seaside resort with attractive homes springing up along the beach, "New" Kino has several modern motels, recreational vehicle facilities, and a few restaurants including the interesting Caverna del Seri. Shore fishing is good, boat rentals are available, and swimming is fun because the high salt content of the water makes floating effortless.

Large Tiburon Island in Kino Bay is the homeland of the Seri Indians and a focal point for these people. Basically nomadic at heart, the Indians never settled into an agricultural subsistence and spend much of their time pursuing the sea turtles that provide a small living for some of them. You'll see many of the Seri (their population is slowly dwindling) in and near towns selling trinkets, especially hardwood animal carvings and shell necklaces. Their gentle, pleasant smiles make it difficult to imagine that years ago they were believed to be cannibals and fierce warriors.

Guaymas—a watery utopia

Guaymas is really three communities; the city is divided from the two resort areas by a mountainous peninsula ending at jutting Cabo Haro. The original port and city face the Bay of Guaymas; 2 miles northwest is Miramar Beach on Bacochibampo Bay; and another 12 miles up the coast is New Guaymas on San Carlos Bay.

The city—a major seaport hub of the Mexican shrimp industry, and fishing capital of the world—sits amidst an encircling range of steep cliffs and mountains. Visitors enjoy the variety of stores, attractive church, and landlocked harbor. Native families bring their children to Las Playitas, a small public beach facing shallow water.

Guaymas is also the terminus of a popular car ferry route from Santa Rosalia in Baja California. The Norwegian-built car ferry, *Diaz Ordaz*, named for a former president of Mexico, is clean and offers excellent service. It is a good idea to have advance reservations; if you don't have them, you can arrange for your passage and find out the cost of shipping your vehicle at the terminal building (cost is based on vehicle length).

To reach Bacochibampo Bay, you'll drive through a long line of private beach homes. Where's the water? It is well hidden by the congested arrangement of hotels, trailer parks, and houses. But remember—all Mexican beaches are public and you'll soon find an access to the rocky shore. Two large resort hotels and one small beach concession offer rooms for rent.

San Carlos Bay, about 5 miles north of Guaymas and about 8 miles west of Highway 15, has become quite popular with American tourists. The multi-million-dollar complex is made up of a luxury hotel, several motels, a yacht club and marina, restaurants, tennis courts, a par 3 golf course, a large recreational vehicle village, a subdivision of seashore homes and cottages, and a small trailer park. There is also a convenient landing strip for private planes.

The waters are filled with an abundant and bewildering variety of game fish. Summer offers the most spectacular fishing, though the weather after May is sometimes oppressively hot. The big runs of marlin and sailfish come in July and August, but game fishing will satisfy the soul of the average angler during fall and winter months. The most exciting (and most crowded) time is during the annual International Deep Sea Fishing Rodeo in July, which marks the peak of the sport-fishing season.

The best way to learn the techniques of game fishing is to charter a boat with a knowledgeable skipper who has been fishing the waters for years and knows where to find the type of fish you're after, as well as the best way to angle for them.

Cabin cruisers complete with light and heavy fishing tackle, bait, ice, ship-to-shore radio, and English-speaking crews may be chartered by the hour or by the day. Rental skiffs and outboard motors are also available; if you wish to take your own boat, it can be launched at Miramar Beach. For big game fishing, though, the larger inboard cruisers are best. Make reservations to charter a boat, especially during the tournament season.

Desert headlands and calm estuaries attract shore fishermen. The most common fish are totuava (up to 100 pounds), corvina, sierra mackerel, roosterfish, and a variety of rockfish. For surf fishing, tackle should be brought from home because not many supplies are available in the stores of Guaymas.

Conchologists enjoy the abundance and variety of shellfish. You can use diving masks to look for them or follow their tracks in the mud at low tide.

The transparent, blue waters of Guaymas are made-to-order for those who enjoy skin diving and snorkeling—very few hazards exist, water temperature and underwater visibility are nearly ideal, and lobsters and turtles are plentiful. Lobsters can be caught most easily on nights when there is no moon or wind because they hide in daylight but feed in shallow water at night.

Besides fishing, Guaymas offers a good spot in which to relax and soak up the sun. If you want to combine exercise with your siestas, try the tennis courts. Or, the swimming, good riding horses, and shopping should keep you occupied.

If you're the self-sufficient soul who likes to do things in an independent way, you'll find ample opportunity and an abundance of free advice in the Guaymas area. Plenty of elbow room along the coastline enables campers to enjoy freedom and solitude, though you'll have to carry your own water.

An annual 4-day carnival begins the end of the third week in February. You'll see parades, aerial acrobats, fireworks, and cock fights. The town is crowded then, so be sure you have reservations.

From Guaymas to Mazatlan

South from Guaymas, Highway 15 threads its way through expansive, scrublike desert with the foothills of the Sierra Madre Occidental always visible to the east. The coastline of the Sea of Cortez is barely discernible on the horizon to the west.

This is Mexico's great agricultural frontier. Here vast acreages of tomatoes, wheat, melons, and other products interrupt the monotony of the wide Sonora and Sinaloa deserts. Cultivation is mechanized, and farming goes on year-round on a large, commercial scale. In the cities you'll see tractor and farm equipment salesrooms full of shiny new machines in quantities larger than what you'd find in the United States.

Many of the cities you pass have come to life in the last 20 years, some of them mushrooming up to surround old adobe settlements.

The highway is generally good, though the pavement has deteriorated in some sections and you'll encounter occasional detours around road-widening and improvement projects. Principal cities along this coastal route are Ciudad Obregon, Navojoa, Alamos (a short side trip from Highway 15), Los Mochis, Culiacan, and Mazatlan.

An agricultural boom town: Ciudad Obregon

Ciudad Obregon is edged by cotton gins, mills, and granaries. Planned before the boom began, Obregon reflects the disorder and incongruities typical of rapid city growth. Yet its streets are well lighted, and some are creatively landscaped. In the spirit of modern urban planning, Obregon's power lines are underground. An impressive church and a brewery highlight sightseeing in town. The Alvaro Obregon Dam, 35 miles north of town, represents the first step in a huge federal irrigation program for this area. Alvaro Obregon, the Sonoran farmer for whom the town was named, was a leader in the Revolution of 1910 and later president of Mexico.

Hunters come to this region (especially from October through February) to shoot the wild ducks, dove, and quail which flock together over the rice fields near town at sunset. Deer, wild turkeys, bears, and wild pigs live in the mountains within 50 miles of Obregon. Arrangements for hunting trips may be made at motels.

Navojoa's old town

An old town dating back to 1614, Navojoa was devastated by a flood in 1914, and subsequently relocated on higher ground. It is a crossroad point for departures to nearby Alamos, to the Mayo Indian village of Yavaros, to isolated Huatabampito Beach, or to other west coast cities down the highway.

Alamos—Mexico's jumping bean capital

If you're looking for a lively little town off the beaten path, don't go to Alamos—the only guaranteed action there is that of the jumping bean. Alamos is known as the major producer of jumping beans—not really beans at all, but little three-sectioned nuts with a tiny worm in each section. It is the movement of the worm that makes this so-called "bean" jump. There's a man in Alamos known as the "Jumping Bean King" because he buys all the beans from the natives who gather them, and then ships them in drums to the U.S. and all over the world. The beans are gathered in mid-summer and must be sold before late September when the worm burrows his way out of the shell, curls up, and dies, unable to exist in his new habitat.

The colonial ambience of Alamos, a fascinating town 34 miles east of Navojoa, pervades all aspects of the town's architecture and even influences the local inhabitants and their activities. Alamos has been declared a colonial monument by the state government, and a conscious effort has been made by its residents to maintain the image the town once had when it was a silver mining center in the late 1700s. Though some of the buildings of Alamos are little more than a century old, they blend to form a collage of colonial antiquity.

Founded in 1540 as a camp for one of Coronado's expeditions, Alamos later became the capital of both Sonora and of what is now the neighboring state of Sinaloa. In the 18th century, Alamos and its suburbs were the world's richest sources of silver.

Moorish arches, delicately fashioned iron grille work, and *portales* (covered walks) are indispensable elements in the Spanish personality of Alamos. Don't miss the graceful fountains, the bright,

A corking good *fishing port,*
Guaymas nestles along bay
some 400 miles north of
Mazatlan.

Arched arcades *fronting*
Alamos plaza offer cool
retreat against noontime sun.

splashy gardens, and the elegant mansions once occupied by silver barons. Art galleries, cantinas, courtyards, leather shops, and the Plaza Mayor, are some of the unique highlights of this treasure out of Mexico's mining past.

To get to Alamos you can drive, fly by private plane, or take a bus. Some excellent inns, motels, and trailer parks are available.

Places to explore near Alamos

Once you've explored the town of Alamos you may want to look at the surrounding country—the tropical forest on nearby Alamos Mountain, the foothill oasis of the great Sierra Madre to the east, old mines and silver smelters, scattered ruins, and the bays and beaches along the coast.

La Ubalama. This cluster of thatched huts is known as a pottery village. It is an easy, leisurely drive from Alamos. Here you'll see women making clay ollas and bowls.

Aduana. This was the great smelting works where Alamos silver was cast into ingots. Today, not more than a dozen families remain in the countryside village. The tall cactus growing from the wall of the church has a special significance. According to legend, the cactus was on the site before the church was built, and an image of the Virgin that appeared on top of the plant pointed out a rich

Train takes high bridge, burros take low bridge in different-paced travel.

silver lode. Every year on November 20 a religious festival attracts thousands of Mayo Indians to Aduana.

Cuchujachi River. Deep pools in this river are hemmed in by bedrock banks, making it a good place for a swim. The 7½-mile road is narrow, rocky, and rough, but passable for the ordinary passenger car. You might see flocks of parrots overhead, ducks in the water, and white-tailed deer in the brush. Great *sabino* trees grow along the watercourse.

Mocuzari Dam. This dam has backed up water and covered the tropical oasis of Aguas Calientes where hot springs once bubbled out of the rocks. Bass fishing is excellent, and you can park a recreational vehicle right on the shore of the reservoir. A visit to this area makes a worthwhile trip if you're interested in Sonora's new agricultural boom.

Mocoyahui and San Alberto Tungsten Mine. For the rough, 30-mile drive to the ruins of Mocoyahui Mission, you'll need a guide from Alamos. Along the way through upland farm country you'll pass burro trains bringing firewood, sesame seed, and oranges to Alamos. You'll see kapok trees laden with masses of silky fibers hanging from open pods.

The bells of the old mission (built about 1728) are supposedly in the possession of Mayo Indians who bring them out for special occasions. The trip from Alamos to the ruins takes about 3 hours. Four miles beyond Mocoyahui is the San Alberto Tungsten Mine, named after its discoverer, Alberto E. Maas, a native of Alamos.

Take off from Los Mochis or Topolobampo

Intriguingly enough, Los Mochis was founded by an American—Benjamin Johnston—who came from Virginia to build a sugar refinery and stayed to lay out a townsite that had the wide streets and square blocks of most American cities. Mr. Johnston also built a magnificent mansion with an inside swimming pool, an elevator, a huge banquet kitchen, and elegant formal gardens.

After Mr. Johnston died in Hong Kong in 1938, the family moved back to the United States; the estate house was abandoned and later torn down, but the gardens are still well worth a visit.

Sugar cane is one of the most important crops in this area, and the Los Mochis sugar mill is the largest on Mexico's west coast. To go through it, drop in at the mill office on the northwest edge of town.

From Los Mochis you can take a rail trip through some of the most spectacular mountain and can-

Alamos ruins *lend Grecian touch to Mexican countryside.*

yon country in the world (see page 28).

Topolobampo, a deep water port on the Sea of Cortez, makes an interesting side trip from Los Mochis. A boat is helpful for touring the surfeit of coves, estuaries, beaches, and islands. The shrimp packing plant welcomes visitors. Sportfishing is excellent if you can go out with one of the local commercial fishermen. Topolobampo is also the eastern terminus for a passenger and auto ferry from La Paz, across the gulf.

Culiacan—Sinaloa's state capital

Culiacan sits in the center of an immense, flat, unbroken, fertile plain that reaches toward the Sea of Cortez. Here the quiet colonial sections of town contrast with modern tractor showrooms and new downtown shops. The town is a blend of desert and tropical elements. Though the surrounding uncultivated land is semiarid, the river banks are green and lush.

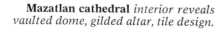
Rugs *create splashes of riotous color along Mazatlan waterfront.*

Mazatlan cathedral *interior reveals vaulted dome, gilded altar, tile design.*

The Golden Coast—
Mazatlan to Manzanillo

When you reach Mazatlan you've crossed the Tropic of Cancer, and you expect glistening sands, leaning palms, and beach resorts. You won't be disappointed.

Resort towns are varied: Fishing is a fetish in Mazatlan; people-watching is the most popular sport in Puerto Vallarta. At Playa Blanca Club Mediterranee the language is French; some off-the-road village residents communicate largely with smiles and sign language.

Paved Highway 200 starts just north of Puerto Vallarta and ends just south of Manzanillo, opening miles of primitive beaches for camping.

Marlin and Mardi Gras in Mazatlan

Long ago Mazatlan overgrew the small peninsula on which it was originally founded and spread northward along a series of crescent-shaped beaches that extend for miles. The main shopping centers, some of the best restaurants, and the older hotels are located in the downtown area. New subdivisions and hotel developments are strung out along the beaches running north.

Connecting it all is the boulevard along the sea wall (malecon) which starts at Olas Altas Boulevard and runs for several miles with several changes of names. In other Mexican cities the evening promenade takes place in the park or plaza; in Mazatlan, it is along the malecon.

Life in Mazatlan is leisurely. Quaint, two-wheel, horse-drawn carts called *aranas* can be hired for sightseeing trips. A three-wheel, three-passenger *pulmonia* (because you can catch pneumonia riding in one) is an open-air taxi similar to a fast golf cart. Benches in the several quiet, shady plazas invite you to sit and surrender yourself to the Mexican sense of manana. Palms, bananas, papayas, mangoes, and flowers give the town a tropical aura.

Shopping is centered around the southern beach, Olas Altas, the public market, and the northern hotel area. At the city market (Mercado Municipal) visit seemingly endless fruit and vegetable stalls and appetizing displays of pineapples, mangoes, bananas, and other tropical delights. Buy curios, try on huaraches, toss a lacy shawl over a shoulder, and bargain to your heart's content.

To watch artisans at work carving, braiding, weaving, or molding, visit the Mazatlan Arts & Crafts Center in northern Mazatlan. The Center is crammed with items from all over Mexico and prices are reasonable. Bring along the children; there's a free zoo with alligators, peacocks, and other native animals behind the Center.

Landmarks include the usual town plaza with old-fashioned bandstand, a yellow-towered cathedral, and some grandiose hills. Atop one of the hills is the El Faro Lighthouse, a rewarding climb for the rugged; underneath, a blue grotto entices visitors in small boats. An ancient observatory on another hill welcomes guests. Farther north, Icebox Hill's tunnels were once repositories for blocks of ice brought by boat from San Francisco and delivered by mule carts to stores and homes.

For a few pesos, daredevil divers leap from the 40-foot El Mirador view tower on the malecon. To the north, gigantic figures of fishermen form a monument to the force of the sea.

To the south is the colorful harbor with docks for fishing vessels, cruise ships, freighters and tankers, the daily ferry to La Paz, and finally, the yacht and sport-fishing anchorage.

Big game fishing developed Mazatlan. Not only do marlin and sailfish swarm in the waters, but the pursuit of these fish is expert and businesslike. Fleets of sleek cruisers cluster at neighboring piers at the docks. Normally as many as four persons fish from a boat fully manned and equipped with everything needed for "billfishing" except muscle. All you need to carry aboard is your camera and a box lunch from your hotel. Make fishing reservations well in advance for March and April.

Local fishermen who catch their fish from dugout canoes hold a market on the beach at the southern end of Plaza Norte.

Other outdoor activities center around the north end of the malecon and the district of on-the-beach hotels (some of them new), condominiums, and recreational vehicle facilities. This is where parachuting, water-skiing, swimming, and sunning take place. Here you can rent bilingual horses who take commands in both Spanish and English to ride on the beach or along a secluded trail.

You can take a boat cruise around the bay, travel through a jungle by inland waterways, or visit an island offshore. Isla de Piedra (Stone Island), only a 10-minute boat trip from downtown Mazatlan, offers one of the most beautiful beaches on the entire west coast of Mexico. You can find someone at Mazatlan's downtown dock area ready to take you across to the island at almost any time of day. (Reach a firm understanding about the cost of a round-trip voyage before you leave the dock, or you may find that the price of the return trip has suffered a sudden inflation.) You won't need a guide on the island; just follow the one and only road past the stick-and-mud houses of the islanders, through tall groves of coconut palms, and over to the beach. Even at a deliberate, sightsee-as-you-go tempo, the walk across the island takes less than half an hour.

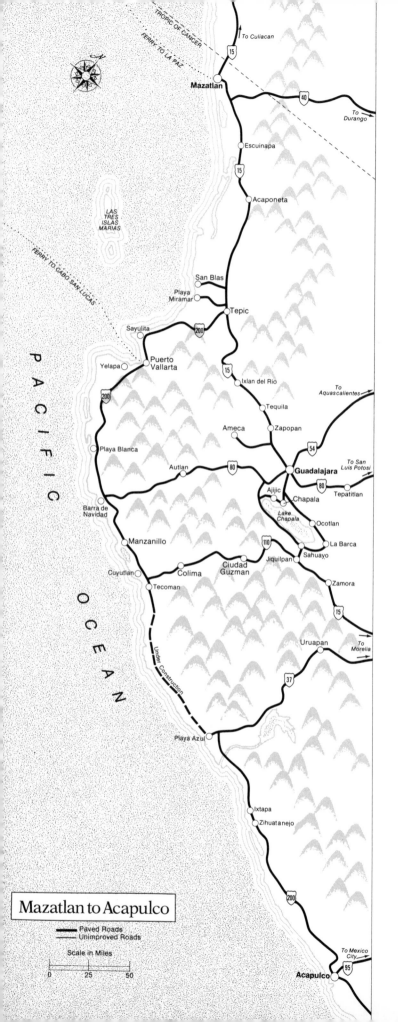

At the beach a thatched-roof pavilion features picnic tables, a juke box, and a refreshment stand. On weekends families from Mazatlan frequently bring picnic lunches over to the island beach, spreading their holiday meal across a rough table in the pavilion. Often jovial, noisy affairs, these gatherings are characterized by much singing and dancing. Beyond the pavilion is the fine white sand of a gently curving beach, uncluttered except for an abundance of large sand dollars.

Tennis and golf are available year-round; check with your hotel for locations and other details. Bullfights usually take place from January to April, but events are also scheduled during the rest of the year. The bullring is right downtown.

Check with your hotel or the excellent Department of Tourism for formal tours to outlying areas. You might want to arrange a private tour with an English-speaking guide. You'll get a look at green and forested back country valleys and mountains on a daylong excursion to Copala, a picturesque former silver mining village. Along the way you might stop at tidy little Concordia to see furniture makers and other craftsmen at work, and to view the richly sculptured small church.

Accommodations range from huge resort hotels to motels and recreational vehicle facilities. Reservations are a must during the Mardi Gras celebrations and are suggested for the winter season.

Festivals range from the weekly Friday Fandango (a street party on Olas Altas sponsored by local merchants) to the Annual International Mardi Gras celebrated during the 5 days before Ash Wednesday. During Mardi Gras you'll see parades, official receptions, colorful floats, dances with exuberant mariachis, and fireworks. Forget sleeping and be prepared for a steep hike in prices.

South of Mazatlan

As the coastal route winds southward the vegetation becomes more varied and lush, and is characterized by ebony, rosewood, lignum-vitae, mahogany, and brazilwood. Palm trees resemble over-decorated Christmas trees because of the yellow, purple, and pink-flowered tropical vines that climb through them.

When the coastal lagoons come close to the highway south of Mazatlan, you'll see bright pink flamingos resolutely standing there in the mud flats. Bananas, papayas, pineapples, mangoes, and citrus fruits grow in jungle clearings. Farms become smaller, and the bigger sophisticated tractors of the north are replaced by simple, uncomplicated farm equipment. Many farmers still plow their fields with teams of oxen.

About 17 miles south of Mazatlan, Highway 40 branches inland across the mountains to Durango, and Highway 15 swings away from the coast. Your only access to beaches from here south is on side roads that lead off to the west. One of the best of these roads leaves the highway about 22 miles north of Tepic and winds down through a luxuriant tropical forest to the old seaport of San Blas.

Sleepy San Blas is a peaceful, quiet, picturesque destination for travelers who shun the luxuries of more tourist-oriented towns.

Tropical jungles and a variety of wildlife surround the village. The beautiful beaches near Matanchen Bay are ideal for sunning and beachcombing; offshore islands abound with colorful tropical birds and offer rewarding finds for shell collectors. Near the fishing area in San Blas you can charter a boat or take an excursion to several remote beaches accessible only by water.

You can drive to San Blas in about half an hour on a good 22-mile, paved road (Highway 54) past thatched huts, small streams, and dense jungle unlike anything else you'll see on the coastal route. Small streams almost always flow near the roadside, and you'll probably see people bathing and doing their laundry along the banks. Marshy flats replace coquito palms and dark estuaries wind through the low vegetation, their banks solidly lined with mangroves too thick to walk through. Exposed roots are encrusted with oysters.

Today, life in San Blas drifts slowly and languorously along. A few small craft, dress, and jewelry shops are scattered among the adobe-and-wattle huts clustered around the church and the rose-scented central plaza. Neat cobblestone streets lined with coconut palms lend a South Seas atmosphere to the area.

During colonial days San Blas was a bustling port; now the impressive customs house near the end of the main street remains as a decaying relic of a bygone era. On the crest of a small hill overlooking the newer section of town is old San Blas, built during the reign of the Spaniards. Hike or drive up here for a look at the crumbling remains of the fort, church, and other small buildings overgrown with vegetation. (Mosquitoes are often numerous here so don't plan a long stay.) You may see some iguanas—scaly creatures sometimes over 2 feet long—inhabiting the ruins.

At the main beach, a wide sandy strip about a mile from the center of town, swimming is good year-round. Along the beach you'll find bathhouses and hotels, and stands selling tantalizing sweets. Accommodations are adequate but a bit below standards usually demanded by American tourists.

A popular excursion is a jungle boat trip up La Tobara tributary. Beginning at the bridge over the San Cristobal River and passing through mangrove swamps and crystal clear jungle pools, the journey takes about 2½ hours and stops at coffee and banana plantations, giving visitors a chance to see

Tequila-the spirit of Mexico

The process of making tequila can encompass a far greater length of time than most imbibers of the Mexican national drink realize. The magic liquid used in producing this renowned drink comes from the *agave tequilana* plant. Also known as the maguey plant, it is better known in the United States by its relatives such as the century plant.

How do you make tequila? It involves several time-honored procedures. First, the spiky leaves of the maguey plant are cut off, revealing only the heart that resembles a huge pineapple. The maguey hearts (some weighing up to 150 pounds) are harvested, put into trucks, and taken to the factory where they are cut up and loaded into giant steam ovens. Inside these ovens the *pinas* (pineapples) are roasted until they reach a consistency enabling them to be shredded easily. The hearts are removed from the ovens, shredded, and pressed in order to extract the juice.

The juice is then poured into large vats where sugars are added and fermentation occurs. After 4 days the distillation process begins; two distillations are needed before the tequila is ready for consumption. Thus, tequila can be ready to market within a week after harvest. For a fine, full-bodied tequila of good quality, though, up to 7 years of aging in wooden casks are required before it reaches a mellow golden color and becomes as velvety as cognac or a fine liquor. The duration of aging time determines the grade of tequila—and its price.

The town of Tequila, about 35 miles northwest of Guadalajara, is the center of the tequila industry and the best place to see Mexico's national drink in the making.

Tequila was founded in 1530 by a Spanish captain, Cristobal de Onate. In 1873 Don Cenobio Sauza founded the tequila industry, using mules to drag the stones that crushed the agave hearts. Today the Sauza family and several other large growers are producing many millions of liters a year for sale to more than 40 countries.

Tours are available if you wish to see the various steps involved in the tequila process. To tour the Sauza distillery, make reservations at the Sauza bottling plant at 3273 Avenida Vallarta in Guadalajara. Even if you're in Tequila without advance reservations, you can often join morning tours of the distillery (Calle Nunez No. 80). The Sauza family estate, located across from the distillery, is also open to visitors.

orchids and other tropical vegetation. Colorful birds such as egrets, herons, and ibises abound, and you might see an iguana or coatimundi.

The best time to go to San Blas is between November and May. Strong winds usually blow across the beach in the afternoon. Summers are hot and humid, though it is sometimes cool enough for a blanket at night. One warning: Take some insect repellent. Though insect control is improving, small gnats called *jejenes* often swarm around the estuaries and beaches until about 9 A.M. and again in late afternoon.

Tepic, an old colonial city with a solid, prosperous look, is the capital of the small state of Nayarit. The main streets are wide and other streets are being widened by cutting away old buildings and adding modern facades that contrast sharply with the old walled cemetery and the arcaded buildings around the plaza. Promenades and concerts in the attractive city park, and soccer games in the stadium at the edge of town provide entertainment for visiting spectators. Points of interest include the cathedral on the main plaza, which was built in 1750 and has two perfect Gothic-type towers, and the Church de la Cruz, once part of the Franciscan Convent de la Cruz founded in 1744. Pay a visit to the state museum, rich in treasures of the past.

The town, situated 3,186 feet above sea level at the base of an extinct volcano, is noticeably cooler than the nearby coast. The broad valley south of Tepic produces sugar cane, corn, and tobacco. A large cigarette factory in town employs many inhabitants. Small banana and papaya groves surround some local native settlements.

Tepic has several adequate accommodations downtown and on the highway near Parque Loma.

New beach developments include Rincon de Guayabitos (probably the most beautiful beach in Mexico), Nuevo Vallarta (a planned resort community), and Bucerias (northern suburb of Puerto Vallarta).

Puerto Vallarta—still unspoiled

The cobblestone streets are as rough, uneven, and jolting as ever; the perilous descents from hillside casas, casitas, and condos are still rugged and scary; and the shops, restaurants, and resorts keep on growing. By some strange grace, though, Puerto Vallarta still retains the charm and simplicity that has made it world famous.

Described in superlatives by most visitors, Puerto Vallarta's environs look more tropical and tidier than those of Mazatlan or Acapulco. Though you'll glimpse much of the native life, the presence of the American tourist is sometimes more obvious because the town is small.

Donkey carts still rattle along the streets among the taxis, autos, and jeeps. Flaming bougainvillea and blue jacaranda hug stucco walls; sweet jasmine perfumes the night. So, if no longer an idyllic retreat, "PV" is certainly one of Mexico's fun spots and a highly picturesque town in a perfect away-from-it-all setting.

The town crowds between the foot of the mountains and beautiful Banderas Bay. To become acquainted, locate the Cuale River, the *zocalo* (plaza), the malecon, and the Church of Guadalupe. The river (which runs in an east-west direction) serves as a natural dividing line within the city, separating the business sections from the south beach. The only bridge across the Cuale provides a scene of constant bedlam rivaling the confusion on any large city's freeway. One of the town's two major shopping districts starts north of the bridge; the other is south on Lazaro Cardenas and parallel streets. Farther up the river loom steep cliffs where luxurious homes cling precariously. One ravine is dubbed "Gringo Gulch" because of the number of Americans maintaining homes there.

In town you'll find a number of deluxe hotels or condominiums for rent. Excellent restaurants often feature both Mexican and American foods. Seafood, especially lobster, is a specialty.

Beaches—lovely, wide, and uncluttered—to the north and south of town are ideal for sunbathing, swimming, water-skiing, hiking, tennis, and horseback riding. Although a few beaches run beside the malecon, swimming is not too good. Playa del Sol, south of the Cuale, has the action; vendors with goods and fish-on-a-stick, thatched-roof snack and cocktail bars, wandering mariachis, and boat and surfboard rentals. Taxis and buses run to and fro.

To the north, an excellent marina adjoins Playa del Oro. It has a number of slips for yachts and for fishing and excursion boats, a concrete dock (where cruise passengers land), a bathhouse, and a terminal building for the Cabo San Lucas ferry.

Tours take you to Mismaloya Beach, a jungle hideaway discovered by Hollywood several years ago and converted into the setting for *Night of the Iguana.* Foliage has obscured most but not all traces of "el set." The view is worth your time, though the beach may be cluttered.

For a novel, all-day excursion that includes swimming, sunning, hiking, lunching, and shopping, take a boat trip to the sequestered fishing village of Yelapa. If you want to linger, make reservations in advance; accommodations are modest and the choice is limited. Living is slow-paced and the people are friendly and hospitable. A handful of Europeans and Americans have made Yelapa their retreat from the bustling modern world.

After lunch you can climb into a hammock under

Extemporaneous oven *roasts fish-on-a-stick to supply Puerto Vallarta beach vendors.*

Filigree-crowned *church tower stands sentinel over passing boats at Puerto Vallarta's popular waterfront.*

a palm umbrella, hike to a nearby waterfall, wade in a warm lagoon, or shop at the small boutique displaying embroidered dresses, handloomed articles, and handprinted cloth.

Highway 200—sunshine route to Barra de Navidad

With the completion of the road between Puerto Vallarta and Barra de Navidad, auto visitors can "resort hop." The 140-mile stretch of diverse coast (a 4-hour drive) is scenic enough to merit a side trip from Puerto Vallarta or Manzanillo, the area's two major destinations. You'll pass through mountain pine and oak forests, rugged high desert, thorn forests, and savannas. Jungles teem with colorful birdlife. Inviting detours can easily prolong your trip.

The highway crosses four major rivers flowing from the Sierra Madre Occidental to the Pacific that are life lines for farming villages and cattle ranches. Bays south of Rio San Nicolas are slated for development. The coast north toward Puerto Vallarta—important breeding grounds for sea turtles—will be kept in its natural state.

Except for the Club Mediterranee at Playa Blanca, resorts are so new that your travel agent may not know about them. But you should have

Look familiar? *Ruins of* Night of the Iguana *set rise above bay at beguiling Mismaloya.*

little problem getting a room on arrival at the handsome new Tenacatita and Careyitos hotels, or at more modestly maintained hotels at El Tecuan, and Cuastecomate. Their prices range from $8 to $60 a night, double occupancy. In addition, several villages offer primitive bungalows or *palapas* (palm-covered shelters) for a few dollars a night. Camping is permitted along most beaches; the only developed campgrounds are about 8 miles south of Rio San Nicolas.

Manzanillo—regal refuge for the rich

Squeezed onto a slender spine of land that separates two bays, Manzanillo is fast becoming the new resort haven for the world's jet setters. This long-ignored coastal town (now one of Mexico's most important ports for trade with the Orient) has turned into a holiday destination for graduates of Acapulco, the Costa del Sol, and the Greek islands.

The entrepreneur-millionaire Antenor Patino is responsible for the resort complex called Las Hadas which includes a marina, several tennis courts, golf course, swimming pools, boutiques and other shops, in addition to the luxury hotel. Cinemas, restaurants, a few small nightclubs and bistros, villas, and the usual shops make up the town. The central hotel complex consists of dazzling white buildings that reflect a Mediter-

Moorish style *marks Las Hadas, gleaming hotel complex on bay near Manzanillo.*

Elevated *Acapulco restaurant provides panoramic view of water activity, high rises, boat (right) beached by storm.*

Parachute, *pulled by power boat, is readied for beach liftoff.*

Shutterbugs and boaters *focus on diver ready to leap from La Quebrada cliffs to ocean below.*

ranean air combined with Moorish overtones.

Manzanillo has everything going for it—vast open beaches, great swimming, excellent fishing (dolphin, marlin, sailfish), and a comfortable climate.

The evolution of Manzanillo to this dreamed-of-resort-for-all is taking its toll on the sleepy, slow pace and low prices of bygone days. But if you're looking for an enjoyable atmosphere, Manzanillo won't disappoint you. The city's paved central streets are narrow, crowded, and often noisy. The waterfront, significantly, is clean and spacious—a place where families stroll at sunset when remnants of afternoon thunderclouds over the distant Sierra Madre cast their reflections on the blue bay. On the high point of land to the west, the tolling of a bronze bell announces the sighting of approaching ships. North and south of town, coconut and banana plantations edge the sea.

The jungle reaches storybook proportions near Manzanillo more than anywhere else on the tropical coast of Mexico. Here it is tall, shadowy, and mysterious, scented and color-splashed with myriad-hued flowers.

Chief attractions are beaches of yellow sand streaked with black on sheltered Santiago Bay and at Las Hadas Cove. Many Mexicans vacation at Manzanillo and at Santiago Beach (also becoming popular with Americans).

Nearby destinations north of Manzanillo include the beach resort of Melaque and the quaint fishing village of Barra de Navidad, both about 38 miles out of Manzanillo. Hardly more than 3 miles separate these neighboring towns but the beaches are quite different. Barra de Navidad, with one of the cleanest beaches along the coast, has deep waters and vigorous waves that attract surfers and waterskiers. Melaque fronts on the more protected bay with calm tranquil water. You'll find some accommodations in both towns. Buy shrimp and fish from seaside stands.

At Cuyutlan, south of Manzanillo, watch for the famous "green roller," an ocean phenomenon which occurs in April or May. At certain times during these months the ocean gathers itself into a huge, hurtling force and rushes toward the beach with a thundering roar. An awesome sight, the "green roller" reaches heights up to 30 feet. Cuyutlan is suggested for daytime sojourns, not for overnight.

Colima, capital of one of Mexico's smallest states, is easily reached by following Highway 110 inland from Manzanillo. A balmy metropolis dating back to 1523, Colima lies at the foot of Mexico's second highest active volcano that erupted last in 1941. Antique car buffs will enjoy the museum 6 blocks south of the city's plaza. For a few pesos you can view 350 beautifully restored cars ranging from 1912 to 1941 models.

Southern Coast contrasts: Acapulco, Zihuatanejo, and Ixtapa

Eventually Highway 200 will link all of the western and southern beaches of Mexico. At the present time, however, Manzanillo is the southernmost major beach reached by this route. To get to Acapulco by road you have to swing in to Toluca or Mexico City and take Highway 95 back to the coast. Jetting to Acapulco is easy from the U.S.; from Mexico City there is a shuttle service with a dozen flights daily. You can also get air service to or from Guadalajara, Puerto Vallarta, and other southern Mexico cities.

Getting to Zihuatanejo (Ixtapa) is not quite so convenient. Daily flights arrive from Mexico City and bus service is available from Acapulco. You can rent a car in Acapulco for the 4½-hour drive through lush, verdant countryside. You'll still see women washing clothes and kids, as well as small pueblos and wayside cemeteries. But go soon; this is an area destined for super-resort status.

Acapulco—still exotic, still the most popular

Acapulco is the big city of coastal resorts with the most hotels—nearly 200—and the most visitors. Its visitor attractions are divided between those for foreigners and those for the many Mexicans who swell the winter population. In spite of the heavy tourist traffic and the wealth of diversions that have been introduced for tourists, the exotic, natural beauty of the area remains.

Winter is probably the best season to visit, but the resort is popular all year (most hotels lower their rates during the off season from May through November). The weather never gets very cold, and the water temperature is always perfect. Vegetation is lush, fragrant, and tropical. Shoppers beware, though—prices are generally higher here than in any other Mexican city (especially from Christmas to Easter).

The town is set at the base of mountains that all but encircle a partially landlocked blue bay. When approaching town along the highway you descend to beach level and hotel row, a long line that reaches in toward the center of town. You'll discover newer resorts (and more expensive ones) on Revocaldera Beach and near lovely Puerto Marquez Bay. The great high-rise structures are the second generation of hotels, air-conditioned and equipped with swimming pools. Across the boulevard—Costera Miguel Aleman—cluster shops, restaurants, and night spots, as well as supermarkets and American quick-food franchise shops.

The boulevard parallels the beach for awhile. At the last center of commerce before the street turns south, a broad, divided boulevard heads inland to where the vast public market complex is located.

The market is fun, whether you're shopping for picnic ingredients or just looking at what may be the most fascinating place in town. Here you'll find unfamiliar groceries, fresh breads, bulk seasonings, and produce both familiar and strange. Flower vendors brighten the courts between pavilions, and truckloads of bananas and other products crowd the streets.

Where the boulevard turns west again you'll see Acapulco's one real antiquity—the 18th century Spanish Fort San Diego—looming on the slope above. This is the heart of town. Enjoy the zocalo, cathedral, and malecon.

Toward the sea is the waterfront park and its seawall extension. Vendors sell curios and crafts in the park's intricate cluster of small stalls. The sport-fishing boats line up at the seawall; excursion boats and cruise ships anchor in the bay.

Beyond the malecon, the waterfront boulevard is less picturesque. You approach the hilly peninsula that shelters the harbor; on its slopes were built the first big hotels and costly houses. Across the peninsula is La Quebrada, site of an observation point over the rocky cliffs of the seaward side of town, where the celebrated high divers leap from a cliff into the water 137 feet below. You get a good view from La Perla lounge in the El Mirador Hotel.

Caletilla and Caleta (original morning beaches) on the low side of the peninsula are the center of water-oriented activity, with a small harbor for sport-fishing boats, glass-bottom boats, and launches for visitors to La Roqueta Island to enjoy the beach, have lunch, or indulge the beer-drinking burros. Parachute rides are popular: the parachute, pulled by boat, lifts you from the beach and takes you for a brief breathtaking bird's-eye tour of the beach.

Several boat excursions—sightseeing trips by day or partying trips by night—explore the harbor or go out to sea and around the peninsula to the dramatic coast of La Quebrada.

Lagoons to the north and south of the mountains enclose the town. Both have boats for fishing and exploring; both are destinations of hunting and sightseeing excursions.

A sports roundup includes miles of public beaches beside a sparkling bay and ocean. Under Mexican law all beach property is public. All beaches and beach hotels offer complete water sport facilities including power and sail boats, pedal boats, surf and paddle boards, and skiing. You'll also find dining and drinking service, cabanas, thatched lounging huts, beach chairs, umbrellas, and beach pads. Sunworshippers find the best beaches from Condesa east to Icacos.

There are four championship 18-hole golf courses. Tennis courts and clubs, including some indoor, air-conditioned courts, spring up like mushrooms.

Angling, particularly for sailfish, is exceptionally good. You can watch greyhound and horse racing at a track near Las Brisas.

The shopping is extensive. There's no need to worry about having the right clothes. You'll find everything you need in town shops or hotel boutiques, though in Acapulco everyone dresses very informally. If you like handcrafts, try Mexican Arts and Crafts on Costera Miguel Aleman. Bargaining is expected with street and beach vendors for baskets, sarapes, beach hats, and junk jewelry.

Night life begins as the day expires in typical tropical fashion. Sounds explode from hotels, nightclubs, and outdoor strolling musicians. Discotheques are popular, entertainers exotic, and a cover charge is usually required. At El Paraiso, on the beach, you can swizzle a drink, eat a meal, or dance the afternoon away.

Zihuatanejo—economical and easy-going

A different experience awaits the visitor arriving in Zihuatanejo from Acapulco. Only 125 miles up the coast, it is a million miles removed from Acapulco's crowded beaches and cosmopolitan air. Nestling at the base of Mexico's Sierra Madre del Sur, the town's protected 2-mile-wide bay is surrounded by low, brush-covered hillsides and coconut plantations. Tame parrots, burros, and laughing children roam dusty streets lined with shops selling mangoes, papayas, corn, and fish. As in other tropical places of its size, the town allows pigs, dogs, and stately Brahman cattle to wander freely among the palm-thatched huts and adobe business houses and out along the water's edge. A trim white lighthouse on a jungle-clad crag far out in the white surge of the sea guards the bay. Outrigger dugout canoes are drawn up on the sand. Parakeets gather in the trees.

Buildings on the main street are small, old, and (in some cases) crumbling. The undemanding pace attracts as many Mexican tourists as Americans. The bay offers both water sports and a slow, warming respite, but sample it while you can because there's a government project underway at nearby Ixtapa aimed at making this a top-flight luxury resort area.

What to do. Playa Principal, the main beach, has rentals for water-skiing, scuba diving, and surfing; arrange rentals in advance through your hotel. You can rent a deep-sea boat with a guide and fish for tuna, roosterfish, and an occasional marlin. At tidepool-studded Isla Grande, a few miles north, cooks will prepare your catch or you can cook it yourself, native-style, on a mainland beach.

The clarity of the water, abundant variety of underwater life, and intricate beauty of its coral reefs make Zihuatanejo Bay a popular place with skin divers. Even if you've never tried the sport before, take along a snorkel and face mask and begin your underwater adventure by floating quietly over the coral reefs. If the appeal of the underwater world becomes irresistible, diving instruction is available. You can rent scuba gear.

From the beach, a few primitive roads invite you to take a short hike into the surrounding jungle with its flowering tropical trees and shrubs and great variety of birdlife.

Shopping is intriguing in the town's small stores. Typically, Saturday is market day. Don't hesitate to bargain.

Where to stay. Zihuatanejo's inexpensive hotels are near the main beach; more luxurious hotels cluster against the cliffs overlooking the lights and less crowded sands of Playa Ropa and Playa Moderas. Though most hotels are not cheap, they are still a bargain by resort standards.

How to get there. Planes from Mexico City service Zihuatanejo-Ixtapa, landing at a modern jetport. Potholes, slow-crossing chickens, and occasional washouts make the drive slow by car or bus up fully paved Highway 200 from Acapulco. Night travel is inadvisable. Air-conditioned buses from Acapulco are a major means of intervillage contact, so be prepared to share in family reunions or to make numerous unexpected stops.

Ixtapa—a new super resort

Fifteen miles north of Zihuatanejo lies Ixtapa where a computer-planned wonder resort is under construction among 5,263 acres of coconut palms, mangroves, colorful flowers, and foliage along 16 miles of beach that, up to now, were known only by tropical birds. Planned are two 18-hole golf courses, tennis courts, scuba diving, deep-sea and lagoon fishing, and an all-purpose marina. Luxurious hotels complete a resort very similar to Cancun on the Gulf of Mexico.

Guadalajara & the Colonial Circle

For many visitors, Guadalajara makes an attractive base from which to explore Mexico's colonial past. To the east is the heartland of the 1810 Revolution of Independence—Guanajuato, San Miguel de Allende, and Queretaro. To the south is Morelia, a living museum of Mexican history, and the enchanting towns of Uruapan and Patzcuaro. In between lies a profusion of colonial villages packed with historical monuments, buildings, and legends. Several of these towns have diligently tried to maintain the colonial ambience and historical authenticity that so often dissipate after years of renovation and new developments.

Guadalajara

Capital of the state of Jalisco, Guadalajara is Mexico's second largest city—and a favorite of many American tourists who find the unique blend of modern and traditional architecture, as well as the tree-shaded residential streets, temperate climate, and cosmopolitan atmosphere a contrast to most of Mexico.

If you have the time and want to explore a place where the best of Mexico is expressed, plan a long stay in Guadalajara. You're not likely to get bored with a place where horse-drawn cabs and caravans of laden burros share the right-of-way with the latest model limousines and sport cars; where street widening (needed to transform a country town into a brisk metropolis) was done only on one side of the street so that only half the ancient buildings had to be removed; where people who hardly gave a passing glance to the erection of an architecturally superior department store pay tireless tribute to the architecturally grotesque cathedral; where the siesta is a jealously cherished ritual that shuts down businesses for 2 hours every working day causing four daily commuter-traffic rushes.

Guadalajara's partial conversion to a sleek metropolis has been attained at some sacrifice of Mexican mellowness, and as you begin to feel at home there may be moments on Avenida 16 de Septiembre or Juarez when you'll have to remind yourself that you're a thousand miles below the border. But Guadalajara still has much that is "old" Mexico, and a very evident enthusiasm for new things has not displaced affection for the old.

Getting around

A slight handicap in learning your way around Guadalajara (and many other Mexican cities) is the division of the city into different sectors so that most street names change as the streets pass from one sector to another.

Guadalajara has four sectors—the boundaries are Avenida Morelos, Calzada Independencia, and Avenida Gigantes. Thus Avenida 16 de Septiembre suddenly becomes Avenida Alcalde when it crosses Avenida Morelos near the cathedral; Avenida Juarez becomes Avenida Javier Mina before it gets to the Mercado Libertad; and going the other way, Avenida Juarez becomes Avenida Vallarta where it passes the university.

Even if you're self-reliant and arrive in your own car, it is a good idea to hire a guide from the government tourist office located in an old convent on Avenida Juarez or through a travel agency for a preview tour of Guadalajara. If you go out for half a day or longer in the city or to visit nearby points of interest, you may want to choose a package itinerary with guide, car, meals, and hotels from the choices offered by a Guadalajara travel agency (or set it up in advance with a travel agent at home).

Taxicabs are plentiful; rates are fixed by a government ordinance.

You won't get much Guadalajaran lore out of the preoccupied driver of a *calandria* as you clip-clop around town, but you might enjoy the experience. These horse-drawn antiques complete with black-liveried drivers once were the private conveyances of well-to-do families. When some vehicles went into public service, their drivers put on yellow armbands to indicate the calandrias were for hire. The armbands must have reminded someone of a yellow-shouldered lark because the carriages have long been known as calandrias (larks or buntings).

For more extensive sightseeing you may wish to join one of the bus tours available in Guadalajara.

Guadalajara's *expansive Plaza de la Liberacion is one of Mexico's most hand-some plazas.*

Morning and afternoon tours last about 4 hours each (with time for shopping) and include the famous pottery suburb of Tlaquepaque in the northern part of the city, as well as the state Arts and Crafts Center (Casa de las Artesanias). The morning and afternoon tours have different itineraries, so you may wish to go on both.·

Don't miss...

From anywhere in the central part of Guadalajara you can walk to most of the important places of historic interest in a few minutes. The Plaza de los Laureles, with its underground parking garage, is a good place to start. Buy a large, detailed street map in a hotel gift shop before you begin.

The cathedral: Be sure to explore the interior, especially beautiful when the huge chandeliers are lighted. Built from 1571 to 1618, partially destroyed in 1818, and modernized in 1944, the cathedral reflects a potpourri of architectural styles and is recognized as the universal symbol of the city.

The churches: The Church of Santa Monica, intricately carved in the Churrigueresque style, was

Brooding beauty *of Orozco murals covers stone walls and ceilings of Hospicio Cabanas. Benches provide "lie-down" viewing.*

completed in about 1720. The churches of San Francisco and Aranzazu both face the shady Jardin de San Francisco—the Church of San Francisco has the most impressive exterior by far, but the Churrigueresque altar in Aranzazu is perhaps the masterpiece of its kind. The Hospicio Cabanas represents the best work of muralist Orozco, whose paintings decorate the chapel of this impressive orphanage, founded in 1829. To facilitate ceiling viewing, benches are available to lie on. Visit the orphanage's 23 flowery patios and see the display of dolls in various Mexican costumes (which are for sale).

The museums: The State Museum located near the central plaza contains art galleries and exhibits covering history, zoology, and archaeology. The original building was constructed in the 17th century as a Jesuit seminary; Casa de las Artesanias, on the northwest corner of Parque Agua Azul, displays crafts from Jalisco; Casa de la Cultura, in the State Library across the street from the park and the flower market, exhibits contemporary art including a great three-dimensional mural by Gabriel Flores on the ceiling of the auditorium dome. Orozco's Museum Workshop displays over 90 works by this well-known artist. Open daily except Monday, it is close to the arch on Avenida Vallarta.

The government buildings: At the Government Palace (Palacio de Gobierno) you're welcome to go in and look around the 17th century building and peruse several powerful murals by Orozco (located near the stairway) that depict historical episodes in the building's history. Above the second floor, a narrow stairway leads to the roof which offers a good view of Guadalajara. The Municipal Palace (Palacio Municipal) is in the colonial style to harmonize with its neighbors. This is the place you go to buy back your front license plate that is taken off your car by a policeman if you park illegally. You can lose an hour that way, but you can also see a truly distinguished mural by contemporary painter Gabriel Flores.

The parks and plazas: The Plaza de la Liberacion is a major result of the modernization of Guadalajara. Two blocks of old buildings were removed to create this long rectangular "square," now rich with fountains and bright flowering *tabachin* trees.

You'll hear the word *tapatio* mentioned frequently around town—it refers to any quality of Guadalajara. Very tapatio is the Plaza de los Mariachis, where mariachi bands gather in the narrow mall to serenade you as you sip sangria or tequila at a parasol-shaded outdoor table. Since they require a small fee for their musical services, check the price per song in advance.

Fountain jets, *colorful plantings enliven front entrance to gracious Degollado Theater.*

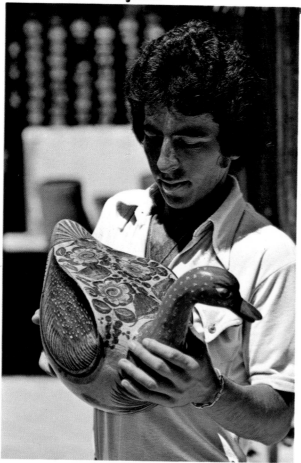

Hand-burnished *clay duck bears finely detailed decoration typical of Tonala.*

The Parque Agua Azul—only two blocks from the Marriott—is a great place to people-watch each Sunday afternoon when a free performance is presented in the outdoor theater. Children will enjoy the zoo and the rides, and the unique spectacle of the many colorful macaws that have complete freedom yet usually stay on their canopied perches suspended over the walks.

Another tree-shaded and fountain-cooled escape from the bustle of the city is Parque Revolucion on West Juarez. Here the Latin dating game, the *paseo*, takes place on Sunday evenings.

Sports and sporting events: Cockfights are legal and have their own arena. At the Santa Rita polo grounds games are played several times weekly; the best matches are at Sunday noon. Perhaps the most colorful and typically Mexican events are the charreadas, Mexican rodeos performed with great skill by dressed-up charros. Rodeos are usually held on Sunday forenoon; you'll have to check the location. The inevitable bullfights are held at the Plaza de Toros opposite the Mercado Libertad, though Guadalajara's burgeoning younger generation must be credited with an overwhelming preference for *futbol* (soccer) and good old *beisbol* (baseball).

Visiting golfers can get a guest card at the Guadalajara Country Club on the northwest side of town, the Santa Anita Country Club on the south-

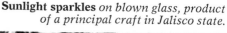

Sunlight sparkles *on blown glass, product of a principal craft in Jalisco state.*

west side of town, and the Atlas Golf Club on the road to Chapala.

The Degollado Theater: To assure yourself of an opportunity to enjoy the elaborate interior, buy tickets to whatever is being performed. The theater's classical facade can be seen from the central plaza. Along with hosting a wide variety of performers, the theater is the home of the famous Guadalajara Symphony.

To discover what's going on when, buy the *Colony Reporter* published every Saturday. It gives the current information on the English-speaking community plus lots of news for the retired.

Places to shop

To put your thoughts in order, go first to the large Casa de las Artesanias at the entrance to Parque Agua Azul, an intriguing museum-salesroom where you can examine many exquisite products identified with various regions of the state. These include furniture, pottery, tinware, glass, ceramic sculpture, and fabrics. Everything's for sale; many items are about half the price of similar articles at home. The prices are generally higher—in some cases much higher—than elsewhere in Guadalajara and in nearby Tlaquepaque and Tonala, but you'll be sure of top quality. You can have your larger purchases shipped directly home.

Mercado Libertad. At few places in Guadalajara can you haggle over prices, but the *Mercado*, claimed to be the world's largest market under one roof, is one of them. After nearly being destroyed by fire quite a few years ago, it has been rebuilt in a more modern style. As you work your way through the overwhelming confusion of merchandise, you'll come upon everything you can think of (and a few things you can't) from renowned Paracho guitars to dried iguanas for witch's brew.

El Baratillo. "The bargain counter" is open for business every Sunday morning. Though most customers are Guadalajarans, more and more tourists who enjoy garage sales or flea markets and haggling and browsing are discovering this market. Of special interest are the dealers in antiques, picture frames, odd pieces of porcelain, and wrought iron. A staggering display of items awaits you—many new, most used—including fake and genuine artifacts, bottles, medicinal herbs, ancient typewriters, and even washing machines. Located on Juan Zavala, a 5-minute drive east of the Mercado Libertad on Javier Mina, this flea market displays 12 long blocks of merchandise. You can always hope that a priceless item has been overlooked and has found its way to the Baratillo.

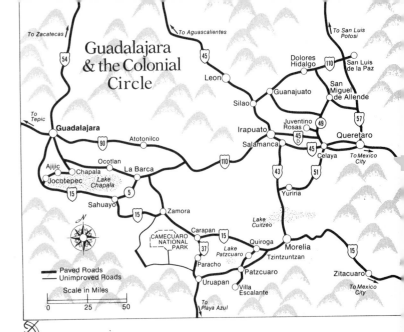

Details at a glance

Getting there and around

Guadalajara is easily reached on many direct flights from the U.S. and Canada. Domestic carriers have frequent service from Mexico City and other large towns.

The highway between Mexico City and Guadalajara (via Morelia) makes a good drive.

Using Guadalajara as a base, you'll enjoy driving your car around the colonial villages. In the city, park it and take cabs, a car and driver, or bus tours for local sightseeing.

Where to stay. Most convenient downtown Guadalajara hotels have had a facelift. In outlying sections you'll discover colonial haciendas or resorts-cum-tennis courts or golf course. In most other towns mentioned, travelers stay in charming old inns, newer hotels or motels, or recreational vehicle parks. Prices are lower in smaller villages.

Climate and clothes. Guadalajara is a city with a sophisticated outlook. At 5,200 feet elevation, the air is clear and bracing. Weather may be warmer in other cities along the route.

For women, pants are acceptable in small towns, though you may enjoy a loose shift if you're visiting in summer. Outside of Guadalajara, men need not bother with a tie.

Cobblestone streets make comfortable walking shoes necessary. Rubber-soled shoes will keep you from sliding on steep streets.

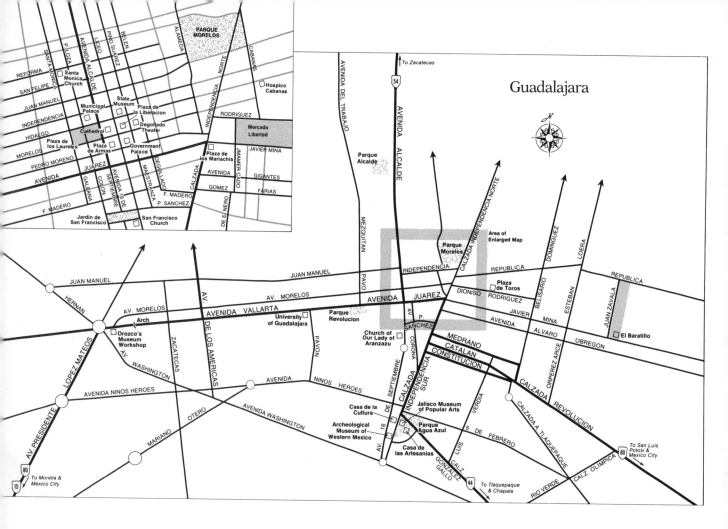

Tlaquepaque and Tonala.

Guadalajara has sprawled east to merge with the pottery town of San Pedro Tlaquepaque and its neighboring pottery village of Tonala. Visit this area to see master artisans at work and to shop for their products, some of which reach retailers in many parts of the world. Not everything is in clay; other cottage industries flourish here also. Go first with a licensed guide from Guadalajara—you miss too much otherwise. If you tire of standing, sit in the plaza and listen to the mariachis.

Plaza del Sol.

Back in Guadalajara, this plaza is Latin America's largest shopping center. This megacomplex, opened in 1969, covers over 12,000 square yards and provides an astounding range of goods and services. It is located in an area of new hotels and motels in the southwestern section of the city between Mariano Otero and Avenida Lopez Mateos.

How are the hotels?

Guadalajara has an outstanding and extensive selection of hotels and trailer parks. Peso for peso there are no better accommodations anywhere—

many are new and most of the rest have been remodeled. Downtown hotels make it easier to get around if you're without a car. The Plaza del Sol area is extremely popular with motorists, as are the other motels and the Camino Real Hotel on the road to Tepic. You'll find accommodations on Highways 15 and 80; the splendid El Tapatio is on Highway 35 en route to Tlaquepaque.

Around town ...

Guadalajara is not noted for its night life, so concentrate on the daytime tours of points of interest around town, either on your own or with a guide.

Barranca de Oblatos (Monk's Canyon). Thermal rivulets plunge down the red walls of this 2,000-foot-deep gorge. Its tropical depths produce much of the fruit marketed in Guadalajara. From the city, follow Calzada Independencia 7 miles to the canyon rim.

Juanacatlan Falls. Visit this waterfall—one of the largest in Mexico—that is at its best from June through September. In the nearby village you can view several iron and textile mills. From Guadala-

Craft towns around Guadalajara

Mexico produces a tremendous amount of exuberant folk art, consisting mainly of handicraft objects designed for household use. The folk art you see in boutiques and souvenir shops derives from the time when each village produced practically everything it needed.

Notably rich in handicrafts is the region around Guadalajara. These craft towns each have their own craftsmen making pottery, baskets, sarapes, or toys for sale to local people in local markets. By visiting these craft towns you'll gain an appreciation for their various styles. Meeting the artist himself also makes a purchase memorable.

Guadalajara is a recognized craft center, partly because so many craftsmen are at work in surrounding communities. If you're visiting Guadalajara, reserve a little time for Casa de las Artesanias de Jalisco. Located at the north end of Parque Agua Azul in a state-operated building, this center both displays and sells regional handicrafts. Here you can see examples of the varying crafts made in each village and begin to discern articles of quality and those that are particularly unique and well made.

About 5 miles southeast of the center of Guadalajara, between Highway 80 and Highway 35, is the well-known craft center with the fun-to-pronounce name of Tlaquepaque (tlockay-pockay). Once known only for pottery—not all of it good—local craftsmen have now branched out into furniture, textiles, glass, and other crafts. The Regional Museum of Ceramics on Avenida Independencia, located in an elegant colonial house, has a collection of pottery from the Valley of Atemajac, including *barro de olor* (odoriferous earthenware) and the unique *petatillo* pottery. Typical of this region, petatillo is recognized by its distinctive, almost oriental,

designs of stylized animals against a background of tile-red slip with white crosshatching. Don't miss the glass factories on Avenida Independencia where you can not only buy glass objects but also watch glass blowers at work. Endless gift shops and boutiques line the main street.

About 2 miles south on Highway 80 and about 3 miles north is Tonala, which produces some of Mexico's most unusual pottery and stoneware. In addition to more practical pieces, its artisans produce many beautifully decorated, hand-burnished birds and animals, and sculptured objects. Small boys often linger around the town plaza, flagging down tourists in hopes of being hired for a few pesos as a guide to one of several ceramic factories.

If you follow Highway 15 south of Guadalajara and continue for 35 miles, you approach Lake Chapala at Jocotepec. This lakeside town is noted for the weaving of sarapes in traditional styles with geometric designs and small flowers in pastel colors on an off-white background, and in contemporary designs featuring birds and flowers in happy patterns typical of the state of Jalisco. For information on individual shops, inquire at the Hotel La Quinta, located about a mile off Highway 15 toward Ajijic. Also known for their weaving are the people of Ajijic, an even smaller community 12 miles farther northeast on the same road. Numerous artists and writers, many of them American, have settled in this quaint, picturesque fishing village on the edge of Lake Chapala. Several boutiques and gift shops in town display high-quality, handwoven cloth and embroidered clothing. Two studios specialize in refined weaving done on hand looms: Helen Kirtland's Studio and Neill James' Studio, both located near Posada Ajijic.

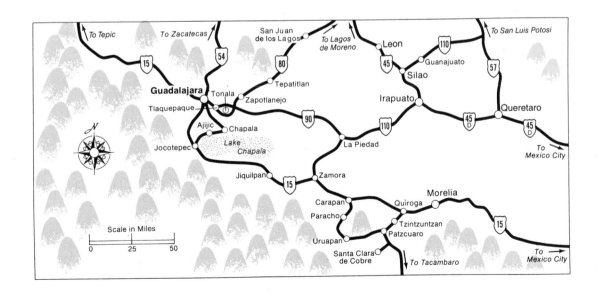

jara take Highway 44 southeast about 14½ miles; then turn onto a paved road for 7½ more miles.

Zapopan. From her 17th century basilica at Avenida 20 de Noviembre and Pino Suarez in this little suburb of Guadalajara, the revered Virgin of Zapopan ventures forth each summer to tour all of the city's churches, returning to her own in October. You can reserve seats at a travel agency for the unusual and emotional return procession on October 12.

Lake Chapala area

Thirty-five miles southeast of Guadalajara lies Lake Chapala, accessible by several good roads. Stretching alongside Highway 15, this hyacinth-dotted lake is the largest lake in Mexico, measuring 65 miles long and 20 miles wide. It is fed by the Lerma River and empties into the Grande de Santiago River. An 18-mile paved road connects the villages that circle the lake. The road from Highway 15—skirting the southern shore to the village of Chapala on the north shore—passes through the picturesque villages of Jocotepec, with its narrow cobblestone streets and a profusion of tropical flora, and Ajijic, where you can buy beautiful hand-loomed textiles. It also passes several residential subdivisions where many of the homes are occupied by retired Americans.

The climate is temperate and mild year-round in the lake region, and the lake is surrounded by mountains. Fishing for sunfish and Chapala white-fish is a popular sport, as are boating, bird watching, and swimming.

Chapala

Traditionally the destination for Sunday outings by Guadalajarans, Chapala has a large community of retired and foreign residents and was popular with the international set long before any of the other lakeshore resort villages. Two private clubs extend their privileges to visitors: one features a golf course, the other is a yacht club. Chapala has several restaurants, most serving the one food item that everyone who comes to Chapala should sample—Lake Chapala whitefish. For quite some time, the pollution of the lake made the consumption of whitefish unwise. The situation has apparently improved, though, and residents and visitors are once again enjoying the regional specialty.

If you continue eastward along the north shore of the lake, you go through the lakeside towns of Ocotlan and La Barca. At La Barca you cross the Lerma River just before it flows into the lake. Then the highway cuts down to Sahuayo and joins Highway 15, or you can continue ahead and join Highway 15 at Zamora, a strawberry town.

Ajijic—lakeside artist's community

Since about 1945 Ajijic has been the home of many foreigners from lively young liberals to quiet, well-known artists. Its international atmosphere, along with its neat, whitewashed buildings and cobblestone streets, make Ajijic a delightful village to visit for an escape from bustling Guadalajara. Shopping is a rewarding adventure; you'll come upon art galleries, weaving studios, and craft shops of all kinds. The retired community represents a large part of the village population.

The fishing village of Jocotepec

Founded in 1528, Jocotepec radiates a quiet contentment with its long history. A few crumbling walls, old colonial architecture, and rough streets bespeak its age and give it a quality that makes it unique among the other lake resort villages. Heavy, handmade sarapes that are white with a colorful central design motif are a specialty of the village. Fishermen's huts and yards of fish nets strung out to dry are evidence of the village's fishing livelihood.

The Colonial Circle

Between Guadalajara and Mexico City, Highway 15 is a paved, two-lane road to Toluca, then four lanes into Mexico City. But it is slow going in the mountainous sections east of Morelia and in the shallow, barren canyons and ravines east of Zitacuaro.

East of Guadalajara you become more aware of Mexico's history through several sights: the wealth of arched aqueducts dating from colonial days; the small farm plots which Indians still till with oxen; huge old crumbling haciendas; burros on their way to market; many small villages dominated by the reassuring presence of the ornate tower of the parish church; and the Tarascan Indians, located in villages around Lake Patzcuaro.

Lakes Chapala, Camecuaro, and Patzcuaro, the falls near Uruapan, and the heavily timbered mountains you pass through on your way into Morelia make this one of the most scenic stretches of all Mexico.

East of Zitacuaro, you leave the cool pine forests for high, semiarid plains. The wind sweeps unbroken across the rolling countryside, hills are covered with sparse grass, and erosion has seriously furrowed the thin, drifting soil. Much of the wide, flat valley of Toluca is divided into small farms, each with its small house of raw adobe and its adjoining stack of fodder elevated on poles. In the windy late winter and early spring, gossamer

On net-draped shore *of Lake Chapala (Mexico's largest), fishermen chop boat channel through water hyacinths.*

Colorful yarn *hangs in hot Uruapan sun to hasten drying after dying.*

clouds of dust hover over the landscape, obscuring the countryside.

Then, just before reaching the Valley of Mexico, the road climbs to its highest point in the Sierra Madre Occidental—10,000 feet—and you go through another stretch of pine and fir forests. Miniscule farms sit in clearings on the steep mountainsides; as you start the descent into the valley, colonies of attractive, expensive homes come into sight.

You can avoid the mountains (though you'll miss some of Mexico's most beautiful scenery) by taking the northern route to Mexico City along a combination of Highways 110, 45, and 57.

South of Leon and the Comanjilla road junction is a small city named Silao. Atop a mountain just east of the city is a huge stone statue of Christ called "Cristo Rey" (Christ the King). The statue can be seen from Highway 45 for several miles in both directions. The mountain on which the statue was erected is said to be the exact geographical center of Mexico—if it is possible to determine the

Like an ivory egg, *Guanajuato nestles among velvet, once silver-rich hills.*

exact geographical center of such a cornucopia-shaped country. A road leads up to the statue from near the Guanajuato highway junction just east of Silao, but this road is unpaved and quite difficult to negotiate. A better road, slightly longer, leaves Highway 110 a few miles east of Guanajuato.

South of Silao and Guanajuato junction, Highway 45 winds into a huge valley which the Mexicans call El Bajio (The Depression). It is the largest of seven valleys that make up the vast Central Plateau and is also one of Mexico's most fertile agricultural areas, providing metropolitan Mexico City with food and dairy products. Down Highway 45 you'll see the Mexican food processing plants of several American companies, largely owned and run by Mexicans—Del Monte, Campbell, Kellogg, Carnation, Ralston-Purina, and others.

Leon—Mexico's sole town

Accorded with generous acclaim as "The Shoe Capitol of Mexico," Leon is a bustling, industrious city in the state of Guanajuato. Shoes aren't everything here; Leon is also well known for all types of leather goods.

The general atmosphere of Leon reflects the city's highly industrialized activities. Prosperous looking and compact, the city has a vigorous commercial air. Stores proclaim the healthy state of the city's economy in well-stocked shelves and windows packed with locally made articles. Leon exudes the bustle and aggressiveness of some U.S. Midwestern farming and manufacturing cities.

You'll probably discover traffic is terrible, and you may find difficulty getting comfortable accommodations. Leon is a large city with many big city problems. Nevertheless, a spacious, wide boulevard runs the length of the city; trees bordering the plaza are trim and lush.

A few miles south of Leon and then 6 miles east on a blacktop road is the popular health resort of Comanjilla. Here, thermal spring waters are piped into large swimming pools and also into the bathtubs and miniature pools of the guest rooms.

Guanajuato—18th century silver capital

Founded by the Spaniards more than 400 years ago, Guanajuato grew into a city of wealth and extravagance during the heyday of its legendary silver mines. It saw some of the fiercest fighting of the War of Independence, then went into a long, slow decline, and has emerged today as a small, stately city with a strangely provocative and medieval European air.

A unique feature of Guanajuato is the subterranean street that meanders through and under the city. The stone-arched tunnel was built on the dry bed of the Guanajuato River and follows the original course of the river for almost 2 miles. One of the continent's greatest floods occurred in Guanajuato in 1905 when the dams at the south end of the city broke during a stormy night. The rampant flood waters cascaded through the nar-

Gently climbing *a hill to its cathedral, San Miguel de Allende is an undisputed gem in Mexico's colonial crown.*

row, ravinelike channel of the unassuming Guanajuato River, drowning thousands of residents.

Guanajuato is a city made for walking. Built where three ravines meet, the city offers the delight of random strolls along the narrow, cobbled byways that wind up the hillsides and turn into flights of stairs when the going gets too steep. You'll find yourself drawn on by the unusual facades of houses (no two alike), beckoned by the filigree of street lamps and overhanging balconies, and diverted by narrow passageways into unexpected squares. And for all your wandering, you're never really lost—the center of town is always waiting for you down the hill.

Sightseeing. Jardin de la Union—a good place to begin a day's exploration—is a delicate and graceful plaza. Here you can sit on ornate wrought iron benches and listen to band concerts each week.

Facing the plaza is Teatro Juarez, a theater in the classic style of the late 19th century. One of Guanajuato's few examples of post-colonial architecture, it once rivaled the opera house in Mexico City in prestige and splendor. Don't miss seeing its opulent, Moorish interior. (The eight bronze figures that top this building are the work of Ohio sculptor W. H. Mullen.)

Next to the theater is the Franciscan Church of San Diego (1784). Its facade is magnificent, though the interior is not especially impressive. A block away you'll come to Plaza de la Paz, dominated by La Parroquia Church, with its baptistry and sacristy dating back to 1696.

Up a narrow alley from this plaza is a comparatively recent building of the University of Guanajuato, designed with a fine awareness of its visual relationship to the colonial town.

La Compania (1747), a beautiful church inside and out, is a part of the university. Its colonnaded dome will serve as a landmark as you stroll about the town.

Handcrafted *iron scrollwork, wooden doors, plastered walls convey colonial character.*

Three other destinations require longer walks: the marketplace (Mercado Hidalgo), with local craft products for sale (Sunday is market day); the pleasant parks by the two dams that hold back the Guanajuato River; and the granary, better known as the Alhondiga. The Alhondiga, scene of a bloody battle in revolutionary days, now houses a regional museum reputed to be one of the most informative and well-organized museums in Mexico.

A roundabout drive (or a steep climb) takes you up the hill behind Teatro Juarez to the Statue of Pipila. At the start of the War of Independence of 1810-1821, the miner Pipila, with a flat stone strapped on his back as a shield, braved enemy bullets and molten lead to set fire to the door of a loyalist stronghold at the granary. Guanajuato became the first major city to fall to the forces of independence.

An attraction you may prefer to miss is the collection of well-preserved mummies at the Catacombs, doomed to exposure because their descendants fell behind on crypt rental fees.

Three miles from the midtown plaza, a church and mine bear witness to the glories of the past. La Valenciana is considered one of the most perfect and elegant churches in Mexico. Its architecture, the craftsmanship displayed in its intricate facade and carved altars, and the impressive view all merit a visit.

Across the highway you'll find the crumbling ruins of La Valenciana Mine, which for half a century poured millions of pesos annually into the treasury of the Spanish vice-royalty and financed the construction of the elegant homes and churches of Guanajuato and its suburbs.

City tours leave from the Juarez Theater in the morning and afternoon. It is best to hire a guide and car—you'll save hours of getting lost.

Shopping. Guanajuato offers many fine shops within walking distance of the central plaza. Quality is generally good; prices are reasonable. Look for silver, brass, crystal, mirrors, and jewelry. Brown is the newest color for local pottery; best place to look is at the marketplace.

Lodging. Accommodations are excellent with many converted colonial buildings providing delightful quarters. Restaurants are not so numerous. The best food is usually in larger hotels. Make advance reservations during the following major fiestas: Virgin of Guanajuato, the last part of May; Corpus Christi, the last two weeks in June; San Ignacio, on July 31; and Purisima at La Valenciana, in early December.

From Guanajuato, you can either return to Highway 45 or continue east to Dolores Hidalgo and San Miguel de Allende.

Dolores Hidalgo—the spark of independence

In this little village, on a Sunday morning in mid-September of 1810, Father Miguel Hidalgo y Costilla, burning with the fire of his obsession that the Mexican people should be freed from the yoke of the Spanish conquerors, spoke to his followers from the front steps of his parish church and exhorted them to take arms against their oppressors. This incident represents the beginning of Mexico's fight for self-rule. Hidalgo is revered by all Mexicans as the "Father of Mexico's Independence."

Several large commemorative monuments have been erected in Dolores Hidalgo, but it is the quiet reverence for the parish church and the historical significance of its well-worn front steps that make an indelible impression on those who visit the town. Hidalgo's house, a block south of the plaza, is now a museum. Also of interest are two ceramic tile factories.

The old church of Atotonilco

Off the highway, between Dolores Hidalgo and San Miguel de Allende, is the village of Atotonilco, at whose parish church Father Hidalgo stopped with his disheveled independence "army" while on his way to battle the Spanish royalists. He took from the church an embroidered tapestry showing the image of Mexico's patron saint, the Virgin of Guadalupe, and made it the banner of his cause.

The plain facade of the sanctuary of Atotonilco belies the fact that it is a treasure house of religious paintings, sculptures, and examples of early Christian-Indian art. Literally hundreds of art works fill the church including stone carvings, miniature murals, statuary, and even poetry.

Atotonilco means "place of hot water." The church was built in 1784 over hot springs; mineral baths are available to the public. Pilgrims come here by the thousands to do penance.

Just south of Atotonilco is the well-known Mexican thermal springs resort of Taboada.

Irapuato's strawberry harvest

First of the several booming cities in the valley of El Bajio is Irapuato, probably most famous as Mexico's strawberry-growing area, with several ultramodern quick-freezing and preserve-making plants. Irapuato produces huge quantities of these juicy, red berries.

In recent years, Irapuato's former drab downtown business section has been transformed into an attractive mall where no automobiles or other vehicles are allowed. The colonial-style development has been built around the town's ancient cathedral and market plaza. The city now has a nine-story hotel, a modern block-square market building, and innumerable shops — all in keeping with the mall's colonial decor.

If you drive into Irapuato, you might want to continue about 30 miles west on Highway 110 to Rancho Corralejo, birthplace of Father Hidalgo. The ruins of the old hacienda where the "Father of Mexico's Independence" was born, and the adjoining humble ranch chapel, are 4 miles north off Highway 110 on a good, slightly narrow, blacktop road. The turnoff is just beyond a branch of the Lerma River, some 6 miles west of the town of Abasolo— site of another of Mexico's larger thermal spas.

San Miguel de Allende—a national monument

Strolling the picturesque streets will be your main pastime in San Miguel de Allende, for this is an exceptionally fine example of a Spanish colonial town — so much so that the Mexican government has made it a national monument in order to preserve its charm. Any buildings that are constructed must be in harmony with the Spanish-style architecture and colonial ambience.

Then. Juan de San Miguel, a Franciscan friar, founded the town in 1542. The "Allende" was later added to the name to honor Ignacio Allende, a hero of the struggle for independence.

San Miguel's narrow cobblestone streets climb the slopes in gradual stages. During a walk around town, you'll see fine old colonial houses, many of them with plaques telling what famous figure was born there, or lived there, or what important event took place inside the thick walls.

Of the dozen churches in San Miguel de Allende, the most unusual is the parish church of San Miguel on the central plaza, which reflects a crazy potpourri of architectural styles. Originally this was a rather plain Franciscan building. It was given its Gothic appearance in the 19th century by an Indian mason who studied postcard pictures of French Gothic cathedrals and then created his own unique version with its ornate towers and pink stone facade.

West of the church is the house where Ignacio Allende was born in 1779. The inscription over the doorway reads in Latin, "Here was born he who is widely known."

Buildings worth exploring include the 18th century Church of San Francisco, which has a 17th century monastery attached to it, and the other group of religious structures on Insurgentes — a photogenic collection of domes, steeples, niches, and scalloped roofs. Inside, examine the "miracle paintings," votive paintings made in answer to a miraculous cure.

Now. The beauty and quiet of San Miguel de Allende have attracted a sizable colony of foreign artists and writers. Instituto Allende, an accredited school of fine arts, attracts students from all over the Americas. The Institute has a beautiful hillside

Easter in San Miguel

San Miguel de Allende celebrates Easter with pageantry and fervor. Colorful religious observances take place during the week preceding Easter, but two of the most spectacular processions occur on Good Friday.

Early that morning the faithful from nearby mountainside villages fill the streets of the old city for church services. They await preparations for the "people's procession."

About 10 A.M., men dressed as Roman soldiers appear, marching in front of a wooden cross and led by a piper playing a haunting Indian melody. Following them are boys painted to resemble lepers, girls carrying their dolls, and other children costumed as shepherds, leading their pets. Life-sized images of various saints are collected from churches, decorated in satin and velvet robes for the occasion, and carried through the streets. You may see a replica of an apple tree with a serpent coiled around its trunk.

Because the procession departs from San Juan de Dios Church and stays mainly on the side streets, it attracts little attention from the downtown population, and business proceeds as usual.

It is a different story for the well-organized late afternoon burial procession. All stores are closed, houses along the parade route are draped with purple ribbons, and people line the main streets hours ahead of time to ensure a good view.

Three young priests bearing candles and a cross lead the pilgrimage. Little girls dressed in white gowns to resemble angels pass by with eyes downcast and hands folded in prayer. In striking contrast are the long lines of solemn, black-clad senoras illuminated by flickering lanternlight. Climaxing the street procession is the special honor guard, bearing a large glass coffin with flowers at its base. By now it is almost dark and the onlookers head for home.

Sunday after Mass is spent in festive celebration. Bands play in the plaza and the citizens wear their finest and most colorful costumes.

Tourists usually outnumber San Miguel's hotel accommodations during this period. If you expect to visit, be sure to make reservations well in advance.

setting on the edge of town. From time to time exhibits of student arts and crafts are displayed. Academia Hispano Americana offers intensive Spanish and related courses. A branch of the National Institute of Fine Arts (Instituto de Bellas Artes) is housed in a former monastery—a handsome, two-story building with gracefully arched corridors enclosing a tranquil, tree-shaded patio.

Because of the many resident Americans as well as visiting teachers, students, and tourists, the city contains many fine shops offering a wide variety of local merchandise, as well as goods from all over Mexico. Interesting art studios abound.

You'll find a charming resort-type hotel, another with colonial charm, nice motels, and other inexpensive accommodations.

Several excellent inns and restaurants are available in town. One of the most unique is the attractive colonial Posada de Ermita, built on the hillside site of the family's home and owned by relatives of Cantinflas, the famed Mexican comedian.

Queretaro—a haven for historians

You reach Queretaro from San Miguel de Allende by ascending a steep hill at the eastern edge of town and then taking a blacktop road at the junction with Highway 57 a few miles north of Queretaro. Or you can travel south on Highway 49 from San Miguel de Allende to Celaya on Highway 45 and then continue to Queretaro on this route (a toll road).

At the northern edge of Queretaro, Highway 57 passes the Mexican plants of four American firms—Singer, Carnation, Ralston-Purina, and Kellogg.

At Queretaro, the route merges with Highway 45 near the town's impressive, modern bullring, and together the two routes proceed to Mexico City (138 miles) on a high-speed road that has been widened to expressway proportions.

Much of Queretaro's charm lies in its history. The townsite was occupied by the Otomi Indians long before the discovery of the New World. It became a part of the Aztec empire in the 15th century and was overcome by Spanish forces in 1531. The "conquest" by the Spaniards consisted of a one-day, weaponless confrontation.

Secret plans for national independence were formulated in this city, and it was here that the Treaty of Guadalupe-Hidalgo was ratified, ceding California, New Mexico, and a portion of Texas to the United States.

Emperor Maximilian and his two faithful generals were executed in 1867 on the "Hill of the Bells" at the western edge of town; the spot is marked by a chapel, the gift of the government of Austria. The constitution under which Mexico is now governed was drafted in Queretaro in 1917.

Today Queretaro exists as a fascinating colonial city with colorful parks and plazas and intriguing old buildings. Plaza Obregon represents the heart of the town, dominated by the Church of San Francisco, with its dome of colored tiles brought from Spain in 1540. The main streets that radiate from this plaza are rich in historical and architectural treasures.

One downtown building of significance is the post office, formerly the government palace. An engraving of this lovely example of colonial architecture appears on the back side of Mexico's old 20-peso bill. Another attractive nearby building, housing La Marquesa Restaurant, was the gift of the Marquis to his bride. The Marquis supervised the construction of the largest of Queretaro's arched aqueducts that carried water from the mountains to the city 400 years ago. Several of these aqueducts still stand—monuments to the engineering brilliance of their builders.

Queretaro is endowed with a reputation as Mexico's center for the gem industry, and around the well-manicured main plaza you'll find several reputable shops that sell opals mined in the nearby mountains. Not all of the stones sold in Queretaro are mined in the area; Queretaro is also a center for gem-cutting, and many of the stones sold locally are from the United States, Brazil, and other countries, but have been cut in Queretaro. You should try to make your purchases only in a well-established shop—the "gems" sold by itinerant peddlers frequently can turn out to be pure "pop bottle."

Celaya—masterpiece of Mexico's Michelangelo

Celaya is probably most famous as the home town of Francisco Eduardo Tresguerras—architect, artist, and poet, often called the "Michelangelo of Mexico." El Carmen Church of Celaya is considered to be his greatest architectural work. Tresguerras is buried in a little chapel of his own design in Celaya's ancient San Francisco Church, the newer altars of which he also designed.

Celaya is also famous as the source of a favorite sweet, *cajeta*, made of goat's milk boiled down with sugar to a thick, gooey syrup. You'll note many cajeta shops along Lopez Mateos Boulevard that cuts through town.

Juventino Rosas—a town for waltzes

Fifteen miles north and west of Celaya nestles the unassuming town of Juventino Rosas, formerly Santa Cruz but renamed in honor of one of Mexico's most famous composers who was born here in 1868. Rosas wrote the beautiful waltz, "Sobre las Olas"

(Over the Waves), which we know in English as "The Loveliest Night of the Year." He received only a few pesos for his composition, and though he wrote many other pieces, none achieved the fame of "The Loveliest Night." He died in poverty at the age of 26 in a Cuban fishing village.

The black gold of Salamanca

If you're in a hurry after leaving Irapuato, you may wish to bypass Salamanca and Celaya and take the modern, limited-access Highway 45-D toll road. The entrance is 3 miles beyond Irapuato. If you continue on Highway 45, the next place of any consequence after Irapuato is Salamanca, best known for the huge Pemex oil refinery located just east of town near the Lerma River. Oil for the refinery comes from Poza Rica in the State of Veracruz. After being processed in Salamanca, oil is distributed to cities throughout the highlands.

Highway 43 runs south from Salamanca to Morelia on Highway 15. Two features of this gently rolling, pleasant, 65-mile trip are the renovated church and monastery at the lakeside town of Yuriria and, 20 miles farther, the 2-mile causeway across Lake Cuitzeo, whose natural beauty is enhanced by the fishermen in dugout canoes scattered over the glassy, mirrorlike surface of the water.

Morelia—for Old World atmosphere

Morelia lies about halfway between Guadalajara and Mexico City, and makes a good stopover midway in the 16-hour drive. Highway 15 turns into the main street of town.

So many of Morelia's elegant old buildings have been preserved that the city is practically a museum of Spanish and Mexican history. Ordinances require that all new construction conforms to the style of the early architecture.

For strollers. Downtown Morelia is an inexhaustible outlet for those who love to use their feet to explore a new town. The most intriguing old buildings are clustered around two central plazas—Plaza de los Martires and Plaza de la Paz. Many visitors think the Plaza de los Martires is one of Mexico's most beautiful. Lacy detail and ornamental ironwork soften the tall, mosquelike arches of its nostalgic old band pavilion; the delicate foliage of stately jacaranda and other flowering trees casts latticed shade across the broad paseo, or walkway. On Sundays especially, Morelia's plaza is full of activity and the atmosphere of Mexico.

It is just a few steps from the Plaza de los Martires to Morelia's lovely old cathedral. Over a century (from 1640 to 1744) was needed to build this graceful, twin-spired building.

From the cathedral, it is an easy stroll to the Museo del Estado. This museum is small enough so that you won't get "museum legs," yet interesting enough to make a visit well worthwhile. Of particular interest is the collection of whimsical, pre-Columbian sculpture.

Morelia's central market is at the end of Valladolid Street, about five blocks east of the Plaza de los Martires. On market days (usually Sunday and Thursday), the market overflows the big central pavilion and extends along Valladolid Street for several blocks. Among the many handicraft articles displayed, huaraches and hammocks are the best bargains.

Near the market is the Casa de Morelos. Besides its historical and architectural importance, the old home contains memorabilia of the famous patriot Jose Maria Morelos.

At the eastern edge of the city you'll see the imposing stone aqueduct with 30-foot-high arches extending down the middle of Highway 15. Nearby is the beautiful Sanctuary of the Virgin of Guadalupe. On the outskirts of town is the neoclassic church, La Iglesia del Nino de la Salud.

Where to stay. Morelia has a languid Old World tempo and charm that appeals to overnight visitors —features that, when combined with sunny days and moderate climate, explain why so many come here for extended vacations.

For short stays there is a charming colonial hostelry facing the plaza, and also several inexpensive hotels. Patrons staying longer usually head for one of the informal, resort-type complexes on the hill overlooking the town. A public golf course adds much to Morelia's recreational pleasures.

Patzcuaro—near an island-dotted lake

Patzcuaro sits on a hilly landscape about 2 miles from the vast 13-mile-long, shallow Lake Patzcuaro. The lake, dotted with a profusion of inhabited islands, is encircled along the shore by several villages whose main communication is by boat. The village dwellers spend most of their time either on the lake fishing or at home producing a variety of handicrafts.

Around town. The 16th century city of Patzcuaro still uses many churches and mansions built in colonial days (1521-1810). Once the political seat of the Tarascan Kingdom and later an important Spanish settlement, Patzcuaro now blends the best of two heritages. At the basilica on the hill, the Colegiata, you can see the Virgin of Health—a compromise entity used to bridge the gap between the pagan beliefs of the Indians and the dogma of the Church. The Virgin, made of cornstalk pith and

Butterfly-net fisherman *heads out for early morning whitefish catch on Lake Patzcuaro.*

Woodchoppers *and laden burros plod purposefully along country road near highway to Morelia.*

orchid mucilage, is revered throughout Mexico and thought to have great healing powers. The Virgin's feast day on December 8 brings visitors from miles around.

Today life in the city is remarkably the same as life was in colonial days. The Tarascan Indians practice a variety of crafts and hold frequent fiestas. *Los Viejitos*—a dance in which men or boys hobble around on canes and wear grotesque masks to make them look like old men—is a traditional dance performed frequently.

Touring. After you've seen the city and visited the Friday market and the excellent museum, you may want to take one of the excursions the region offers such as boat trips to some of the islands, and a 15-minute ride to the top of El Estribo for a view of the city and lake. Janitzio Island is a classic for photographers; the butterfly-net fishermen provide ideal early-morning subjects. Boat or automobile trips are available to some of the villages around the shore (Chupicuaro, Erongaricuaro). Consider taking a 12-mile trip south of Patzcuaro on paved Highway 120 to Santa Clara del Cobre (Villa Escalante), where several small

Final touches *give high sheen to lacquer tray in Uruapan.*

copper foundries produce graceful urns, pitchers, and pots.

Shopping. Best buys in this region include lacquerware, silver jewelry, pottery with fish designs, ceramic animals, red-checked wool fabrics, woodenware, and copper. An excellent place to find everything at bargain prices is in Tzintzuntzan, a small village about halfway between Patzcuaro and Quiroga; the market is on both sides of the highway.

Specialties. At restaurants, ask for the delicate and delicious pescado blanco, a small, almost transparent whitefish caught in the lake. The fish are a nationally known delicacy of the Patzcuaro region.

For a taste of colonial life, you can stay at a renovated hacienda or a colonial-style motel.

Handpainted lacquerware in Uruapan

About 48 miles from the Highway 15 turnoff at Carapan, Uruapan exudes an air of drowsy remoteness. The town is set in a verdant, floral landscape —a burgeoning mixture of pine, cedar, oak, and

Painter *captures cool vista at Lake Camecuaro Park.*

ash, with banana, avocado, mango, and other tropical plants and trees. Uruapan is another of Mexico's extremely lush areas awarded the title of "the flower garden of Mexico."

Lacquerware — especially trays and masks — is produced in several small shops in Uruapan and the surrounding area. The best work has engraved designs cut through layers of lacquer. Guitars are made in Paracho, on the highway 15 miles south of the junction town of Carapan. Be on the lookout, too, for beautiful wooden articles, especially those made of cedar.

Uruapan's pride is its unique park, Parque Nacional Licenciado Eduardo Ruiz. Tree-shaped paths lead along a meandering, cool river and up to its headwaters — a series of bubbling springs. Local residents often bathe in Bano Azul, one of the river's pools. Coffee and banana plantations and orange groves surround the area and provide ideal settings for picnics, picture taking, and siestas.

For another purely relaxing excursion, ride out about 6 miles to Tzararacua Falls. The waters of the Cupatitizio River gush from many points around a natural stone amphitheater and drop about 90 feet into a pool surrounded by tropical trees, plants, and flowers. Rustic, circular rest houses on a trail to the pool make cool picnic spots.

Quietude and emptiness are the two prevailing qualities you'll sense at Paricutin now. It has been quiet since 1943 when the volcano pushed its way 1,700 feet up from the corn fields in the valley floor. You can drive out to view the weird, blackened landscape. If you're possessed with a greater curiosity, you can explore the lava fields on horseback. It is a 24-mile round trip on a cinder-surfaced road from Uruapan.

An icy swim in Lake Camecuaro

Half a mile off the highway from the humble village of Camecuaro (8½ miles beyond the town of Zamora) is Lake Camecuaro, a little-known but refreshing and idyllic spot where you can stop for a picnic lunch, take a restful boat ride, or walk around and stretch your legs. On Highway 15 watch for a small sign pointing out the spur road leading south to the lake. The half-mile road is paved, but the road at the lake itself is rough (you can park at the entrance to the lake park and walk through the grounds).

Lake Camecuaro is narrow and only about half a mile long. Giant cypress trees protrude upward from the clear, azure water. Pristine white ducks glide among the gnarled roots, and usually there are a few bronzed Mexican boys swimming in the shaded water. If you join them, you'll find that they are a hardy bunch—the water is incredibly cold. It comes from springs that flow out of the ground a short distance back from the shore.

Golden Angel *atop Monument to Independence seems to direct traffic on Paseo de la Reforma.*

Mexico City... Road's End

A tour of Mexico City, the country's capital, can be telescoped to fit into almost any tight vacation schedule. Or you can slowly savor and meticulously explore the city—with its metropolitan population of 12 million—if your time is unlimited. Mexico City lies in a mountain-rimmed valley 7,400 feet above sea level. On a rare clear day, you can see the snow-capped volcanic peaks of 17,591-foot Iztaccihuatl (ees-tak-*see*-watl) and majestic 17,893-foot Popocatepetl (po-po-kah-*teh*-petl) about 35 miles to the southeast.

With all of its big-city problems, Mexico City can hold its own along with any exotic foreign city. It is a place of hustle and bustle; its charm lies in its profusion of color and sound.

Mexico City marks the beginning and end of all major highways. Kilometer miles to anywhere in the country are measured from this city.

Getting around

For greater enjoyment of the myriad delights of Mexico City, read up on it before you go. If you're the independent type, you may prefer to wander through the city armed with a guidebook, a map, an English-Spanish dictionary, and your own self-inspired itinerary. On the other hand, at your hotel or any travel agency you can engage the services of an official, government-authorized guide (ask to see his credentials) who will take you in his car, or drive yours, wherever you wish to go.

To get advice, assistance, and helpful literature, or to register complaints on prices or services, consult one of the two following agencies: the Ministry of Tourism at Juarez 92 (just east of its intersection with Paseo de la Reforma), or the Tourism Department of the Mexico City Chamber of Commerce, Reforma 42.

Public transportation—buses and the Metro system—is inexpensive, and satisfactory once you learn your way around. Taxis vary in type and rates, and will give you more flexibility than public transport.

The automobile—patience and courage

At first, Mexico City traffic is apt to dampen your enthusiasm for driving. Streets in the older sections of town are narrow, one-way, and congested. On the wider streets cars move fast, and the traffic circles (*glorietas*) at intersections along many main thoroughfares may give you the sensation of being caught in a revolving door. Taxi drivers, darting in and out of traffic with split-second judgment, are particularly skillful at sizing up the intentions of others. Bicycle and motorcycle riders who weave between cars are a constant menace in traffic. As in many European cities, motorists sometimes use only their parking lights when driving at night.

Street signs are black-on-white. Streets often change names every few blocks. Watch for the small blue and white *transito* (direction) and green and white *preferencia* (right-of-way) signs on the walls of buildings at corners. Traffic is regulated by lights at most intersections; at others a policeman may be stationed in the center. When he faces you or has his back to you, you must stop; when he turns his side to you, you may proceed.

Traffic and security police wear light blue uniforms. A small flag on the chest or shoulder of an officer's shirt indicates that he speaks the language of the country the flag represents. Official car watchers, whose only pay is in tips, are clad in khaki.

As you enter the city on a major highway you may be accosted by individuals who offer to guide you to your destination. Mexican travel authorities strongly recommend that you do not employ these or any other unauthorized guides.

It is important to park your car in a safe place because Mexican car insurance doesn't cover the loss of component parts. When you park on the street or in a parking lot—even when an attendant is in charge and you lock up the car—don't ever leave clothing, cameras, or other valuables exposed inside the car; lock them in the trunk or, even better, take them with you.

At often very crowded downtown parking lots, you must leave your keys in the ignition or deliver them to the attendant so the car can be moved if

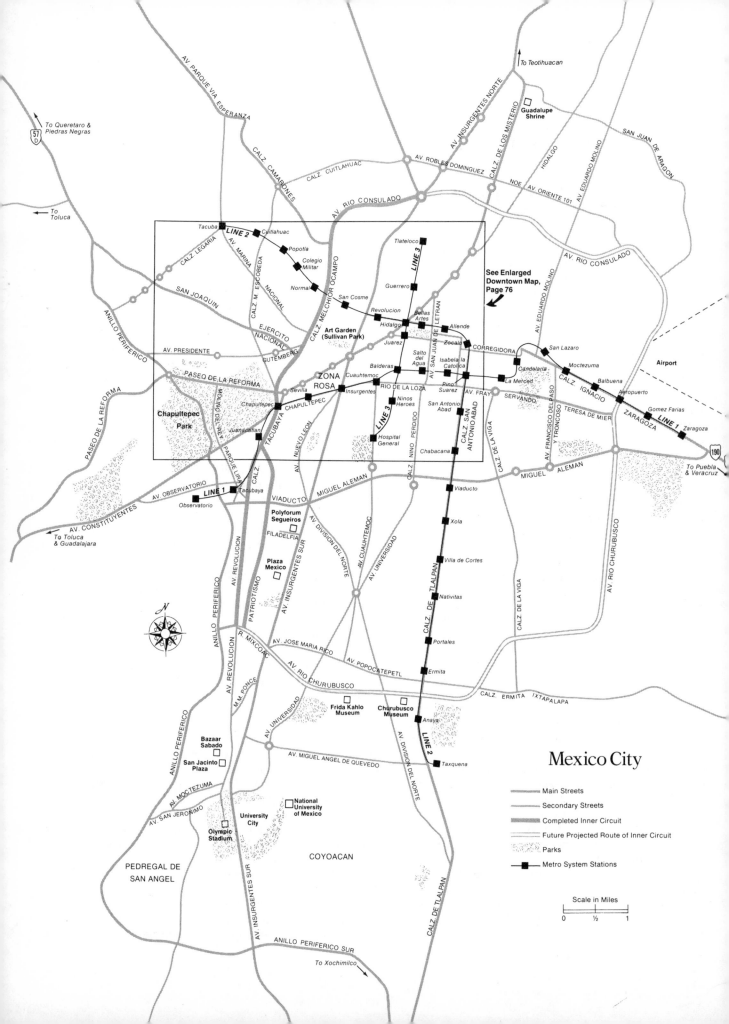

Mexico City

To Queretaro &
Piedras Negras

To Toluca

To Teotihuacan

Guadalupe
Shrine

LINE 2
Tacuba
Cuitlahuac
Popotla
Colegio
Militar
Normal
San Cosme

LINE 3
Tlatelolco
Guerrero
Revolucion
Bellas
Artes
Hidalgo
Allende
Juarez
Zocalo
Corregidora
San Lazaro
Moctezuma
Balbuena
Candelaria
Aeropuerto
La Merced
Balderas
Salto
del
Agua
Isabela la
Catolica
Pino
Suarez
Gomez Farias
Cuauhtemoc
Rio de la Loza
Zaragoza
Ninos
Heroes
San Antonio
Abad
Chabacana

See Enlarged
Downtown Map,
Page 76

Airport

Art Garden
(Sullivan Park)

ZONA
ROSA
Sevilla
Insurgentes
Chapultepec
Chapultepec
Tacubaya
Juanacatlan

Chapultepec
Park

Hospital
General

LINE 1
Tacubaya
Observatorio

Viaducto
Xola
Villa de Cortes
Nativitas
Portales
Ermita
Anaya
Taxquena

LINE 2
LINE 1
Zaragoza

Polyforum
Segueiros
FILADELFIA
Plaza
Mexico

Frida Kahlo
Museum
Churubusco
Museum

Bazaar
Sabado
San Jacinto
Plaza

National
University
of Mexico
University
City
Olympic
Stadium

PEDREGAL DE
SAN ANGEL

COYOACAN

To Puebla
& Veracruz

To Xochimilco

	Main Streets
	Secondary Streets
	Completed Inner Circuit
	Future Projected Route of Inner Circuit
	Parks
■	Metro System Stations

Scale in Miles

0   ½   1

Details at a glance

How to get there

All main roads lead to Mexico City. Mileage is measured from the city to all other parts of Mexico. Drivers enjoy good highways, scenic variety, and sufficient gasoline (if you plan ahead).

By air. Mexico City is reached easily by air from most large U.S. cities. Connections to other cities go through the capital. In addition to Aeromexico, Mexicana, and U.S. carriers, several foreign lines offer service.

Bus and train. National Railways of Mexico departs from border towns. Pullmans and reserved seats are usually available. Greyhound and Continental Trailways operate a variety of motorcoach tours. Check with a travel agent for details.

Getting around. Driving in Mexico City is nerve-razzling. Park your car and use local transportation. Taxis, buses, and *peseros* (jitneys that travel main city streets for 2 or 3 pesos) are plentiful. Servicio Delfin, the city's newest bus service, offers air-conditioned coaches with no overcrowding.

English-speaking guides with private cars cluster around hotels. Settle the price in advance. Hotel tour desks usually offer excursions to main points of interest. A half-day city orientation provides a passing glance to attractions you'll want to explore in detail.

Riding the Metro, the city's subway, is an experience. Attractive, clean, noiseless, decorated marble stations (many with archaeological treasures) may change your image of underground transportation. Don't attempt the trip during rush hours.

Accommodations. Hotels come in a wide assortment: budget to deluxe, colonial to resort with pool. Most are centered around three locations: downtown, along the Reforma, and in the Zona Rosa. Confirm reservations in advance.

Climate and clothes. Mexico City's weather is springlike the year around. The rainy season extends from May to October, often limited to afternoon showers.

Dress is sophisticated in this cosmopolitan city. During the day women wear pants suits and dresses, men are attired in suits or sports jackets and slacks. Leave shorts for resorts. Evenings are dressy and often cool—you'll want to bring a jacket.

necessary. On the street, try to park near a uniformed car watcher and tip him a peso or two when you leave. Meters that register up to 4 hours have now been installed on many streets. A 50-centavo coin entitles you to park for 24 minutes; one peso gives you 48 minutes. Don't leave your car parked on the street overnight. You can always arrange to park in your hotel's own parking area or in a nearby public parking garage.

Taxis—tips on all types

You'll probably find taxis the most convenient way to get around in Mexico City. All taxis have meters and drivers are supposed to use them. If the driver fails to put the flag *(bandera)* down when you enter the cab, politely remind him to do so. The law stipulates that you pay the meter reading if you hail the cab on the street; the fare is higher if you call a taxi from a stand. You may pay anywhere from 5 to 30 pesos (a tip is not expected) for a taxi ride to a downtown destination, depending on whether you use a cruising or cab-stand vehicle. Though plentiful, taxis are sometimes difficult to find. If this is the case, call one from a cab stand listed under *sitios* in the yellow phone directory. The fare will be higher, according to the distance the taxi has come in response to the dispatcher's call. You can also arrange for hourly or daily taxi rates.

Up and down the 3-mile main route from Chapultepec Park to the Zocalo (down Paseo de la Reforma, Juarez, and Madero, and return via Cinco de Mayo, Juarez, and Reforma), you can take a *pesero* or peso cab (jitney). This is a euphemistic term, for the one-peso fare is a thing of the past; all jitney fares are now two pesos and up. When the driver has room for more passengers, he holds his left hand aloft. You simply alight at the stop nearest your destination. There are many pesero routes in the city, but the Chapultepec-Zocalo route is the one of greatest benefit to the tourist.

The Metro: fast and convenient

Since 1970 Mexico City has had a new transportation system—the Metro or subway. Construction was initiated in 1967, and excavations unearthed parts of the ancient city of Tenochtitlan. For a glimpse of some of the archaeological finds, get off at the Pino Suarez station where a small, round Aztec pyramid was left in place in the terminal lobby. Unlike some dark, dreary underground tubes, the Metro is well lighted and gaily decorated.

At present, there are three lines (see map on page 68), with others in the planning stage. The Metro operates between 6 A.M. and 12:30 A.M.; a ticket costs about 10 cents including transfers.

Present plans call for the construction of a network of ground-level railways for electric trains that will connect outlying areas of the Federal District with the subway terminals.

Buses—bargain travel to almost anywhere

Buses are still one of the most convenient ways to travel in the city—provided you know your way around. They serve almost every section of the capital, but will take at least twice as long as a taxi. Ask about bus routes at your hotel. Bus stops are indicated by a small, elevated sign with the word *parada* on it. Fares are very low, and service is usually available until midnight.

Around the Zocalo

Since 1325, when the Aztecs established their capital of Tenochtitlan on an island in Lake Texcoco, the area of the *Zocalo*, Mexico City's huge downtown plaza, has been the seat of government and religion for the entire country. Upon the Spaniards' arrival in 1519, the island (with an area of only 165 square blocks) was linked to the mainland by broad causeways and an aqueduct that brought fresh water from the western shore of the lake. Tenochtitlan had an estimated 80,000 inhabitants.

The conquerors were amazed at the beauty of the palaces, the luxury of their furnishings, and the impressive grandeur of the great ceremonial center immediately north of today's Zocalo. But during their 80-day siege of the capital in 1521, they systematically razed the Aztec structures and, upon the rubble, built a Spanish town.

Your visit to Mexico City, therefore, might well begin where the post-Conquest history of Mexico began so many years ago.

Measuring 790 feet on each side and bordered by four broad streets, the Zocalo itself has had a colorful career. After the Conquest it became the very center of colonial life. Market stalls selling wares of every description filled it until 1789. A gallows stood in front of the National Palace; at one time fountains marked the four corners of the plaza. The Zocalo has been the site of a bullring, a park, and until about 30 years ago, the terminal for bus and streetcar lines. Now, because large crowds frequently assemble there, it is a barren expanse of concrete blocks broken only by a flagpole, mobile planters, and a subway entrance.

Coming into the plaza from Avenida Madero, you'll see the Hotel Majestic on the righthand corner. Its roof garden restaurant is a good place to eat or drink while you enjoy the panoramic view of the Zocalo and the historic buildings that face it. For the night of September 15—the eve of Independence Day—the hotel is booked far in advance by those wanting a box seat for the spectacle staged in the plaza when as many as 300,000 people gather to hear the President repeat the Grito or call to arms given by Miguel Hidalgo in 1810. Elaborate fireworks and the pealing of the cathedral bells follow the ceremony.

Turning right on the west side of the square, you pass through the *Portales*, a broad arcade in which merchants maintained permanent stalls from 1524 until some time after Mexico won its independence from Spain in 1821. Small shops and cafes now operate there, opening onto the arcade.

The two Municipal Palaces stand on the south side. The Old Palace, built in 1532, was almost destroyed by rioters in 1692. In addition to the city offices and archives, it also housed the Royal Mint established in 1536, the first in America. The New Palace, between 20 de Noviembre and Pino Suarez, was inaugurated in 1948. Both buildings are now devoted to over-all administrative functions.

The Supreme Court building at the southeast corner of the square was completed in 1940. Of greatest interest to visitors is Jose Clemente Orozco's powerful mural, a satirical critique of the judiciary.

The National Palace, a squat, three-story building, occupies the entire east side of the Zocalo where the Palace of Montezuma once stood. The official headquarters of Cortez erected there was purchased by the Spanish king in 1562 to serve as a residence for the viceroys. Maximilian had improvements made, and the building was enlarged when Porfirio Diaz became president. It wasn't until 1927 that the third story was added. The central balcony and the niche above it together form the focal point of the facade. In the niche hangs Mexico's Liberty Bell, rung by the president at 11 P.M. on September 15. Below the balcony, the main entrance gives access to the great stairway where, in 1929, Diego Rivera painted one of his finest murals—"Mexico: Yesterday, Today and Tomorrow." Behind the Palace, at Moneda 13, is the Museum of the Cultures with exhibits depicting the history of art throughout the world.

A fragment of one of the pyramids that stood in the Aztec ceremonial center may be viewed at the corner of Seminario and Guatemala, across from the rear of the cathedral. Beside it is the small Ethnographic Museum, with a scale model of the ancient ceremonial center.

The magnificent Metropolitan Cathedral, on the north side of the plaza, has detractors who claim that it suffers from an overabundance of architectural styles resulting from a 200-year construction period. Be that as it may, it continues to be the

Diego Rivera's mural *in the National Palace depicts turbulent history of Mexico.*

Indian *ceremonial dancers perform on the zocalo fronting Mexico City cathedral.*

Downtown Mexico City *street vendor sells lunch snacks.*

Love for color *shows in cathedral illumination on special holidays.*

most important Catholic church in the New World, housing a multitude of religious art treasures. Recently it has been totally renovated, from foundations to bell towers, in keeping with its status.

Erection of the first cathedral was begun by Cortez in 1524, 3 years after the Conquest. Foundations for the present cathedral were laid in 1573, and work continued as funds permitted; the awe-inspiring Altar of the Kings was not completed until 1737.

First-time visitors should take special notice of the cathedral crypts (entrance on the west); the Altar of Forgiveness and the Choir, almost destroyed by fire in 1967, and now restored with painstaking care; the four huge oval paintings by Miguel Cabrera above the two side entrances; and the 85-foot-high Altar of the Kings, a glory in gold leaf, at the end of the central nave. Chapels of great artistic merit line the two lateral naves.

The Monte de Piedad or National Pawnshop stands at the northwest corner of the Zocalo, on the site of the palace where Hernando Cortez and his men were housed upon their arrival in 1519. The present mansion was constructed in the early 18th century and, in 1836, became this hemisphere's oldest credit institution. Anything except perishable goods may be pawned; if not redeemed within a specified time, articles are offered for sale here or at one of the numerous branches throughout the country. Good bargains can often be found.

Along Avenida Madero

When a number of Franciscan friars arrived from Spain in 1524, Cortez granted them four square blocks of land on the western shore of the island capital. Then he ordered a narrow street to be cut through from the Zocalo so that the friars might have easy access to church and government offices. The street was first called San Francisco, and members of the aristocracy built their mansions along its 6-block length.

Eventually, as in all large cities, commerce began to move out to the less congested suburbs, leaving the downtown area to decay. Since 1970, however, the city government has rejuvenated all streets leading into the Zocalo from the west including eliminating unsightly signs and cables; sand-blasting, painting, and repairing building facades; paving the streets with octagonal red tile and the sidewalks with pink stone blocks; planting trees and shrubbery; and installing colonial-type street lighting.

A stroll down Avenida Madero—renamed to honor the leader of the Revolution of 1910—is a delightful journey into the past.

Rebozos carry tiny passengers and groceries, leaving shoppers with free arms.

Colorful costumes, *intricate dances, and native music highlight world-renowned Ballet Folklorico performances.*

Blue and white *tile-faced facade distinguishes House of Tiles—once a palace, now a restaurant.*

The Church of La Profesa, corner of Isabel la Catolica, was built by the Jesuits in the 16th century. Here, in 1820, members of the clergy and other Spaniards plotted to defeat Mexico's bid for independence by bringing in a European prince to rule the country. Among the plotters was Agustin de Iturbide who, after consummating Mexico's independence through guile, was to proclaim himself emperor.

The Palace of Iturbide, just 2 blocks west at Madero 17, is an elegant building. Completely restored in 1972, it now houses the offices of a financial institution. Its construction as a private dwelling was begun in 1779 by the Count of San Mateo. When Iturbide entered the city in triumph on September 27, 1821, the building's owner invited him to make the palace his home. After having himself crowned emperor in July, 1822, Iturbide continued to live there, but only for 10 months—until he was forced to abdicate and fled into exile. The following year, when he attempted to reenter Mexico, Iturbide was captured and executed.

The Church and Monastery of San Francisco, nestling behind the Latin American Tower, played a dominant role in the spiritual and social life of the people from 1524 until the 1850s. The four square blocks ceded to the Franciscans by Cortez were bounded roughly by today's streets of Madero, San Juan de Letran, Venustiano Carranza, and Bolivar. There the city's first church was built in 1525. The present church, the third to stand on the site, dates from 1716. Recent excavations permit a complete view of the lovely facade and reveal that the heavy structure has sunk 12 feet into the spongy subsoil.

The House of Tiles, directly across the street at Madero 4, is one of the city's downtown show places. Another palatial residence, the building was erected prior to 1708 as the town house of the Counts of Orizaba. The facing of Puebla tiles it wears was added in 1737. For many years the exclusive Jockey Club occupied the building. Then in 1919 the first Sanborn's restaurant was installed in the spacious patio, where it continues to operate today.

The Numismatic Museum is just west of Sanborn's across narrow Condesa Street on the second floor of the Guardiola Building. The 20,000-piece collection includes duck quills filled with gold dust; cacao beans and jade beads used as media of exchange before the Conquest; coins brought in by the Spaniards and those they minted in Mexico during the colonial period; money coined by insurgents during the War for Independence and, a century later, the Revolution of 1910. Admission is free; hours are 10 A.M. to 4 P.M., Monday through Friday.

The 44-story Latin American Tower, on the opposite corner of Madero and San Juan de Letran, has suffered no damage from sinking or earthquakes despite its height and weight since construction in 1956, because it is built on a concrete slab resting on pilings anchored in solid rock 100 feet below the surface. Water is injected around the pilings to maintain the level of the building. The 42nd floor is a *mirador* (scenic lookout) commanding a superb view of the entire valley; the Muralto restaurant and cocktail lounge occupy the floor below.

Avenida Juarez

Continuing westward, Madero becomes Avenida Juarez. The first building on the right after crossing San Juan de Letran is the Palacio de Belles Artes, home of the world-famous Ballet Folklorico, the National Symphony orchestra, and classic and modern ballet companies. It is also the opera house. Information on all events appears in *The News,* Mexico City's English-language daily, and in give-away tourist publications. Some of the best murals ever painted by Orozco, Rivera, Siqueiros, and Tamayo adorn the stairwell and walls; special art exhibits are held in the various salons. Your eyes will be caught by the 22-ton glass mosaic curtain by Tiffany, installed in 1910.

Begun in 1904 and built on land reclaimed from Lake Texcoco, the massive marble structure has sunk 6 feet below street level. The sinking has caused spectators' seats to tilt forward; at performances you may feel that you have to hold on to keep from falling out of your chair.

Alameda Park, immediately west of the palace, is two by four blocks in size and the largest green area in downtown Mexico City. Establishment of a park on the one-time lake bed was decreed in 1572. In 1973 the park was completely refurbished—its broad walkways paved with pink stone blocks, its several fountains cleaned and repaired, and its numerous classical bronze and marble statues burnished. Comfortable benches and attractive lighting fixtures were placed along the paths and on the periphery of the park.

Early in the colonial era the stake for burning victims of the Holy Inquisition was set up on the west side of today's Alameda. Throughout the 19th century the park was enclosed by a wall and reserved for the upper classes who promenaded there on Sunday in carriages or on horseback. Sunday in the Alameda is also the subject of Diego Rivera's mural (1947) in the lobby of the Hotel del

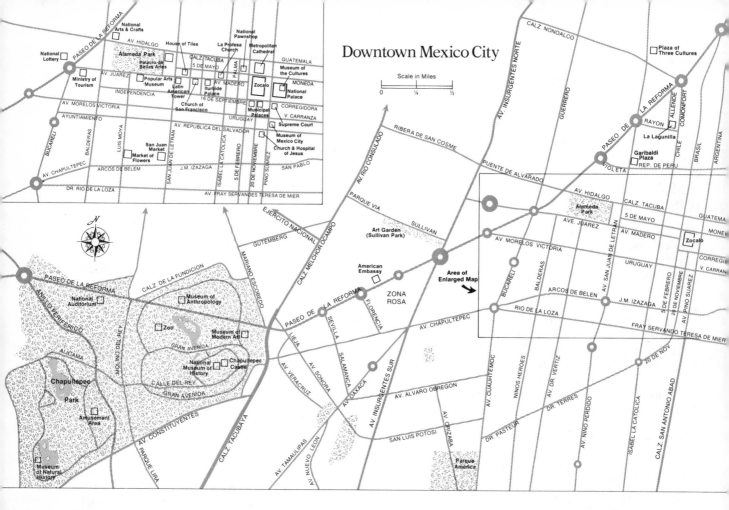

Prado, across the street at Juarez 70. You'll enjoy the mural's (and the park's) colorful Sunday sprawl.

Midway along the Juarez side of the park stands the imposing Juarez Hemicycle, dedicated in 1910 to Benito Juarez, president of Mexico during the War of Reform and the Empire of Maximilian.

The Museum of Colonial Paintings, facing the west side of the Alameda at Mora 7, is housed in the 16th century Church of San Diego. Hidalgo Street borders the park on the north, and at No. 85 is the Hotel Cortez, dating from 1780. It was built by the Augustinians as an inn for pilgrims beside one of the causeways that linked the capital to the mainland.

One block east, two 18th century churches, San Juan de Dios and Santa Veracruz, face each other across a small sunken plaza.

The National Museum of Popular Arts on the south side of Juarez next to the Hotel Alameda occupies the old Church of Corpus Christi, part of a convent founded in 1724 for noble Indian women. On the south side, too, is a profusion of jewelry and handicraft shops.

Popular arts are well represented at two locations in the last block of Juarez before its intersection with Paseo de la Reforma. On the ground floor of the Ministry of Tourism, Juarez 92, sales exhibitions lasting from 4 to 6 weeks are offered. Each is devoted either to one type of craft object from different areas of the Republic—textiles, ceramics, basketry, woodworking, and so on—or to the varied products of a single state.

Across the street at Juarez 89 is a new museum-salesroom, opened in 1974. The setting, a charmingly restored colonial building, started life as a convent. Today, its two spacious floors are filled with a vast array of popular arts chosen for their authenticity and superb workmanship. The National Handicrafts Fund operates the museum and also arranges the six to eight exhibits staged each year in the Tourism Ministry.

Paseo de la Reforma

Stately Paseo de la Reforma was laid out by Maximilian, who reigned as emperor of Mexico from 1864 to 1867. Having established his royal residence in Chapultepec Castle, Maximilian desired a direct route to the National Palace and traveled it in an ornate carriage drawn by six buff-colored mules. At that time the roadway was known as Carlotta's Promenade.

From its intersection with Juarez westward to the park, the Paseo is punctuated by several impressive monuments. Where the two streets cross stands the oldest of them all—El Caballito (Little Horse), the bronze equestrian statue of Charles IV of Spain. A magnificent work of art, the statue was cast in Mexico in 1802 and first stood on the Zocalo. It is the horse (as the statue's affectionate name implies) that has captured the public's imagination, not the rider, who remains anonymous to most.

On the traffic circle in front of the Fiesta Palace Hotel is a splendid monument to Christopher Columbus, placed there in 1877.

Cuauhtemoc, last emperor of the Aztecs, keeps his vigil at the Reforma-Insurgentes intersection from a rather complex pyramidal monument of three bodies, completed in 1887. Surmounting the whole is the heroic figure of 22-year-old Cuauhtemoc in full battle dress, his spear at the ready.

Most beloved by Mexicans of all the Reforma monuments is the Independence shaft on the traffic circle where the Hotel Maria Isabel Sheraton and the United States Embassy stand. Begun in 1902 but torn down in 1906 because of a faulty foundation, the monument was completed in 1909 on pilings driven 70 feet through the spongy subsoil to solid rock. Aside from the weight of the 150-foot column, the foundation supports the 8-ton gilded angel poised on the shaft's tip. After the severe earthquake of 1957 hurled the angel to the marble flooring at the base of the shaft, and during the many months required for repairs, the benches around the traffic circle were occupied continuously by the monument's devoted admirers.

Once the lovely fountain of Diana the Huntress graced a traffic circle at the entrance to Chapultepec Park, but fountain and circle were forced to give way to the march of progress and construction of the vital inner-city expressway, some sections of which have been completed. Now that the section passing the park on the east is completed, Diana again presides over her fountain in a small park nearby, on the north side of Paseo de la Reforma.

Pink Zone

The Pink Zone—Zona Rosa—is to Mexico City what the central plaza is to a provincial town. Bounded by Paseo de la Reforma, Insurgentes Sur, Avenida Chapultepec, and Florencia, the Zone covers an area of roughly 18 square blocks. Within its confines are numerous restaurants of all types, nightclubs, hotels, travel agencies, art galleries, and shops and boutiques in infinite variety selling everything from colorful paper flowers to designer clothes and handsome wearing apparel in kid or suede.

It is the ideal place to window shop, to run into friends or new acquaintances, to see and be seen. High fashion prevails on these streets; even the trees are pink.

Chapultepec Park

If you entertain the notion of "doing" Chapultepec Park in a day, forget it! This vast cultural and recreational center covers more than 2,000 acres. It is bounded by Avenida Constituyentes on the south-southwest, extends westward in an irregular form beyond Molino del Rey Street and the peripheral

Days of the Dead: cause for celebration?

The streets and markets of Mexico around Halloween time may surprise you with their great array of confections and simple toys or figures with skull, skeleton, or coffin motifs.

They're for the Days of the Dead, celebrated November 1 and 2. This Mexican holiday is a curious blending of the Christian All Saints' Day and a pre-Hispanic feast day. The figures reflect the unique Mexican attitude toward death: serious, but also mocking and humorous.

Downtown shops display paper flowers and unusual Halloween-style trappings. Bakeries feature a special bread (pan de muerto). Markets sell children's dolls and masks, toy coffins, and miniature skeletons.

Many Mexican families gather to eat an elaborate meal. Often an altar is set up with burning candles and zempasuchitl (the flower of the dead). The special bread, tamales, turkey mole, pulque, and confections are offered in the belief that the souls of the departed will return to enjoy the meal.

If you visit any of Mexico's cemeteries on this day, you'll see families and friends gathered to chat while cleaning and decorating the graves.

Days of the Dead celebrations are of special interest in Lake Patzcuaro's island village of Janitzio. Residents bring food to the cemeteries and keep an all-night vigil. Hundreds of candles burn on the graves, making a spectacular sight.

highway, and in some places overflows Paseo de la Reforma on the north. On the east, the park relinquished a portion of its land for construction of the Melchor Ocampo section of the inner-city expressway.

Located within the park's boundaries are four of the country's finest museums, three lakes with boating facilities, a variety of playground equipment, a Coney Island-type amusement park with all the usual rides plus one of the largest roller coasters to be found anywhere, and several miniature railways. There are also flower gardens, a number of handsome fountains and sculptures, and miles of quiet walkways shaded by centuries-old cypress trees (ahuehuetes). The park is closed to auto traffic on Sunday.

The Zoo houses some 2,000 birds and animals of several hundred species. The newest inhabitants are two giant pandas—a gift of the People's Republic of China—who were a year old in September, 1975, when they took up residence in their special air-conditioned quarters. The zoo is closed on Mondays.

The Museum of Modern Art is the freeform building on your left as you enter the park by Paseo de la Reforma. It was built in 1964 and sits in sculpture-filled gardens. Permanently displayed in Salon I are the works of Jose Maria Velasco, Mexico's talented and prolific 19th century landscape painter. In Salon II the artists of a later period, 1900-60, are represented including canvases by Orozco, Rivera, Tamayo, Siqueiros, Dr. Atl, and others. The works of contemporary painters, active since 1950, are on view in Salon III. Special exhibits by artists of all nationalities are mounted from time to time. Open 11 A.M. to 7 P.M. daily, except Monday.

The National Museum of Anthropology, a miracle of architecture and museum planning, is easily identified by the 168-ton figure of Tlaloc, the rain god, standing at the entrance to a tunnel leading to the parking area. Pedro Ramirez Vazquez was the architect of this splendid structure, perhaps the most modern and functional museum in the world.

Off the spacious lobby, on the right, is the temporary exhibit hall with its ingenious mechanisms for lighting and display. At the rear of the lobby, opposite the ticket counters, is the Orientation Salon. Here, a light-and-sound spectacle presents the chronological sequence of Mexico's ancient cultures in capsule form in 23 minutes. The recorded lecture is in Spanish, but the display of pictures, bas-reliefs, figurines, and scale models of pyramids and temples is easily understood without the commentary, and serves as a valuable introduction to the exhibits awaiting you inside the museum.

As you enter the door into the mammoth patio, remember that the museum's treasures occupy 100,000 square feet of floor space on two floors; a complete view of the interior entails a 3-mile hike. For your convenience, each salon on the ground floor opens onto the patio where stone benches enable you to rest. A stairway on the lefthand side of the patio leads down to a restaurant. There are several restrooms.

The patio's outstanding feature is a 5,300-square-yard "umbrella" on a sculptured bronze column. From it falls a refreshing cascade of water that is also a cooling device for the water that flows through the museum's mechanical systems.

Open Tuesday through Saturday, 9 A.M. to 7 P.M.; Sunday and holidays, 10 A.M. to 6 P.M.; closed Monday. You may find it rewarding to devote more than one day to your exploration of this museum.

A roadway through the park begins directly opposite the Anthropology Museum and leads to the Hill of Chapultepec and the castle that crowns it. There the National Museum of History was installed in 1934.

Chapultepec Castle, begun in 1783, was originally intended to be a weekend resort for the Spanish viceroys. But the War for Independence intervened, and the castle was not completed until 1841 when it was designated as a military academy. It was the last bastion to fall to the invaders during the U.S.-Mexican War of 1847. Then came Maximilian and Carlotta, who made the castle their private residence, adding many of the beautiful features it possesses today. Subsequent presidents of Mexico—with the exception of Benito Juarez—resided there until Lazar Cardenas decreed that the history museum should be installed in the castle.

The eastern portion of the building displays the rich furniture and furnishings left behind by Emperor Maximilian. Notice Carlotta's exquisite bathtub. In the museum proper, the history of Mexico is depicted in various salons. Aside from their fascinating exhibits, several salons are adorned with murals by O'Gorman, Reyes Meza, Gonzalez Camarena, and Siqueiros. Open daily 10 A.M. to 6 P.M.; closed Tuesday.

The Museum of Natural History, far out Constituyentes just before reaching Dolores Cemetery, is on the roadway on your right. Spectacularly modernistic in architecture, its exhibits are universal, not exclusively Mexican. Note especially the Rotunda of Illustrious Men (and women). Open 10 A.M. to 5 P.M., Tuesday through Saturday; 10 A.M. to 8 P.M., Sunday; closed Monday.

Sweeping staircase *dramatizes Modern Art Museum entrance.*

Curtain of water *cascades from umbrella roof in central patio of Museum of Anthropology in Chapultepec Park.*

The National Auditorium, west on Reforma (left-hand side) shortly before its intersection with the peripheral highway, is the scene of classical ballet performances, jazz concerts, and other cultural programs presented chiefly by troupes and bands from abroad. International sports events are also staged there. Check *The News* (English-language daily) for details.

On Sundays and holidays Chapultepec Park is filled to overflowing with family groups. That is when vendors of balloons, soft drinks, candies, and tacos reap the richest harvest. But there are many things going on every day in the park, making a leisurely visit well worthwhile.

For those who shudder at the prospect of traversing so much ground on foot, first-class buses operate out of a terminal at the rear of the Museum of Modern Art. After winding through the old section of the park, the buses emerge onto Constituyentes, enter the new section by its main entrance, work their way north to the Reforma, and then return to the terminal. There are scheduled stops all along the route.

Glistening bunches *of flowers, washed by afternoon shower, sell for only pennies.*

Other places of interest

Many visitors find other attractions scattered throughout the metropolitan area—some historical, some symbolic of the city's everyday life, others unique to Mexico. You're sure to make discoveries of your own. Here are a few suggestions to get you started:

Museum of the City of Mexico. On the northeast corner of Pino Suarez and Republica de El Salvador, midway between the Zocalo and the Pino Suarez subway station, stands the magnificent town house of the Counts of Santiago de Calimaya. Its foundations were laid in the 1530s, but the known history of the mansion begins in 1775 when it was totally restored by the count of that epoch.

The building is impressive because of its elegant simplicity and the excellence of its stone carving. Notice the massive stone serpent's head that once adorned the Aztec ceremonial center and is now embedded in an exterior wall of the building.

Massive Tlaloc, *outdoor exhibit at Anthropology Museum, represents god of rain.*

In 1960 the mansion was declared a national monument and, after restoration and adaptation, it became the Museum of the City of Mexico. Ground-floor salons depict the pre-Hispanic history of the Valley of Mexico, from man's appearance in the Valley up to the defeat and destruction of Tenochtitlan in 1521. Second-floor exhibits transport the visitor through the colonial and independence periods to present-day Mexico City. From the last corridor you can look down upon an ingeniously illuminated scale model of today's metropolis. Open 9:30 A.M. to 7 P.M.; closed Monday.

Church and Hospital of Jesus. Diagonally across the street, on the southwest corner of the intersection, stands the oldest hospital in the Americas, founded by Cortez in 1524 on the spot where Emperor Montezuma greeted him upon his arrival 5 years earlier. In continuous operation since its founding, the hospital now occupies a square block with newer facilities surrounding the colonial core which is still in use. Under the terms of his will which provided financial support for the institution, Cortez stipulated that the hospital be directed by his descendants.

This stipulation was respected until the 1930s when the government took over the administration of the hospital from an unworthy scion of the family. An inexpensive health care plan for those not covered by social security and unable to pay for private insurance is now in effect. The hospital is endowed with all the latest equipment.

In the Church of Jesus Nazareno lie the remains of the conqueror, Cortez. Cortez died in Spain in 1547, leaving instructions that his body was to be returned to Mexico 10 years later. After being moved from place to place, the remains were finally interred in the church in 1794, but hatred of the Spaniards reached such a pitch during the War for Independence that they were removed and hidden in another part of the church. Persevering historical investigators rediscovered the remains in 1946, and they are now entombed in the north wall of the sacristy. The church is open to visitors.

Garibaldi Plaza. If you're addicted to mariachi music, and the louder the better, Garibaldi Plaza is the place to find it: 6 blocks north of Madero, 1 block east of Santa Maria La Redonda (northward extension of San Juan de Letran), between Honduras and Peru streets. The plaza and the numerous restaurants and night spots on its perimeter were completely refurbished in 1973. Groups of musicians begin to gather there about 10 P.M., and the later it gets the more music there will be as mariachi bands that have been performing elsewhere join in the fun. Remember—you pay if they play.

Fancy ropework *and riding mark charreada. Losing sombrero during show loses points for charro.*

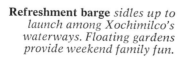

Refreshment barge *sidles up to launch among Xochimilco's waterways. Floating gardens provide weekend family fun.*

Always on Sunday

Any visit to Mexico City should be planned to include at least one Sunday, for certain activities of major interest can be indulged in only on that day.

Bullfights are, for many, among the chief reasons for coming to Mexico. In the capital they take place in the world's largest bullring, Plaza Mexico on Insurgentes Sur, which seats 50,000 fans. The formal season begins around December 1 and lasts for 3 or 4 months. That's when prestige matadors fight brave bulls weighing in the neighborhood of 1,000 pounds. During the rest of the year, younger, less experienced *novilleros* fight smaller bulls.

When you buy your tickets—which you should do in advance through a travel agency, but can do at the bullring—specify whether you want to sit on the *sombra* (shady side) or the sunny side. Sombra seats are more expensive. Shun the ticket scalpers! The exciting spectacle begins promptly at 4:30 P.M.

Xochimilco, perhaps the second most popular Sunday destination, is about 15 miles southeast of the downtown area. Several hundred years before the Conquest, the Xochimilcas established a land base and floating gardens aboard rafts of varying sizes, long since anchored by plant and tree roots. They developed a thriving trade in green goods with the island capital of the Aztecs. When the lake was drained, the constantly enlarged raft-islands and the canals dividing them remained to become a colorful Sunday recreation area.

Nothing floats there now but canoes and gondolas. Until recent years each gondola proudly wore its name emblazoned in fresh flowers across the front of the canopy; unfortunately, now plastic flowers are used to form the names.

You can visit Xochimilco at any hour of the day, but Mexican family groups go in the afternoon and that's when the holiday spirit reaches its peak. Along the banks are a number of restaurants where your boatman can put in. (We recommend taking a lunch.) Authorized hourly rates for boat rides are posted at the docks. Agree on the charges before you set off.

Art buffs will enjoy a stroll through the Art Garden, one block west of Insurgentes and two short blocks north of Reforma. Between the hours of 10 A.M. and 3 P.M. every Sunday, some 250 artists struggling for recognition display works including paintings in all media, etchings, drawings, and sculpture.

In 1972 the small area, formerly Sullivan Park, was totally reconditioned as an outdoor art gallery. Broad, winding, beige and pink pathways serve as exhibition halls. There are eight splashing fountains, three large bird cages with a variety of colorful and musical birds, landscaped gardens and shade trees, and many benches where you can sit and watch the passers-by. An underground parking garage occupies the section of the park fronting on Insurgentes.

Charreria, a strictly Mexican institution, and its creature, the charreada, are the progenitors of the Western-style cowboy and the rodeo. Neither cattle nor horses were known in Mexico until after the Conquest in 1521 when those who had won the land for Spain were rewarded with immense haciendas, which they stocked with imported livestock. The tasks of everyday ranch life, as well as the maneuvers required to round up, cut out and, in general, herd cattle gave rise to new and complicated skills that were gradually refined into what became known as *charreria*, the art and showmanship of the man on horseback.

The charreada, as a public spectacle, dates from 1921. The huge haciendas were broken up by the Revolution of 1910 and, once the dust had settled, nostalgia led the dispossessed haciendados to form the National Association of Charros. Most of the feats performed are wellknown to rodeo fans, but these two are peculiarly Mexican: the *coleo* or *coleada* where, within a specified time, a charro must overtake a wild steer and throw it by twisting its tail *(cola);* and the *paso de la muerte* (pass of death), where the rider must pass from the back of his own mount to that of a wild bronc while riding at a full gallop.

Charreadas are usually held Saturday and Sunday mornings at Charros del Pedregal, Camino Santa Teresa No. 305. Call 573-11-69 before planning to attend; some events are not open to the public.

A new charro ring will soon be built in Chapultepec Park.

La Lagunilla, long known as the Thieves' Market, is an open-air Sunday mecca for antique hunters. Located on Rayon, between Allende and Comonfort streets, the market is open from 9:30 A.M. to 4:30 P.M.; for the best selection you'll be wise to go in the morning.

It is sometimes possible to come upon a real find at the market, and it helps if you can distinguish between genuine and make-believe antiques. If there's a crowd, beware of pickpockets.

San Juan Market. Five blocks south of Alameda Park, at Ernesto Pugibet 21, is the San Juan food market, an epicure's paradise. Its vast array of delicacies is assembled by purchasing choice produce in the capital's wholesale markets, underwriting the production of non-Mexican fruits and vegetables in truck gardens near the city, and importing fine foods not available within the country. All the ingredients for international cuisine are available there, as well as the components necessary for succulent Mexican dishes. San Juan's reputation is such that the bulk of its sales are made by telephone to luxury hotels, gourmet restaurants, and foreign embassies.

Siqueiros Polyforum. On the righthand side of Insurgentes Sur, on the grounds of the towering Hotel Mexico, stands the Siqueiros Polyforum, a 4-story, 12-sided exposition hall covered with the dramatic acrylic murals of David Alfaro Siqueiros. The 12 panels each illustrate one phase of the artist's theme, "Humanity's Progress on Earth and in the Universe."

The underground level offers a select display of traditional and modern handicrafts for sale including furniture, ceramics, crystal, and textiles. A glass elevator and a winding stairway lead to the ground floor and cupola. At ground level is an exposition of Mexico's urban development plans for the future. The cupola is adorned with a continuous relief painting by Siqueiros that can be viewed from a revolving platform accommodating up to 1,000 persons. The Polyforum is open daily, except Tuesday, from noon to 10:30 P.M.

A visit to the suburbs

On the southern outskirts of the metropolis, three suburbs and University City form a section of particular interest to visitors. Two of these areas, Coyoacan and San Angel, are very old; the other two, the campus of the National University and the Pedregal residential section, are ultramodern. All four can be covered in a day by car; drivers or guided tours are available at all major hotels. More time is needed to explore in a leisurely manner the many places that will attract your attention.

Coyoacan. Once an Indian kingdom, Coyoacan means "place of the coyotes." After the Spanish conquerors had razed the Aztec capital, they withdrew to Coyoacan until the island city could again be made habitable. Almost overnight Coyoacan became a Spanish town, and many buildings of the 16th and 17th centuries not only remain standing but continue in use today.

Plaza Hidalgo and the Centenario Garden together form the main plaza of Coyoacan. The house

said to have belonged to Cortez (but doubtful because it dates from the 17th century) faces this shady, flower-filled area.

On the walls of a chapel in an adjoining patio are modern murals depicting the Conquest.

Across the plaza from the so-called Cortez house stands *La Parroquia* (Parish Church), constructed in the 16th century. To the right of its facade an arch gives access to the monastery of which it was a part.

Two other 17th century homes bear the names of Pedro de Alvarado and Diego de Oraz, two of Cortez' top lieutenants. The houses are both Moorish in appearance, similar to the one attributed to Cortez. But if either Alvarado or Oraz ever lived in the houses originally erected on the sites it was only briefly, for they were both fully occupied elsewhere in consummating the Conquest.

At some distance from the central plaza are two museums well worth a visit. One is the Frido Kahlo Museum on the northeast corner of Allende and Londres, established in the home the artist shared for 25 years with her husband, Diego Rivera, until her death in 1954. Open daily, except Monday, from 10 A.M. to 6 P.M., it displays the works of both artists plus archaeological pieces collected by them.

The other is the Churubusco Museum installed in the Churubusco Monastery at the corner of General Anaya and 20 de Agosto. The first building raised by the Franciscans in 1524 was rebuilt and enlarged in the 17th century and again in the 19th. During the U.S.-Mexican War of 1847, the monastery became a fortress, falling to the invaders on August 20, 1847. Now a museum devoted chiefly to relics of that war, it is open Monday through Saturday, 10 A.M. to 8 P.M.; Sunday, 9 A.M. to 2 P.M. and 3 to 5 P.M.

University City. Inaugurated in 1953, the modernistic campus of Mexico's National University extends east and west of the highway over an immense flow of lava erupted by the volcano Ixtle in about 200 B.C. The campus is an outdoor gallery of mural art expressed in every medium by leading Mexican muralists.

Clearly visible even before you enter the campus is the 10-story, wrap-around, polychrome stone mosaic mural on the Central Library, for which Juan O'Gorman was both architect and artist. On the west side of the highway, the daring stone mosaic decoration carved and painted on the stadium was designed by Diego Rivera. Facing the stadium is the rectory, adorned on three sides by Siqueiros; the central mural is unique for its 3-dimensional massiveness. Other muralists whose works enhance campus buildings include Messeguer, Eppens Helguera, and Chavez Morado.

Of special attraction to those interested in Mexican flora are the university's Botanical Gardens where exotic plants from all regions of the country are on view in two greenhouses and three acres of exterior plantings. The orchid and cacti collection is south of the stadium, over a clearly marked roadway. Cacti are arranged in a natural lava rock setting; the orchids in a ground-hugging conservatory. Tropical rain forest plants grow under simulated natural conditions in a conservatory east and south of the Olympic swimming pool. In all, more than 2,000 species are displayed, each tagged with its botanical name and the area from which it comes. The gardens are open every day of the year.

The National University was founded in 1551 by royal decree in a building on the Zocalo just north of the National Palace. As the number of students increased, each professional school moved to quarters of its own. When the present campus was inaugurated it drew together students from schools by then scattered all over the city. In 1975—only 22 years later—enrollment stood at 245,000. Now dispersal is again in process, with the establishment of branch universities in the most remote areas of the capital and in nearby towns.

Jardines del Pedregal. West of the university stadium are the *Jardines del Pedregal,* "Gardens of the Lava Flow"—an extension of the same flow upon which the campus is built. To reach this incredible residential area, return north on Insurgentes Sur to San Jeronimo, taking off to the left just beyond Avenida Universidad.

The Pedregal must be seen to be believed. Its modernistic architecture incorporates black lava stone into homes and landscaping with dramatic results. The weird, beautiful trees and flowers that flourish on their rocky beds complete the otherworldly atmosphere.

Here there are no pre-Hispanic or colonial monuments; only the uncommon beauty that sprang from the fertile imagination of a group of architects in the late 1940s.

San Angel. Your eyes will be drawn first to the enormous pile of El Carmen Church and Convent, built by the Carmelites in 1615-17. Services continue to be held in this church resplendent in gold leaf, Puebla tile, and oil paintings. In the thick-walled convent, the National Institute of Anthropology and History maintains a museum of colonial art and workshops where authentic copies of pre-Hispanic ceramic figures and jewelry are manufactured and offered for sale.

San Jacinto Plaza, a long block west of Revolucion, is surrounded by some of San Angel's oldest buildings. The 18th century Casa del Risco on the east side, for example, was a private residence until recent years. Now it is a museum displaying all the furnishings of a bygone era—furniture, paintings, chandeliers, and chinaware. Set in one wall of the patio is the huge fountain that gives the

The Olmec, Mexico's mother culture

Thirty years ago considerable mystery surrounded the Olmecs. Today, though, archaeologists agree that these people were the initiators of all that became known as "high culture" in pre-Colombian Mexico, and that their homeland was in the jungles of the present states of Veracruz and Tabasco on the Gulf Coast.

Their name comes from the Indian word *ulli,* or rubber, and means "inhabitants of the country of rubber." Their beginnings date back to around 2000 B.C.

Stone was scarce in their jungle home, and that prevented the Olmecs from developing a lasting architecture. Structures found at La Venta, San Lorenzo, and Tres Zapotes are basically of earth or mud—temple bases arranged around plazas, forming ceremonial centers. The stone they were able to bring into the area was used for carving colossal figures, notably the so-called "baby-face" heads.

But while their architecture was poor, not so the Olmec intellectual and artistic skills. They not only developed a numbering system, a calendar, and hieroglyphic writing, but also became masters at carving stone and jade. Remarkable in their culture was the deification of the jaguar; feline motifs on pottery, figurines, and masks all signal Olmec influence.

The Olmecs, as an ethnic entity, disappeared about the beginning of the Christian era. Groups of Olmecs wandered and merged with other peoples, spreading Olmec achievements throughout Mexican territory—into Oaxaca, the central highlands, as far north and west as Colima and Guerrero on the Pacific Coast—even to Guatemala and El Salvador. The Maya, for instance, based their calendar system on the original Olmec invention; refined by the Maya, the calendar became the most exact ever devised in mankind's history.

Today, La Venta, Tabasco, close to the mouth of the Tonala River, is one of the few Olmec sites that can be visited easily. Earth mounds can still be seen as well as a few stone monuments, but most of the sculptures unearthed have been removed for display at La Venta Park, in Villahermosa, Tabasco.

house its name because it forms a fantastic *risco*, or cliff, of multicolored tiles and fine porcelain pieces.

On the front of a building on the west side of the plaza is a bronze plaque unveiled in 1959, which reads: "In memory of the Irish soldiers of the heroic St. Patrick's Brigade, martyrs who gave their lives for the Mexican cause during the unjust North American invasion of 1847." The names of 68 officers and enlisted men follow.

Archives of the Library of Congress reveal, though, that these "martyred heroes" were actually deserters from the U.S. army who, in July, 1847, signed agreements to serve in the Mexican army in exchange for land grants. Many of them came from San Patricio, Texas—hence the name "St. Patrick's Brigade." After their capture and court-martial by U.S. forces, 23 were hanged, and 24 were lashed, branded, and dishonorably discharged. The fate of the rest of the men is not known.

Also on the west side of San Jacinto Plaza is the Bazaar Sabado, or Saturday Bazaar. It occupies a 17th century mansion from which the sleeping Santa Ana barely escaped with his life on the day U.S. troops took San Angel. On Saturdays only, from 10 A.M. to 8 P.M., some 100 craftsmen, Mexican and foreign, display their creations—many of contemporary rather than traditional design—running the gamut from exquisite silverware and jewelry through clothing and textiles to furniture. There is a restaurant on the patio.

If you haven't yet had lunch (or if it is time for dinner) try the charmingly different ambience of the San Angel Inn, Palmas 50. The early 18th century manor house of a 90,000-acre hacienda, it became a restaurant in 1963 and offers international cuisine. Dining is indoors or on the broad terraces that surround a lovely patio filled with flowers.

Exploring San Angel on foot through the winding cobblestone streets is a thoroughly enjoyable experience, if you are comfortably shod. The area was "discovered" in the 18th century by viceroys, members of the nobility, and high churchmen. Since it is higher and somewhat cooler than downtown Mexico City, San Angel became a fashionable spot for rest and recreation, especially in the summer. Many of the homes built by aristocrats still stand, mostly behind high walls, of course. Home and garden tours are arranged by the Ladies' Club of San Angel; ask your travel agent, or inquire at the American Book Store, Madero 25.

The city's diversions

A highlight of Mexico City's nighttime entertainment is the show given every Wednesday at 9 P.M.

and on Sunday at 9:30 A.M. and 9 P.M. at the Palace of Fine Arts. Known as Ballet Folklorico de Mexico, it is one of the liveliest and most satisfying combinations of Mexican music, dancing, costumes, and staging that you'll see anywhere. Try to get tickets at least a day ahead of time, preferably from a travel agent; they may sell out early during heavy tourist seasons.

Many of the most elegant nightclubs, shows, and restaurants are concentrated in the Pink Zone. The larger hotels elsewhere in the city all have one or more nightclubs or bars with afternoon and evening entertainment.

Every Monday, Wednesday, and Friday night there is a drawing at the National Lottery Building, corner Juarez and Rosales, to determine the day's lottery winners. You'll have more interest in the proceedings if you've bought a ticket or two from a street vendor. Prizes range from hundreds of pesos to millions. (U.S. customs regulations prohibit bringing lottery tickets into the United States.) Often some entertainment enlivens the lengthy proceedings in which the most active participants are small, uniformed page boys who call out the winning numbers they draw from revolving cages. The complete list of lottery winners is published the following day in the morning newspapers.

Jai-alai is played every night of the week except Monday and Friday at Fronton Mexico, facing the Monument to the Revolution. Usually, the games begin at 6:45 P.M. The greatest spectator interest centers on the betting, which is confusing to the novice. On every play the odds change, and "bookies" pace back and forth in front of the stands exchanging money with the bettors by means of a cut-open tennis ball attached to a long pole. Those who prefer a less strenuous betting system can use the windows in the lobby, where bets may be placed on the final outcome of the game or on quinellas.

Movies are very popular and well attended in Mexico. Current films, including some not yet released in the United States, are available. Sound tracks on all foreign films, including American, are in the original language, with Spanish subtitles. You'll find the programs of the best movie houses listed in the entertainment section of *The News*, Mexico City's English-language daily.

Hipodromo de las Americas is the capital's beautiful racetrack on the northern outskirts of the city. Races are held on Tuesday, Thursday, Saturday, and Sunday afternoons all year round—except from mid-September to October 12. Tuesday racing is discontinued during the summer.

Soccer or *futbol* (a faster, more agile game than U.S. football) is the most popular sport in the world and is played with verve to capacity crowds.

Monumental mosaic designs *like Juan O'Gorman's give unique look to Mexico's National University.*

Size is no particular advantage in soccer but stamina is, since the same 11 players who start a game for each team usually finish the match too. Mexico has soccer comic books, sand-lot soccer, and little league soccer—all indicative of the national preoccupation with the sport. In Mexico City, big-league games are played in the Estadio Azteca (seats 108,000) out on Calzada Tlalpan, Thursday evenings and Sunday mornings. Occasionally additional games are scheduled. Tickets may be purchased at the stadium.

Eating well

Like all metropolises, Mexico City has an abundance of excellent restaurants specializing in many different cuisines. But since it is here that you can savor Mexican food as it is prepared on its home ground, take a look at Mexican cuisine first.

Check with your hotel for suggestions about restaurants noted for outstanding native dishes.

Forget the familiar taco and enchilada and try some new exciting item on the menu instead. Don't overlook the seafood. Most restaurants have menus in both Spanish and English; otherwise ask your waiter for explanations.

One of the world's few great, distinctive cuisines, Mexican cooking has been refined over a period of several thousand years. Though simple in its beginning—based on corn, beans, and squash—by the time of the Conquest preparation was so complex and ingredients so varied that the Spaniards were amazed.

While the discovery of New Spain meant that Europe's table was enriched by such Mexican foods and flavors as corn, tomatoes, avocados, chiles, chocolate, and vanilla, it also gave new direction to Mexican cuisine. The Spaniards brought with them oil and animal fats, adding another cooking process—frying. They also introduced cattle, hogs, and sheep (thus also milk, butter, and cheese), as well as sugar and rice. These new ingredients were rapidly incorporated into Mexican fare, and the wonderful result is your gain.

You'll also find Mexico City a delight for continental dining—from Arabian to vegetarian. No matter what the restaurant's specialty, you'll probably find delicious tropical fruits on the menu. Hot sauces are always available upon request. Mexican beer is extremely good, and these Mexican brands of wine come well recommended: Santo Tomas, Hidalgo, Terrasola, and Domecq.

Meals cost about the same as you would pay at home for equivalent food and service. Tourists have been exempted from the 15 percent restaurant tax, but to benefit from that exemption you must show your tourist card and passport *when you ask for the bill.*

Leisurely mealtimes are the rule. The usual lunch hour is from 2 P.M. on, dinner from 9 P.M.

A restaurant's atmosphere adds to a good meal. Several excellent choices are Hacienda de los Morales (elegant dining in an 18th century manor house), Prendes (operating since 1892 in a building of the old San Francisco monastery), or Del Lago Menor and its more expensive counterpart Del Lago Mayor (both on lakes in Chapultepec Park).

Teotihuacan's *Pyramid of Moon (background) dominates many smaller shrines.*

Nearby attractions

You can make these excursions on your own, via bus tour, or with a car and driver-guide. Though none are very far from the city, you should figure at least a half day for short trips, a full day for others.

Teotihuacan and Acolman. Teotihuacan, 25 miles northeast of Mexico City via a toll road that takes off from the Laredo highway on the outskirts of the capital, is an archaeological site so majestic that the Aztecs, who came upon it several centuries after its abandonment, named it the "City of the Gods." Its urban area covers 8.7 square miles and, at the height of its glory (about 200 to 600 A.D.) the inhabitants numbered between 100,000 and 200,000. The magnificent ceremonial center and some of the outlying palaces and priestly dwellings have been restored, and the zone is open every day.

The largest and oldest monument is the Pyramid of the Sun. It was constructed in about 100 B.C. over a long, sinuous, sacred cave—the relics found there prove that the site had been populated for two centuries or more before the pyramid was built. Including the sanctuary that once stood on its summit, the pyramid is 230 feet high, the tallest so far discovered on the American continent.

The broad Avenue of the Dead, 1.5 miles long, runs precisely parallel to the Pyramid of the Sun. On the north it terminates at the Plaza and Pyramid of the Moon (considerably smaller and erected some time after that of the Sun). To the south it passes in front of the huge enclosure erroneously called the Citadel, and there it ends. In reality, the so-called Citadel was a ceremonial complex; the

Energetic climbers *atop Pyramid of Sun appear as mere dots. View is across Avenue of the Dead.*

Shopper can be sure *that turkey she buys at outdoor market near Mexico City is fresh.*

Reverent *pilgrim to Guadalupe shrine bends to kiss portrait of Virgin.*

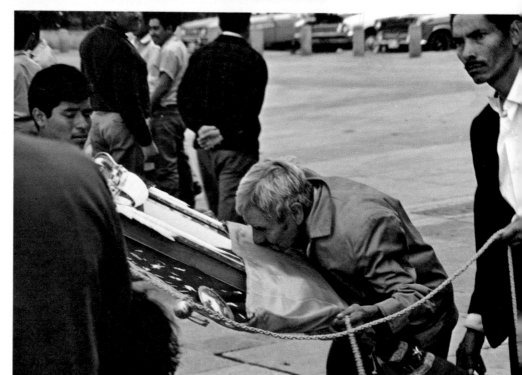

ancient Mexicans worshiped their gods in the open air.

On the eastern side of the square court stands the Temple of Quetzalcoatl (Plumed Serpent), the facade covered with superbly carved stone heads of feathered serpents and the rain god Tlaloc.

Facing on the Plaza of the Moon and along both sides of the Avenue of the Dead are numerous small, flat-topped pyramids and temples. At the southwest corner of the plaza stands the Palace of Quetzalpapalotl. Completely reconstructed, it exemplifies the sumptuousness of the palaces of that era. On the walls of some chambers are traces of the mural paintings that once covered all pre-Hispanic buildings.

When Teotihuacan was in its heyday, it drew religious pilgrims from as far away as Yucatan and Central America. During that same period it was also the most important trading center in the Mexican highlands.

Several good restaurants operate in the archaeological zone, including one installed more than 50 years ago in a mammoth grotto. There is a small, good museum.

From October to May, every night except Wednesday, a light-and-sound spectacle in English is presented at 7 P.M. The script incorporates the legends that sprang up with respect to Teotihuacan, place of mystery. Warm clothing and a lap robe are essential. Tickets are available from travel agencies.

Just off the toll road, about 6 miles south of Teotihuacan, is the handsome, fortress-type Church and Monastery of Acolman, established by the Augustinians in 1539. Probably its most interesting feature is the severely simple, beautifully executed plateresque facade—the purest example of that style in Mexico. In the interior of the temple under many layers of paint, colossal 16th century frescoes in three colors—red, black, and yellow—were discovered during renovation. They resemble those found in more ancient Italian churches. A collection of religious art is exhibited in the monastery. It is open every day.

Texcoco and Chiconcuac. Texcoco is due east of the northern suburbs of Mexico City but, for the time being, it must be reached by one of these two roundabout routes: north almost to Acolman Monastery and then south to Texcoco, or southeast on the Puebla highway to Los Reyes and then north. The latter is a shorter drive of about an hour and a quarter.

A direct route across all that remains of once vast Lake Texcoco is under construction as part of a government reclamation project. When completed it will cut driving time in half. The salty soil of the old lake bed, dry during the winter months, is being reconditioned to permit farming and reforestation. Part of the 66-square-mile area is to become a recreational center. All this will not only put an end to the dust storms that plague the capital in the dry months, but will avert the threat of flooding in the rainy season.

It was in Texcoco (then on the eastern shore of the lake) that Cortez, after being ignominiously routed from the Aztec capital in 1520, assembled 13 brigantines for another assault. Timbers were cut in Tlaxcala and carried across the mountains to Texcoco by 8,000 Indian bearers; by April, 1521, the warships were ready for launching. Four months later, the Conquest was an accomplished fact.

Texcoco now has 70,000 inhabitants. Sunday and Monday are market days, and the market is famous for *barbacoa* (deep-pit barbecued lamb), ceramics and textiles of distinctive styles and designs, and blown glass.

Chiconcuac is less than 10 minutes north of Texcoco over a narrow dirt road. Before the Conquest, Chiconcuac was also on the lake shore—a tiny village that even then specialized in weaving, delivering its goods to market by canoe. Today it is a town of 11,000, and the volume and variety of its textile products in wool and acrylic fibers are unsurpassed anywhere.

In more than 50 shops along the main street you'll find blankets, wall hangings, and sarapes; handmade hooked or shag rugs; sweaters in any style for men, women, and children in a wide selection of colors; *jorongos*—sarapes with a slit in the center to put your head through—as well as shawls, overblouses, stoles and *rebozos* (a long scarf). For anything knit or woven, Chiconcuac is the place, and prices are right.

Guadalupe Shrine and Tlatelolco. A short distance inside the northern city limits is the Basilica of Our Lady of Guadalupe, Mexico's patron saint. This is often a stopping place on the way to Teotihuacan. En route, via the northward extension of Paseo de la Reforma and about 16 blocks beyond its intersection with Juarez, you can also visit the Plaza of the Three Cultures. You can't miss it because from the time you start the drive north, the high-rise buildings of the Tlatelolco housing project will dominate the horizon. Turn left around the traffic circle, and then west onto Calzada Nonoalco, the southern boundary of the project. Turn right at the first corner and the plaza is on your right.

Below street level are the excavated remains of pyramids and platforms, a small portion of Tlatelolco's ceremonial center. Behind the plaza is the attractive 16th century Church of Santiago Tlatelolco and adjoining it, the College of the Holy Cross, completed in 1536 for the sons of Indian

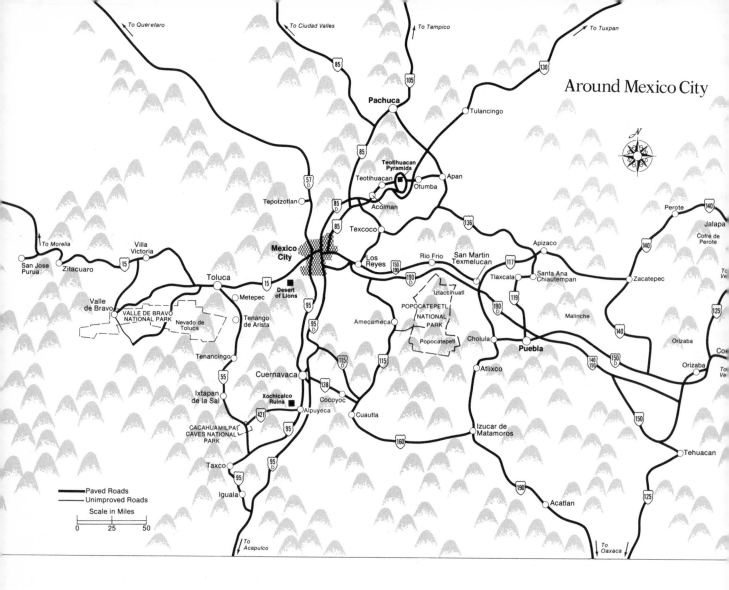

nobles. It was in this college that Fray Bernardino de Sahagun, aided by survivors of the Conquest, completed a monumental work by recording in Nahuatl the history and customs of the Aztecs.

Returning to Paseo de la Reforma, continue north to Villa de Guadalupe by either Misterios or Calzada de Guadalupe. As you approach the enormous plaza in front of the Basilica, you'll note the new Basilica on the left. The old Basilica, dating from 1709, is to become a religious museum.

It is said that on December 9, 1531, a young Indian convert named Juan Diego was on his way to Mass in Tlatelolco when a vision appeared in his path—the Virgin Mary, dark-skinned and clad in the robes of an Indian princess. It was her desire that Juan should go to the Bishop, relate his experience, and express her wish that a chapel be erected there, on Tepeyac Hill, where she might minister to her Indians.

The Bishop was understandably skeptical. On the following day the Virgin again appeared to Juan and repeated her instructions. Still unconvinced, the Bishop requested that Juan bring him proof of the Virgin's identity. Reluctant to embarrass both the Virgin and himself, Juan remained at home on December 11. On the 12th, though, he set out in haste for Tlatelolco to fetch a priest, for his uncle was gravely ill. As he had feared, he again encountered the Virgin and had to tell her of the Bishop's demand.

Unperturbed, she sent Juan to gather the roses she said he would find growing on the desolate hillside. Then she assured him that there was no need to worry about his uncle, who had recovered his health, and asked Juan to take the roses immediately to the Bishop. When Juan opened his cloak in the prelate's presence, its inner side contained a portrait of the Virgin. Satisfied at last that a miracle had occurred, the Bishop ordered construction of a chapel on Tepeyac Hill; the sacred painting was placed above its altar.

The Virgin of Guadalupe became Mexico's patron saint. Her portrait, in a heavy gold frame, hangs over the altar of the Basilica. Skeptics continue to assail its authenticity, but experts have confirmed that the "canvas" is genuinely of 16th century Mexican manufacture, and that in 1531 there was no one in Mexico capable of painting such a portrait. As for the paints, they have so far successfully defied analysis.

Mexico City's Christmas season begins with midnight Mass in the Basilica on December 11, when thousands of the faithful crowd the church and atrium. After an all-night vigil, they sing *Las Mananitas* (Happy Birthday) to the Virgin at dawn on the 12th.

Tepotzotlan. Amid the wealth of religious art and architecture that is Mexico's heritage, the Church of San Francisco Javier in Tepotzotlan is outstanding, a masterpiece of ultrabaroque magnificence. Drive 25 miles north on the highway to Queretaro; the church tower is visible on your left. The National Museum of Colonial Arts and Handicrafts was installed in the monastery after renovation and restoration in 1959. Church and museum are open from 10 A.M. to 6 P.M.

Every year, in a patio to the left of the church, the *pastorela* is presented nightly from December 16-23. It is an ingenuous version of events surrounding the birth of Christ, conceived by Spanish nuns during the Middle Ages. Tickets can be secured from travel agencies, and the cost includes dinner, pinatas, village bands, and a *posada* or reenactment of the Holy Family's search for shelter. Dress warmly! A restaurant, Hosteria del Convento, in the same patio is open every day for lunch and dinner, serving favorite Mexican dishes.

En route to Tepotzotlan you'll pass several bustling industrial suburbs, one of which houses the Mexican plants of such well-known American firms as Ford, Goodyear, and Monsanto. (When the factories in this area end their day shifts, this highway is crowded with workers returning to the city; time your return to avoid this rush hour.)

West to Toluca to market

Friday is market day in Toluca and the drive from the capital is well worthwhile, even if you only absorb the local color. The countryside is beautiful and you can enjoy the surrounding baths, spas, and resorts by venturing only a little farther.

One way to get there is to go through the Desert of Lions (neither a desert nor filled with lions), a national monument and park, via Highway 15 en route to Toluca. Discover ruins, secret passages, and cool pine forests in which to picnic.

Toluca—brisk city by a huge volcano

Nestled in the center of the green Valley of Toluca is the bustling commercial city of Toluca. The invigorating, brisk weather typical of this flat valley is an inevitable result of its high altitude of almost 9,000 feet. Nevado de Toluca, an extinct, sometimes snow-shrouded volcano, towers over the city. Within its walls, the crater of the 15,000-foot volcano ensconces two lakes filled with rainbow trout —for the warm-blooded angler. Views are spectacular on the road into the volcano's crater.

Most visitors spend hours at the market in Toluca. The old market downtown is no longer; the new modern market, opened in 1973 south of the city just off the peripheral highway, is open every day. Friday is the day when merchandise floods the

Cave exploring at Cacahuamilpa

The great caves of the world embody the same characteristics—they are ageless, yet ever-changing as mountains and glaciers. Water trickling and seeping dissolves the rock in such mysterious ways that cave explorers seldom feel sure they've found every passage or palatial chamber.

In their dazzling complexity, the Caves of Cacahuamilpa (Las Grutas de Cacahuamilpa, pronounced ka-ka-wha-*meel*-pa), though not well-known outside of Mexico, rank right along with Mammoth Caves in Kentucky and Carlsbad Caverns in New Mexico. The Mexican government has now made them easier than ever to see. As you stroll the 1¼ miles of concrete walkways, electric lighting illuminates great rooms more than 100 feet high and 200 feet long, and stalactites and stalagmites up to 7 feet long.

Cacahuamilpa is 95 miles south of Mexico City via Highway 55 from Toluca, or 20 miles northeast of Taxco on a side road branching off the main highway between that city and Cuernavaca. At 3,360-foot altitude, the caves are close to springs, rivers, and falls. Near the caves are a swimming pool, a parking area, and restaurants.

Though the caves were discovered about 130 years ago, they still have not been fully explored. A cross marks the grave of the Englishman who discovered the caves long after the Indians who once inhabited them had left. Lured on by the intrigue of his discovery, he disappeared into the caves never to return.

Official national park guides lead scheduled tours daily. For larger groups of visitors, special tours at other times can be arranged for a slightly higher admission charge. Tours take about 4 hours.

Outside the entrance, local people sell attractive containers shaped like water birds and canes with forked tops, all carved from native woods.

adjoining plaza. The popular arts section is installed in one of the permanent buildings.

Also worth a visit are the Museum of Popular Arts on Highway 15 at the eastern entrance to Toluca, and the Museum of Carreria (horsemanship) downtown. Archeological pieces from the Toluca area and the entire state of Mexico now reside at the Museum of Teotenango, 11 miles south of Toluca on Highway 55.

Linger in a spa in Ixtapan de la Sal

This popular spa and resort, noted for its luxurious mineral baths, lies south of Toluca on Highway 55. The busiest season is winter when tourists from colder climes flock here for relaxing sessions at the thermal baths.

There are two towns—old town, purely Mexican, rustic, and bright with tropical vegetation; and Nuevo Ixtapan, beautifully landscaped, with a huge luxury hotel as well as more modest establishments. A public bathhouse, outdoor pools, and individual "Roman" baths adjacent to the big hotel serve all visitors, for a fee.

San Jose Purua—baths and bubbly streams

West of Toluca on the road to Morelia is the turnoff to San Jose Purua, one of Mexico's most celebrated spas. (Don't attempt to take a trailer down the steep road.) Here you'll find Balneario San Jose Purua perched on the edge of a canyon in a lush, tropical setting of flowering trees, bubbling streams, waterfalls, and quiet ponds. The hotel has several thermal spring swimming pools, and some of the rooms have private mineral baths. Reservations are an absolute must. The area is mountainous, interspersed with arid plains.

Valle de Bravo—weekend resort

Roughly 80 miles southwest of Toluca or 2½ hours from Mexico City, Valle de Bravo can be reached on a mountainous, paved road. The town slopes down to the shores of an artificial lake constructed as a huge hydroelectric project to benefit the surrounding region.

The area of Valle de Bravo, including the lake, has become an increasingly popular resort. On weekends, Valle de Bravo comes alive. Hordes of visitors from Mexico City come for picnics near the two waterfalls (the Molino River and Velo de Novia), walks into the shady, verdant woods, fishing for the abundant trout, water-skiing, and yacht racing. There is an outstanding golf course and, of course, the accommodations are excellent.

French, Americans, and Canadians, as well as the wealthier Mexicans, escape into the modern-colonial vacation and retirement homes neatly arranged around the lake. The romantic, restful attitude of the resort enables the frantic weekend visitor and the local inhabitant to lead their separate lives. Valle de Bravo is an arts and crafts center noted for its pottery.

Country clubs and rustic inns provide lodging and entertainment in this resort of orchids and butterflies. Hopefully, strict government building codes will help to maintain the still unexploited atmosphere of the area.

The return from Valle de Bravo to Highway 15 can be made by an alternate paved route that unfortunately has somewhat deteriorated. Although an airport has not as yet been constructed, a helicopter pad is available for service to Mexico City.

The Golden Triangle

Mexico City-Cuernavaca-Taxco is one of the most popular package tours sold in the U.S. From Taxco you can continue on to Acapulco (see page 43) on the fast superhighway and return to the capital by air. The toll road between Mexico City and Acapulco bypasses Taxco, but you can turn off to reach this intriguing colonial town. Or you can reach Taxco by taking the older, more winding Highway 95 all the way from Mexico City. Maintained as a toll-free road, it is about 20 miles longer and much slower. The two routes join at Iguala.

Taxco is a popular overnight stop. Since most tourists going to Acapulco include this stopover on their itinerary, you'd be wise to have confirmed reservations. Cuernavaca also has excellent accommodations and is likely to be less crowded.

Cuernavaca—a top garden spot

Capital of the state of Morelos, Cuernavaca impresses visitors more with its lush, gardenlike personality than its bustling, metropolitan character. Visitors who don't have much time to spend in the various regions of Mexico will appreciate the colorful town of Cuernavaca—it is a mixture of all the best Mexico has to offer.

Tropical in atmosphere, Cuernavaca provides a large number of Americans and residents of Mexico City with a popular weekend and holiday retreat.

Shimmering pink blossoms, rainbows of flowering vines, an intoxicating melange of scents that drifts over the walls of hidden gardens, and trees bedecked with splashes of reds, oranges, blues, and yellows, all create the experience that awaits the visitor to Cuernavaca.

The Borda Gardens were once the epitome of the town's elegance and tropical atmosphere. At the gardens you'll find a grand old mansion, a mirror pool, fountains, and the exotic but sadly neglected gardens. The mansion, once the summer home of Maximilian and Carlotta (1864-1867) now houses an arts and crafts shop, an art gallery, a small museum, and a restaurant.

During your stay be sure to visit the medieval palace-fortress known as the Cortez Palace on the main plaza. The building was constructed by Hernando Cortez in 1526 after the Spaniards occupied the town. Restored by the National Institute of Anthropology and History, the palace contains a museum, and a mural by Diego Rivera.

The Cathedral of Cuernavaca has a beautifully restored, modern interior; the exterior reflects the bold architectural style of the palace. During colonial years, missionaries used the cathedral (then a monastery) as a departure point for their missionary work in Asia. For a special treat, attend the Mass on Sunday and absorb the unique, spine-tingling experience of hearing inspirational music played by a mariachi band.

Cuernavaca offers a wide assortment of shops specializing in shoes and *huaraches* (sandals), silver, and handblocked and handloomed fabrics. Possibly the best reason for visiting Cuernavaca, and one you won't want to miss, is the dining. Both Las Mananitas *(numero uno)* and Las Quintas are outstanding and you'll find a number of new restaurants opening all the time.

Little hotels, hidden behind the walls, are all excellent bases from which to visit the nearby attractions—the Caves of Cacahuamilpa, Lake Tequesquitengo, and the ruins at Xochicalco.

Taxco—tied to its silver heritage

With twisting streets and red-tiled roofs, Taxco hangs on a steep mountainside as if someone had planned it as a movie set of an Old World village. It is one of Mexico's most colorful towns, and a favorite subject for artists and photographers. The Mexican government has designated Taxco as a national colonial monument.

Taxco is immersed in its silver heritage. Representing the center of Mexico's silversmith trade, Taxco has been molded by silver mines, silver barons, and the silver industry of modern times. Silver was first discovered in the area by Cortez in 1522, paving the way for the arrival of a French miner, Jose de la Borda, who created his own silver empire in the 18th century. A few crumbling, ghostly mines testify to his good fortune and subsequent wealth. The silver industry evolved to its present status about 50 years ago after being revitalized by an American, the late William Spratling. Today, you'll find silver showrooms and workshops all over town—though little silver is actually mined around Taxco any more.

Taxco's streets, hills, buildings, and shops are

Twin towers *of Taxco's gorgeously baroque church, Santa Prisca, backdrop tree-shaded plaza.*

best explored on foot. (One suggestion—wear tennis shoes to avoid slipping.) Taxco is another of those towns whose streets are mostly one-way and change names frequently. Cobblestone streets and narrow passageways lend a feeling of authenticity to the colonial atmosphere so well established by the town's architecture.

Taxco's hotels, for the most part, cling to the hills around town, providing luxurious views of the nightly fireworks in the square below. The local tourist office provides general information and a map of the town. Make sure your reservations are confirmed in advance.

East of Mexico City

Every long-distance traveler who gets caught in a frantic sightseeing schedule develops a desperate thirst for a refreshing change of pace, and that's what you'll get on the trip from Mexico City to Veracruz. This adventure can be approached as a loop drive—down by way of Puebla, Orizaba, and Cordoba, and back by way of Jalapa, Perote, Apizaco, and Texcoco. The loop starts from a region overflowing with churches, pyramids, and other monuments so typical of central Mexico. Slowly, the emphasis of the trip shifts to a seductive, tropic atmosphere that lulls even the most hardened traveler into a relaxed mood—even one who, anywhere else, would want to see "everything" in as little time as possible. The drive will submerge you in a rich variety of landscapes and climates—green valleys and desert on the plateau, pine forests, subtropics, and tropics. Though you can drive this loop in 2 days, you should really take more time. Off the heavily traveled tourist track, the roads are nevertheless paved all the way. One very rewarding feature of this loop drive is the opportunity to see five of Mexico's most famous mountains—Popocatepetl, Iztaccihuatl, Malinche, Pico de Orizaba, and Cofre de Perote.

November through February is the dry season, though you might get caught by a *norte* (overcast sky and a cold wind that blows sand from the dunes around Veracruz); the rest of the year it is hot in the morning with showers in the afternoon, but the land is at its greenest. The toll road that connects Mexico City with Cordoba is a high-speed but highly scenic highway. If clouds permit, you'll

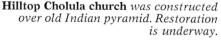

Hilltop Cholula church *was constructed over old Indian pyramid. Restoration is underway.*

Tiled dome *of Sanctuary of Los Remedios sparkles in sunlight. Cholula is a city of churches.*

see 17,761-foot Popocatepetl and 17,343-foot Iztacci-huatl—both majestic and snowcapped year-round. Once over the crest (which, incidentally, is the Continental Divide), you slowly descend into a green, fertile valley.

Tlaxcala—Cortez and his Indians

Capital of Mexico's smallest state, Tlaxcala is set in the hills of an area steeped in history. A cross-road of Indian trade routes and cultures, this region reveals the influence of high-culture groups from the beginning of the Christian era. Most famous of these were the Tlaxcaltecas for whom city and state were named. Allies of Hernando Cortez in confronting their common enemy, the Aztecs, the Tlaxcaltecas gave him their constant support, particularly during the battle of Lake Texcoco in 1521 when the final Spanish victory over the Aztec empire was achieved.

Weaving is an important craft in this region; vibrantly colored sarapes and woolen fabrics are produced here. The area around Tlaxcala and nearby Santa Ana Chiautempan is one of Mexico's most prolific wool centers. Top quality tweeds, handwoven sarapes, and rugs are sold in San Martin Texmelucan, Huejotzingo, and also at a government-sponsored market along the toll road at Rio Frio.

Cholula—Christian churches in an Indian city

Cholula, just off Highway 190 about 18 miles beyond San Martin Texmelucan, is a town of churches. Here, as elsewhere, the Spaniards built churches over structures sacred to the Indians. You can visit some 39 chapels in close proximity, and many more are not far away. Most notable is the Sanctuary of Los Remedios because it was built atop Cholula's main pyramid, a mile in circumference at its base. Not a true pyramid but an acropolis composed of numerous structures, it was fashioned over a period of several centuries beginning about 100 A.D. Tunnels allow you to explore some sections.

The ancient city has been under study and restoration for many years. A museum at the excavation site houses a collection of fabulous Cholulteca pottery, a polychrome lacquer-type ware decorated with intricate designs.

Cholula is also the location of an impressive new campus of the University of the Americas that moved here from its outgrown facility on the western edge of Mexico City.

Puebla—Talavera tile from a Spanish town

Puebla is one Mexican city that has retained much of its Spanish heritage. Its modern architecture contrasts sharply with the many colonial buildings, some of which are among the oldest on the North American continent.

The city's plazas, especially the main plaza, are ideal vantage points from which to absorb the beauty of the polychromatic tilework used on a number of the town's buildings.

Puebla has always been an important ceramics center. Even before the Spaniards arrived in Mexico, Indians of the area were accomplished potters, utilizing the nearby clay deposits for the manufacture of earthen kitchenware. After the Conquest, potters from Toledo, Spain, brought their famous Talavera pottery techniques to the newly founded city of Puebla.

Talavera ceramics of varying quality are still available. The best Puebla pottery and dinnerware, artfully designed and beautifully glazed, feature bold geometric designs of conventionalized patterns against a milky white background. Bright blue or yellow appear most frequently in the principal design, often accentuated with secondary patterns in contrasting tones of green, red, or brown. Colored designs applied thickly after glazing give the finished product a somewhat irregular, bas-relief effect that emphasizes its handcrafted appearance. Most of the ceramic manufacturers maintain their own display and salesrooms at or near the place of manufacture. A single family usually operates the small-scale *fabrica* (work area) in a courtyard; the display or salesroom is often located within the family home.

A profusion of ornate and intricately deco ated churches are located in Puebla. Two not to miss are the cathedral, with its carved marble doorways, and the elaborately gilded Chapel of the Rosary in the Church of Santo Domingo.

A thirst-quenching stop in Tehuacan

Though the toll road bypasses Tehuacan, you might want to make a side trip to this mineral springs resort nestled at 5,500 feet. Tehuacan's invigorating, refreshing climate and the nearby natural springs inevitably have made it a popular resort. This area is also the source of much of Mexico's bottled water. The bottling plants of two well-known companies are near town and offer tours for visitors, as well as all the refreshing spring water you can comfortably consume.

Tehuacan's pastoral, luxuriant atmosphere is enhanced by jacaranda, bougainvillea, *casahuate* trees, and myriad birds whose chattering awakes you with the rising sun.

On the road to Tehuacan, you'll see Mt. Malinche off to your left just beyond Puebla. Unlike Popocatepetl and Iztaccihuatl, Malinche is snowless year-round. It was named for Cortez' Indian mistress.

Stone-walled village *is surrounded by expanses of stark scenery typical of northeastern Mexico.*

North & East to the Gulf

Travelers from the East Coast of the United States have a choice of highways to use to reach Mexico City or some of the pleasant towns along the Gulf of Mexico. Even West Coast drivers often take the interior route, Highway 45, to the country's capital.

The northcentral and northeastern sections of Mexico are not exactly filled with tourist destinations but a few highlights deserve mention.

In this chapter we follow the four main routes south, calling attention to some of the attractions along the way.

Along Highway 45

Some consider the northcentral area of Mexico, traversed by Highway 45, dull and monotonous. Part of it is. For at least half the way—between Juarez (you are crossing from El Paso) and Durango—the country is flat and semiarid, with practically no variation in the mile after mile between towns and villages.

But whenever you come to a sign proclaiming *Poblado Proximo* (inhabited neighborhood), the land suddenly comes alive. Boys riding bicycles, men leading burros, children playing in dooryards, bougainvillea spilling over garden walls—these are small but satisfactory compensations for the highway monotony.

At times the unrelenting sameness of the road gives way to a narrow village street that threads past old buildings, tree-shaded plazas, and vendors selling melons or rebozos, revealing the fragments of northcentral Mexico you'd been expecting as you drove the first 600 miles or more through the cattle country below the border.

Mexicans call the southern portion of the highway (between Guanajuato and Mexico City) "La Ruta de la Independencia" (The Route of Independence), because it was along this route that Father Miguel Hidalgo marched with his ragged army to overthrow the Spaniards. Hidalgo was executed in Chihuahua on July 30, 1811. He is revered by the Mexicans as the "Father of Mexico's Independence."

Highway 45 never drops below the 3,752-foot elevation at Ciudad Juarez, where it begins. It climbs the long and high Mesa Central at grades so moderate as to be almost imperceptible much of the way, making this route a good one for trailers.

You can cut east toward the coast by taking Highway 49 at Ciudad Jimenez. This route bypasses Hidalgo del Parral and Durango, taking you through Torreon and Rio Grande and then to Fresnillo, where you pick up Highway 45 again. Highway 49 is a good paved road. Fill your gas tank at Jimenez; the next town, Gomez Palacio, is 145 miles away.

Chihuahua!

One of the largest cities in all of northcentral Mexico, Chihuahua owes its earliest beginnings to the rich silver strikes that were made in the nearby mountains in the 18th century.

Parts of the city are quite modern looking, but the older sections of town contain some fine examples of colonial architecture. Among them are the State Capitol (Palacio de Gobierno) on Hidalgo Plaza, on the grounds of which Father Hidalgo was executed in 1811 during the War for Mexican Independence; the Federal Palace (Palacio Federal), also on Hidalgo Plaza, where Hidalgo was held prisoner while awaiting execution; and the immense cathedral facing the zocalo, or public square (Plaza de la Constitucion). Explore the wide boulevards (Paseo Bolivar, Avenidas Victoria, Cuahtemoc, and Caranza) lined with ornate colonial mansions, and the narrow downtown streets with thick-walled adobe houses whose windows are barred, roofs turreted, and courtyards enclosed for protection from the Apache Indians who once plagued this region.

Among the attractive parks are Lerdo de Tejada where Sunday concerts are held, and Parque de Mortero, at the end of Avenida Matamoros. Parque de Mortero surrounds an ancient Spanish mill and arched aqueduct.

Another place of interest is La Quinta Luz, the home of Pancho Villa's widow, Senora Luz Corral. Open to the public, it houses a collection of weapons and personal effects of Mexico's 20th century guerrilla-revolutionist. Combination villain and benefactor—a sort of Mexican Robin Hood—Villa and his band of terrorists ranged across the northern states, ostensibly serving the cause of *La Revolucion*. They robbed trains, captured towns and cities, and ambushed and plundered the countryside at will. Villa's reputation still survives, but mostly because of his colorful exploits (made even more colorful by the U.S. press) rather than for his noble service. (To capture Chihuahua, for example, he disguised his army as burro drivers.) When the revolution ended, Villa dropped into obscurity for a time before he was ambushed and shot in Parral in 1923. One of the most interesting items in La Quinta Luz is the old Dodge touring car in which Villa was assassinated.

Another unusual building worth a visit is the great Victorian mansion on Bolivar Boulevard that now houses the Chihuahua public museum.

From Chihuahua you can take a spectacular rail trip through the mountains and canyons of the Sierra Madre Occidental to the town of Los Mochis on Highway 15 (see page 28).

Ciudad Camargo—in the heart of cattle country

Ciudad Camargo is an old but progressive Mexican town. Operating from a modern headquarters building, the cattlemen's association is central to the town's activities. A large meat-packing plant, located at the southern edge of town, refrigerates and ships meat throughout Mexico and the United States. It also sends hides to Leon and utilizes the rest of the animal in making fertilizer. Other industry in the area includes a textile plant, a flour mill, and several cotton gins.

In this bustling and businesslike town, the highlight of the year is the fiesta for its patron saint, Santa Rosalia. Starting early in September, the 8 days of celebration include dances, horse races, cockfights, and other entertainment. An 18th century, mission-style parish church named after Santa Rosalia is 4 blocks east of the highway.

Three miles from Camargo are the hot springs (Ojo Caliente and Ojo de Jabali) whose waters were known to the Indians for their curative power.

Many sportsmen visit Camargo for the black bass fishing at nearby Boquilla Dam. The Boquilla Dam blocks the Conchos River to create an irregular body of water some 40 miles in length. Water from the dam turns the turbines of the big hydroelectric plant that furnishes part of the power for cities as far distant as Juarez. This body of water was named Lake Toronto after it was stocked with fish brought from Canada, but the area is better known as La Boquilla.

Spring months are considered best for fishing.

During July and August the lake is closed to fishermen; strong winds in February and March often make the water too rough for small boats. Many sportsmen bring their own boats which can be easily launched from the sloping shore. Boats may also be rented by the day. The best fishing spots are several miles up the lake from the dam.

Primitive mining town of Hidalgo del Parral

Virtually cut off from the world until Highway 45 was completed, Hidalgo del Parral has remained an isolated, primitive town. Until the arrival of the highway, the town had few visitors other than miners. (Most travelers still tend to use Highway 49 to Fresnillo via Gomez Palacio, rather than Highway 45.) Rich metallic ores were first discovered around here in the middle of the 16th century —and the mines are still producing.

The townsite is hilly; streets are narrow and steep, and most of them are one-way. Mule-drawn wagons are a familiar sight.

Six churches are scattered throughout the town —all of them with bullet holes in their stone walls. A large 18th century church on the plaza, La Parroquia, is worth a visit to examine the richly embellished interior and gilded altar screens.

The general store at one end of Plaza San Juan de Dios was formerly the house in which Pancho Villa lived before his assassination. His grave holds a headless corpse, a morbid reminder of a grave robbery several years after his burial. Villa's widow has tried, without success, to remove his body to an impressive, ornate crypt in Chihuahua.

The Palace of Pedro Alvarado, near the Plaza San Juan de Dios, is an elegant mansion built and lived in by a lucky 19th century miner who struck it rich in the silver mines.

The Municipal Palace (Palacio Municipal) is known for the rather bizarre clock tower that surmounts the north corner of the building.

Durango—Hollywood's favorite backdrop

As you approach Durango, the road climbs up to this tidy, prosperous-looking city on a high, flat plain (elevation 6,314 feet) among barren mountains about halfway between El Paso and Mexico City.

Durango reflects an openness of design and a provincial atmosphere that are atypical for a city of its size. The streets are wide and paved; the zocalo is gracious and well kept. One of the most pleasant cities on Highway 45, Durango has several large parks, a few smaller parks, and a riverside promenade. The massive cathedral, with its yellow facade, has magnificent vaulted ceilings. Inside the

Government Palace (Durango is the capital of the state of Durango), the walls of an entire inner courtyard are decorated with murals.

Industries in the Durango area include ranching and cattle raising. Iron mining, which draws from one of the richest deposits in the world (located on a nearby hill known as El Cerro de Mercado), is the most important industry in the area.

In recent years, Durango has become the setting for many movies, mostly Westerns. If you arrive during the shooting of a large production, accommodations may be difficult to find.

From Durango, one of Mexico's most scenic roads —Highway 40—winds up and over the Sierra Madre Occidental to meet Highway 15 just south of Mazatlan. A good, paved road for its entire length (about 200 miles), Highway 40 is not a particularly fast route. With a few quick stops for pictures or picnics, it takes about 6 hours to reach Mazatlan. Sheer drop-offs from the side of the road restrain any inclination to hurry. Besides, the breathtaking views are so awe-inspiring that you'll want to stop to look or photograph often, if visibility permits.

Before you leave Durango, get picnic provisions and fill your gas tank. Eating places along the road are few and not particularly tailored for spending hours indulging in a luxurious picnic. Gasoline pumps are located at El Salto, El Palmito, Concordia, and at the junction of this road with Highway 15. Because of the thousands of sharp curves and steep grades, this route to Mazatlan is not recommended for tourists driving trailers and motor homes.

Shortcut to Fresnillo

If time is crucial to planning your itinerary in Mexico, utilizing Highway 49 to Fresnillo instead of Highway 45 will cut hours off your driving time. By taking this route, you leave Highway 45 at Jimenez (where you'll find fair accommodations) and by-pass Hidalgo del Parral and Durango.

From Jimenez to Gomez Palacio, the highway pursues a monotonously straight path. *Vados* (flash flood channel dips) occur intermittently over the route, but they are shallow and well-engineered and can be traversed at reasonably high speeds.

The colonial city of Gomez Palacio (Mexico's soap-making capital) is just across the dry Nazas River from Torreon. Mexico's youngest major city, Torreon was founded near the end of the last century. Gomez Palacio and Torreon both have adequate accommodations and restaurants that offer Mexican as well as American repasts.

This general area is known as La Laguna because it was formerly a huge lake—or more correctly,

Details at a glance

How to get there

Covering this large stretch of territory is best done by car, although commuter plane service links Mexico City and the larger cities—notably Monterrey.

Buses travel back and forth from border towns to Mexico City, and trains from Ciudad Juarez and Nuevo Laredo make frequent stops along their runs. A fast overnight Pullman train runs between Monterrey and Mexico City.

Getting around. Public transportation is available in some areas, but you'll explore this region best by car. Self-contained campers are ideal.

Accommodations. Pace yourself to reach a good-size town for overnight stops. Not much is plush, but clean rooms are available. Check with a travel service like AAA or Sanborn's for best locations.

Climate and dress. If possible, plan trips for spring or fall. The northern section is desertlike and can be quite hot, while the gulf side may be very humid.

Plan your wardrobe for comfort. Bring a jacket for unexpected cool evenings in high country, and a swimming suit for cooling off in a pool.

several large lakes. The fertile, rich soil yields bountiful crops of cotton and grains when given ample irrigation. Several dams have been built in the mountain headwaters of various rivers in the area to provide the irrigation required for the production of crops.

Leaving Torreon and Gomez Palacio, Highway 49 joins Highway 40, by-passing the suburban town of Lerdo and leading on to Cuencame, where Highway 49 cuts south, passing through the town of Rio Grande. The road continues on until it merges with Highway 45 at La Chicharrona Junction, a few miles north of the old mining town of Fresnillo.

Nombre de Dios—Spanish ghost town

Thirty-five miles south of Durango is the humble, time-worn farm settlement of Nombre de Dios, the first Spanish settlement in the state of Durango. Today, only ghostly shadows inhabit this 400-year-old farm, though sometimes an occasional figure can still be seen lingering amidst the crumbling walls. It is worth the short detour off the highway to drive through the cobbled streets and past ancient courtyards planted with tropical fruits.

Past the detour a dusty road sign informs you that you're crossing the Tropic of Cancer. Ten miles south, Highway 45 merges with Highway 49. At Fresnillo (now by-passed), a flat, dusty city greets you with gigantic slag piles of tailings from silver mining and grey smelters with a regiment of black smokestacks that dwarf the unassuming church spires.

Ruins of "Seven Caves"

Twenty-seven miles farther, Highway 45 combines with Highway 54 from Saltillo. Four miles beyond is a traffic circle and a monument commemorating the construction of the highways in this area. The junction with Highway 54 to Guadalajara is another 4 miles south. The ruins of La Quemada are an easy 28-mile side trip via this road. This outpost is of a civilization much older than that of the Aztecs. Ruins on the hillside include remnants of a few columns, a temple, a palace, and a public square with steps. La Quemada means "Place of the Seven Caves;" natives call it Cerro de los Edificios. It is always open; you pay a few pesos to visit it.

Zacatecas—the pink city

Approaching Zacatecas you sweep down into a canyon and drive under the lofty arches of an ancient stone aqueduct dating back to the 1700s. At one time Zacatecas was one of Mexico's most difficult cities for the motorist to negotiate, but now a divided boulevard by-passes the town and

drivers no longer have to experience the annoying sensation of rattling along the narrow cobblestone streets.

This sloping townsite is 8,200 feet above sea level. Parts of town are so steep that instead of streets, stone steps climb the canyon walls. The faint pinkish cast radiated by Zacatecas is the cumulative result of the local sandstone used in most of the buildings. The town has a magnificent cathedral whose huge facade is intricately and meticulously carved; its vaulted interior is supported with stalwart stone columns. The marble altar testifies to its Italian origin.

A favorite attraction in Zacatecas is the intriguing summit of Cerro de la Bufa, a mountain northeast of the city. A blacktop road has been built to the top of "La Bufa," where there's an ancient chapel (1728) and a demure plaza. The view from atop "La Bufa" provides an all-encompassing panorama of the surrounding countryside. The road to the summit starts near the university at the south end of town; ample parking is available.

Music boxes in Guadalupe

Another small town on Highway 49 is Guadalupe, and it is worth taking time out of your driving schedule to meander through its narrow, quiet streets. The focus of your wanderings will be the old Convent of Guadalupe, housing numerous works of art and hand-printed books. The buildings are open to visitors for a minimal admission charge. It is sometimes possible to prevail upon a guide to admit you to the small chapel, which is lavishly decorated with gold leaf.

At the southern end of Guadalupe is an unusual factory where music boxes are made (and sold), along with an assortment of other beautifully inlaid articles. Items are not cheap; try to find someone who speaks English to answer questions and to help bargain.

You're in hot water in Aguascalientes

South from Guadalupe on Highway 45 is the state of Aguascalientes. The colonial city and state capital of Aguascalientes is a railroad center for this area. Industry and crafts (especially sarapes, linen work, and hand embroidered cotton) contribute greatly to the livelihood of this modern city. The making of wine and the distilling of brandy are other important industries in this grape-growing area.

The name of the town refers to the town's location near thermal springs. These springs provide an opportunity for visitors to indulge themselves in a languorous afternoon of mineral baths and swimming.

Tarahumara Indian *hunkers down for a brief rest during infrequent visit to Chihuahua.*

Pink sandstone buildings *and sloping setting add to Zacatecas' charm.*

Mexican shorthorns *lie placidly beside highway in Durango state.*

For many years the townsite was a small outpost in Chichimeca Indian territory; the Chichimecas were hostile and warlike, making the conquest of the area by Pedro Alvarado nearly impossible. Only after many futile attempts and frustrating defeats was he successful. Don't miss the Government Palace, a mansion of the 1600s belonging to the Marquis de Guadalupe.

San Marcos Fair, the spring festival of Aguascalientes, is celebrated in late April for about 2 weeks. An occasion in honor of the city's patron saint, the San Marcos Fair features dancing, fireworks, cockfighting, and bullfighting. Accommodations will be difficult to obtain during the celebration.

Through the Northeast

The three routes that take you through northeastern Mexico from the border are Highway 57, Highway 85, and Highway 180. These highways are all in reasonably good condition.

A faster route to Mexico City than the Pan American Highway (Highway 85), Highway 57 is the alternate route to the interior of Mexico from the east coast of the United States. Driving is easier, for the highway does not climb and wind through mountainous regions as the Pan American Highway does. The road is very good—paved all the way.

From the border towns of Piedras Negras and Ciudad Acuna, just across the Rio Grande from

Eagle Pass and Del Rio respectively, it is a pleasant drive over gently rolling countryside to Monclova, where Mexico's largest steel mill is located. At Monclova, Highway 30 to the southwest goes to Torreon and is an excellent short cut for motorists heading for Mazatlan on the west coast of Mexico.

Eight miles south of Monclova, just beyond the small mining town of Castanos, Highway 53 runs southeast to Monterrey.

Sarapes in Saltillo

Encompassing a vast plain at a mile high elevation, Saltillo reaches to the low hills, offering views of higher mountains in every direction. Saltillo is the prosperous capital of the state of Coahuila—a popular stopping place in summer because of its relatively cool climate.

Founded in 1555, Saltillo retains much of its Spanish colonial character. At one time it was the capital of most of the state of Texas when that part of the United States belonged to Mexico.

"Downtown" runs chiefly along the two one-way streets of Victoria and Aldama, from the central plaza west for about half a dozen blocks to the shady Alameda. The State Capitol building (Palacio de Gobierno) faces on the plaza; across from it is the Cathedral of Santiago with its 200-foot tower and richly carved facade.

In several small factories you can watch the weavers at work on the brightly colored sarapes characteristic of Saltillo. Skilled craftsmen fashion articles of silver, tin, brass, and copper. You'll also

Intricately *carved cathedral tower is Saltillo landmark.*

find craftwork and souvenirs from many other parts of Mexico.

You have to look carefully so you won't miss the market on Allende. As in a normal business block, the street is lined with small shops. The main part of the market is inside a tall, barnlike building, and has three levels. This is Saltillo's all-purpose department store. Here you can buy food, clothing, hardware, and all the types of handicrafts sold in town, as well as more utilitarian items such as pottery for use as cookware.

The Interamerican University (La Universidad Interamericana), just a few blocks from the Alameda, attracts many students from the United States, especially in the summer. The state also maintains a university and a technological institute in Saltillo; a school of agriculture is located a short distance to the southwest.

The Mexican plants of the International Harvester Company and Honda are located in Saltillo.

Wine and the Battle of Buena Vista

Highway 40 runs east from Saltillo to Monterrey on a fine divided expressway (eliminating many of the wicked curves that formerly marked this well-traveled route), and west from Saltillo to Torreon through large expanses of desert. About midway between Saltillo and Torreon, a few miles south of an oasis junction called Paila, is the wine-making town of Parras de la Fuente. Nearby is the popular resort named Rincon del Montero, fed by springs that give this small area a verdant appearance in

marked contrast to the desolate countryside around it.

Southwest of Saltillo, Highway 54 heads for the desert past the old mining town of Concepcio del Oro to Zacatecas, beyond which you can continue to Guadalajara. Just southwest of Saltillo, along Highway 54, is the almost forgotten site of one of the confrontations of the U.S.-Mexican War—the Battle of Buena Vista. (The Mexicans call it the Battle of Angostura—the name of a village nearby.) The battleground where the clash between Mexico and the United States occurred is 10 minutes from Saltillo. A small, weather-beaten shaft marks the rocky spot on which the battle took place on February 23, 1847.

The captivating ghost town of El Catorce

West of Matehuala is the tranquil ghost town of El Catorce, once a prosperous silver mining community that boasted a population of 40,000 in its heyday. Now, only a handful of residents remain, and the attractive churches, public buildings, and residences are slowly crumbling.

The town's name is said to have come from a band of 14 bandits (*catorce*=14). These infamous bandits continuously raided the trains that transported silver from the mines. The Mint Building (Casa de Moneda) stands as a ghostly reminder of the high volume of silver ($3 million annually in silver ore) produced by the mines in the region near El Catorce.

For ixtle, visit the Matehuala region

In the desert around Matehuala there are veritable forests of several species of agave and yucca which are the source of various fibers, all generically known as *ixtle*, and the basis of Matehuala's all-important industry. Finer quality fibers are used mainly for sacking and for decorative pieces such as place mats and wall hangings. Coarser fiber is made into packing material, brush bristles, and door mats. Ixtle is also used for upholstery filling. Once pounded and shredded, it is wound into hanks that are tied in knots, soaked in water, allowed to dry, and then untied. The resulting curled segments provide the necessary resiliency for the filling.

Food, lodging, and gasoline are available here. You can ride a slightly antiquated bus up to El Catorce.

South of Matehuala, you'll start seeing the *nopal* or tuna cactus, the fruit of which is quite delicious. Natives gather the fruits and sell them along the highway. The fruit is also used to make a regional sweet—*queso de tuna* or tuna "cheese."

About 50 miles south of Matehuala, at an unassuming placed called Huizache Junction, Highway 80 from Antiguo Morelos (on the Pan American Highway) joins Highway 57, and the two routes continue as one to San Luis Potosi.

San Luis Potosi—historical and industrial

The largest city along Highway 57 is San Luis Potosi, capital of the state of the same name. The main highway by-passes the city by a mile or so; if you make the side trip into town, you'll consider your time well spent.

A rich mining center since the 1600s, San Luis Potosi is also a modern industrial city and a major rail center. Here, too, is the Mexican plant of another well-known U.S. firm—Allis Chalmers.

The local bazaar, Hidalgo Market, offers good buys in rebozos, locally made pottery, and regional handicrafts. The Chamber of Commerce displays an interesting selection of crafts from the state— and it is all for sale. You'll probably have a chance to sample prickly pear or tuna cheese here.

Of interest, also, are the cathedral, the Church of Our Lady of Carmen, and the famous Caja de Agua

—the small, round wellhouse designed by Tresguerras which serves as the hub of the city's water system.

South to rebozos and fighting bulls

Twenty-nine miles south of San Luis Potosi is the tidy town of Santa Maria del Rio on the banks of the languorous Santa Maria River. This community is known throughout Mexico for its rebozos. For generations its women have been weaving beautiful silken "Santa Maria rebozos"—highly prized by the ladies of Mexico. Recently, because the Mexican government became concerned that the art of weaving "Santa Maria rebozos" might die out as the older women of the town passed away, a special school was established to teach young girls the art. Tourists are invited to visit the school on the main plaza; you can purchase rebozos and other colorful handicrafts made by the children.

A few miles beyond Santa Maria del Rio is the Rancho Santo Domingo, where for three generations the Labastida family has bred fine fighting bulls. These big beautiful black animals of Rancho

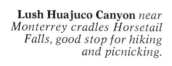

Lush Huajuco Canyon *near Monterrey cradles Horsetail Falls, good stop for hiking and picnicking.*

Santo Domingo are in great demand by the largest bullrings of Mexico. Tourists are welcome to visit the old hacienda and the rancho's own little chapel. Senor Javier Labastida, the American-educated grandson of the founder, is sometimes on hand to act as a guide.

Farther down the highway is the junction with Highway 110 to Dolores Hidalgo and Guanajuato. Near Dolores Hidalgo, Highway 49 branches south to San Miguel de Allende.

Monterrey—beer and buildings

You can reach Monterrey from many directions, but if you're driving south from the U.S. you'll probably take Highway 85 from Laredo. The first 45 miles south of the border are long and monotonous. South of Vallecillo, though, the road climbs gradually into the foothills of the Sierra Madre before dropping down into the industrial city of Monterrey, capital of the state of Nuevo Leon, and probably Mexico's leading manufacturing center.

Bustling, increasingly modern Monterrey retains much of its colonial charm despite being an industrial city. Historical landmarks are scattered throughout the city as reminders of its original 17th century settlers.

At the northern edge of town are the modern buildings of the state's streamlined, progressive University City. In the downtown area, in addition to a dozen ultramodern skyscrapers, are the attractive colonial-style government buildings, the cathedral, and the modern Federal Palace (Palacio Federal), which affords a fine view of the city from its tower.

Interesting buildings deserve a visit, and you should plan to spend some time at the cathedral on Zaragoza Plaza, built between 1790 and 1840; the Municipal Palace (Palacio Municipal), a 17th century colonial-style city hall; the ultramodern Purisima Church with impressionistic statues of the Apostles; and El Obispado (the Bishop's Palace), located on the west side of the city. Built in 1785, the palace served for years as a residence for church dignitaries. During the U.S.-Mexican War, it functioned as a fort where Mexicans resisted American troops; it was also occupied by Pancho Villa during the Revolution of 1910.

Monterrey has two bullrings. The best season is from November to March, but during the summer, bullfights are sometimes staged on Saturday nights under the lights. After a day at the bullfights, you may enjoy a cooling drink at the Monterrey country club, Valle Alto Golf Club; tourists can pick up a visitors' card at the Chamber of Commerce.

Monterrey is the heart of Mexico's beer industry. The country's largest brewery, Cuauhtemoc Brewery, on the outskirts of town, offers guided tours for visitors. Tourists are served free samples of the brewery's products—Carta Blanca and Bohemia beers—in a wooded beer garden.

Because of Monterrey's industrial boom, its population has been on the increase for the past couple of decades. In addition to the state university at the north end of the city, privately endowed Monterrey Institute of Technology at the southern end of town is as attractive as its cross-town rival and as highly regarded in educational circles.

Nearby areas to visit include the Garcia Caves and La Boca Dam. The Garcia Caves are about 30 miles northwest of Monterrey. A labyrinth of spectacular limestone caverns, the caves are open daily to visitors. A little funicular railway makes hourly trips daily from an excursion depot (5 miles northeast of the village of Villa de Garcia) to the entrance of the caves. The State Tourist Department operates the tram and conducts tours of the caverns. The funicular round trip and tour take about 2 hours.

La Boca Dam can be reached by taking Highway 85 south for about 25 miles. Here you can refresh yourself by enjoying one of several available water sports: swimming, boating, and water-skiing.

Picnic at Horsetail Falls

Highway 85 enters Huajuco Canyon south of Monterrey and follows the canyon for about 20 miles. The area is one of the most lush and fertile in all of Mexico.

Twenty-four miles south of Monterrey is a short but rewarding detour off the main highway to the very popular resort area that features an idyllic waterfall called Cola de Caballo, or "Horsetail," which spills in delicate ribbons for 225 feet down a mossy, fern-draped precipice. This is a perfect retreat for a picnic.

You leave the main highway at the south end of the village of El Cercado and follow a 4-mile, paved, privately owned toll road through orange groves and sugar cane fields into the forested foothills of the Sierra Madre. At the end of the drive is the resort complex of cottages, dining room, and swimming pool. Here you'll be greeted by the resident company of guides who will take you (for a reasonable fee) to the falls by burro, saddle horse, or horse-drawn cart—or, if you prefer to go without a guide, you can walk the ¾-mile path from the resort to the falls.

The scent of orange blossoms in Montemorelos

Montemorelos, just off the highway about 50 miles south of Monterrey, is Mexico's largest orange-growing district. Fresh oranges and glasses of thick, pulpy orange juice are sold along the road.

At Montemorelos the highway is joined by Route 89 from China (pronounced *Chee-nah*), a popular short-cut road to Mexico from the border cities of McAllen, Texas, and Reynosa, Mexico.

Linares—a scenic by-pass

The largest town between Monterrey and Ciudad Victoria, Linares is the center of an extensive farming, ranching, and citrus-growing area. Linares was founded in 1712 as the Bishopric of San Felipe de Linares. Two churches, the Church of Senor de la Misercordia and the Parochial Church, both face their own plaza.

At Linares, Highway 60 takes off to the west. After winding through scenic Santa Rosa Canyon, it climbs up and over the majestic Sierra Madre to a junction with Highway 57 about midway between Saltillo and Matehuala. A popular short-cut route for motorists from southern Texas gateways, the highway enables you to reach Highway 57 without going through the metropolitan cities of Monterrey and Saltillo.

The country becomes more tropical south of Linares; towering mountains are omnipresent on the right side of the horizon.

Ciudad Victoria and Mexico's first president

Ciudad Victoria is the capital of the state of Tamaulipas, one of Mexico's most industrialized states, which extends in a narrow strip along the Rio Grande and then follows the Gulf of Mexico south as far as the coastal town of Tampico.

The city's name comes from that of the man known as Guadalupe Victoria (born Felix Fernandez), whose ardent faith in Mexican independence eventually brought him the distinction of being Mexico's first president. His assumed name had popular appeal: Guadalupe for Mexico's patron saint; Victoria for victory. Together with other patriots like Miguel Hidalgo, Jose Maria Morelos, and Vicente Guerrero, Victoria fought against Spanish rule.

Perhaps they most bitterly resented the Spanish *haciendados* who owned vast tracts of land together with those who worked it, in a relationship resembling the feudal system of medieval Europe. When the war ended in 1821, the insurgents' attempts to split up these haciendas failed; "land" was again a battle cry of the Revolution of 1910.

Natural fibers are an important crop in this region, and are used both for industrial purposes and to make the colorful hammocks and other decorative objects sold on the streets and in the markets.

Highway 85 is joined at Ciudad Victoria by Highway 101 from the Texas towns of McAllen and Brownsville. An extension of Highway 101 is open from Ciudad Victoria to the southwest over the Sierra Madre, offering some spectacular scenery before straightening out on the high mesa.

South to the tropics

South of Ciudad Victoria, the highway descends sharply and the country becomes increasingly lush and tropical. You cross the Tropic of Cancer 24 miles south of Ciudad Victoria. Vegetation becomes more dense, and masses of colorful vines, thick, tangled forests, and groves of mango, banana, and avocado trees pervade the area. Fragrant flowers bloom profusely everywhere. The beautifully brilliant *flamboyant* (royal poinciana) trees are scattered among the vegetation, brightening the greenness with vibrant splashes of red.

The somnolent, tropical village of El Limon, only 197 feet above sea level, is the center of a vast, rich agricultural district. A sampling of the crops of this region would include sugar cane, cotton, spring tomatoes, and peppers.

From Ciudad Mante, Highway 80 runs southeast to Tampico, one of Mexico's most important seaports. The road is paved, and a few miles out of Ciudad Mante it passes Mt. Bernal, better known as Mt. Sombrero because of its close resemblance to a Mexican hat.

Fifteen miles south of Ciudad Mante, Highway 80 goes southwest to Huizache Junction where it joins Highway 57 for its continuation to San Luis Potosi.

Eighteen miles west of Antiguo Morelos, and then 10 miles north on a gravel connecting road is one of Mexico's most popular spots for natural beauty—El Salto Falls. Unfortunately, modern society's need for electricity has diminished El Salto's majestic grandeur; a power project has harnessed the falls, and water now flows over the brink only during the rainy season.

Ciudad Valles—agricultural shipping center

Until Highway 85 came to Ciudad Valles, the place was just a sleepy little village. One of the oldest cities in the state, Ciudad Valles was founded as a Spanish outpost in 1533. Located near the Sierra, it provides an ideal shipping point for the products of the region: cattle, sugar cane, citrus fruits, and coffee. Most of the products are distributed to other cities within Mexico by railroad.

Until the opening of Highway 57, Ciudad Valles was the most popular tourist town between Monterrey and Mexico City, and its hotels were filled to capacity every night. Now, with many tourists taking the other, faster route to Mexico City, the hotels along Highway 85 have far fewer customers —which accounts for the slightly bedraggled, dusty appearance of most of them.

From Ciudad Valles, Highway 70 goes west through well-engineered Sierra Madre passes to a little oasislike citrus town called Rioverde, and on to San Luis Potosi.

From Ciudad Valles, Highway 70 also leads east to Tampico. Just off this road, about 10 miles east of Ciudad Valles, is the well-known resort of Taninul, a popular spa for many years. Not far away are the ruins of important Huastecan archaeological sites.

Tamazunchale—Huastec country

One of the most scenic sections of Highway 85 is between Ciudad Valles and Tamazunchale. Exotic tropical vegetation grows luxuriantly along the highway. The quaint old town of Tamazunchale lies at the foot of the Sierra Madre Oriental on the south side of the Montezuma River. Butterflies and birds are the town's most popular inhabitants; tourists, especially those who enjoy bird watching, may see the unusual species of the area. Don't miss the 16th century church and the unusual market offering tantalizing tropical novelties. Tamazunchale is generally considered the capital of the somewhat isolated Huasteca Indians, who live for the most part in the nearby mountains.

Just south of Tamazunchale, the road begins to rise from the tropical valley to the top of the Sierra Madre, climbing about 5,000 feet in 60 winding miles. Fog can be dense during the earlier morning hours and again in the later evening hours, so it is advisable to make the ascent during daylight.

Mining towns along Highway 85

Some of the most spectacular views to be seen along Highway 85 are from points between Tamazunchale and Jacala, a mountain mining town.

Zimapan, to the south, is a colonial mining town established when lead and silver deposits were discovered after the Conquest. It is still active.

South from Zimapan is Ixmiquilpan, where you can enjoy a rest stop and visit one of Mexico's oldest and grandest churches and convents, built by the Augustinians in 1550.

The highest point on the Pan American Highway is reached just north of Colonia Junction, near the old mining city of Pachuca, where the highway reaches an elevation of 8,209 feet at a community called Hacienda de la Concepcion. Here the Americans living in Mexico City have erected a monument as a "good neighbor" gesture to the Mexicans. From this point the highway gradually descends into the great Valley of Mexico.

A short cut along the coast

Another route traversing northeastern Mexico skirts the coastline from McAllen-Brownsville, Texas, to Tampico in the state of Tamaulipas. Providing little of scenic interest in the arid country south of the border cities of McAllen and Brownsville, the route begins with either Highway 97 from Reynosa or Highway 101 from Matamoros. The two highways meet at the junction community of El Tejon and continue south as Highway 101 through San Fernando to Ciudad Victoria. The 83 miles to Ciudad Mante are driven on Highway 85, the Pan American Highway.

At Ciudad Mante, Highway 85 connects with Highway 80 and continues east as Highway 80 until you reach Tampico. You may take an alternate route to Tampico and cut mileage and save time by taking Highway 180, a coastal short-cut route. It takes off from Highway 101 about 25 miles south of the town of San Fernando and proceeds south to the town of Soto la Marina and on to the farming city of Aldama. From Aldama the highway takes you to the small town of Manuel at the junction with Highway 80, where the road continues on to Tampico. The road is paved and saves nearly 100 miles over the older route via Ciudad Victoria and Ciudad Mante.

Tampico—on the Gulf of Mexico

Just beyond Ciudad Mante, you turn left onto Highway 80 for the drive to the seaport and oil town of Tampico, where you have your first glimpse of the Gulf of Mexico. Tampico is one of Mexico's biggest and most dynamic seaports. The port itself is inland on the Panuco River, and the city has grown up on a half-dozen hills amidst several freshwater lagoons.

The banks of the river are peppered with refineries and oil tanks. The Panuco River is also heavily fished by local commercial fishermen. From the 1870s until foreign-held oil properties were expropriated by the government in 1938, Tampico was the center of operations for British, Dutch, and American oil companies. Elegant homes of the petroleum magnates still stand outside town.

Today, Tampico is appreciated by tourists who come to fish the coastal waters for such game as snook, trout, snapper, and yellowfish. Hunting is also a popular sport for visitors; duck, quail, and turkey can be taken. Arrangements for fishing charters are made through your hotel. Hunting trips can also be arranged through your hotel or a tour operator.

One of the largest Pemex refineries is at Ciudad Madero, a suburb to the north of Tampico near the mouth of the Panuco River.

Southern Mexico

Southern Mexico encompasses an area unknown to many visitors. Most tourists arriving in Mexico City, Puerto Vallarta, and Acapulco never penetrate the southern states. Yet these states offer rewarding experiences that are missed by those who prefer more developed metropolitan areas to the more primitive regions. Here you'll find modern seaports, small fishing villages, broad expanses of sandy beaches, groves of tropical fruits—bananas, pineapples, papayas, mangoes, avocados, coconuts, and oranges—exotic birds, historically interesting cities, and many of Mexico's greatest archaeological sites.

Nowhere else in Mexico can you see Indians who have retained their cultural characteristics in such pristine form as the Zapotecs, Lacandons, Chamulas, and Zinacantecos. The archaeological sites of Palenque, Mitla, La Venta, Monte Alban, and El Tajin leave you with lasting impressions of the early civilizations of southern Mexico, an area so vital to the understanding of ancient Mexico. Anthropologists in search of the earliest culture in Mexico's history focus on this region, studying the artifacts of the Olmecs.

You'll find travel in the southern area enjoyable year-round because of the mild winters and warm summers. (A few places, such as the Isthmus area, become extremely humid and hot during the summer.) Tropical vegetation, especially from Tampico southward, is dense and lush. Fauna of the area provides an insight to unusual species; *quetzals* (Guatemala's national bird, regarded by the Mayas as a religious symbol), egrets, jaguars, and tapirs all roam here, particularly in the state of Chiapas.

South from Tampico

Motorists have a choice of two routes south to Tuxpan — Highway 180 down the coast, or Highway 105-127 through Panuco and Tempoal.

The short route is down the coast on Highway 180, but you've got to cross the wide Panuco River on a car ferry, which is big and businesslike. The long line-up of cars and trucks waiting their turn to board the ferry can be a bit discouraging, though—and the steady pounding of huge Pemex oil field equipment has ruined the road in places.

The older route across the bridge over the Panuco River at Panuco has been rebuilt from Panuco to Tempoal, and you drive through ranching and sugar cane country and pleasant, rolling foothills. Beyond Tempoal the road is uneven and hilly. At Alazan Junction the two highways meet and go on into Tuxpan on a blacktop road.

South of Tuxpan at Poza Rica the road splits, and the right fork is Highway 130 that winds through beautiful mountain country to Pachuca on Highway 85—one route to Mexico City. From Tuxpan, you can take Highway 180 down the coast to Veracruz.

Tuxpan—fishing for tarpon is great!

Tuxpan is known as a quiet paradise for tarpon fishermen. Tarpon can be caught from the river at any time, but the peak season is in June. The most important activity of the port town, though, is cattle and petroleum shipping.

Four miles to the east of Tuxpan is the Gulf of Mexico and a beautiful beach. Delicious tiny shrimp, taken from the nearby lagoons and served with a hot sauce *(salsa picante)*, are a specialty of local restaurants. An attractive, divided riverside drive adds to the charm of this tidy fishing port.

A bridge across the Tuxpan River takes you to the smaller river town of Santiago de la Pena on the south shore. You then head southwest through verdant tropical country peppered with gas flares from oil wells.

Poza Rica and Papantla

Soon you arrive at one of Mexico's leading oil towns, Poza Rica, or "Rich Hole." This booming town has one industry—a huge Pemex oil refinery.

Because of the town's sudden growth, most buildings testify to the haste in which they were built. Oil is king here, and if you happen to forget for a moment, the penetrating stench of petroleum will soon remind you.

Overwhelming vastness *dazzles visitors exploring Monte Alban ruins and gazing down to Oaxaca valley 1200 feet below.*

Ten miles south of Poza Rica on an alternate highway to Papantla are the ruins of El Tajin, a site rivaling any of the other major archaeological zones in Mexico. Around 800 A.D. the Totonacs settled here, but the site was inhabited as early as the 5th or 6th century.

The seven-story Pyramid of the Niches with 364 exterior niches certainly reigns as the most important building. Counting the door to the temple on top as another niche makes 365, probably representing the days of the solar year. In front of the pyramid is a tall steel pole around which the famed Flying Pole Dancers *(voladores)* from Papantla perform on special occasions. Today, Papantla is the main trading and cultural center of the Totonacs.

A major industry around Papantla and the nearby town of Gutierrez Zamora is the growing and processing of vanilla beans. In June, you'll see the voladores perform as part of a week-long fiesta celebrating the sale of last year's vanilla harvest and praying for rain for this year's crop.

On to Veracruz

At Gutierrez Zamora a bridge over the placid Tecolutla River replaces the former ferry. The highway then proceeds alongside the gulf for about 20 miles, past sandy dunes and beaches, through Brahma ranching country and magnificent groves of coconut palms.

At an old lighthouse junction called El Faro, you have a choice of two routes to Veracruz. Highway 180 continues down the coast; on the other highways you wind inland by way of Teziutlan, Perote, and Jalapa.

The coast route follows the Gulf of Mexico. South of Nautla, the highway clings to the coast, skirting the azure gulf and tranquil lagoons on one side and verdant foothills on the other.

Snow-shrouded *Mt. Orizaba, Mexico's highest peak, shows face briefly amidst clouds.*

Seventy miles south of Nautla and 2 miles to the west is Zempoala, the last capital of the Totonacs. Its architecture, though notably inferior to that of El Tajin, embodies a building material not found elsewhere—rounded boulders from river beds. Its cemeteries are worthy of note; tombs are miniature temples about 4 feet high.

Veracruz—the untourist town

Lighthearted Veracruz is different from other Mexican cities, and the difference quickly becomes apparent. You feel the heat (after the April rains come) as a palpable thing, and one experience with it helps you understand the paradoxical combination of vivacity and indolence you sense in tropical people. The warm climate and fruitful land favor both the rich and the improvident; the palm-thatched shack is never far from the palatial town house, and everyone from *peon* (laborer) to *presidente* gathers under the arcades.

Above all, you'll notice that Veracruz has not made the special preparations and provisions for tourists found in most cities in Mexico. Veracruz is for itself. Insights into the lives of the people are there to appreciate; unselfconsciously, the people live out their lives.

Noise in this city—where shutters are more common than glass windows—seems magnified in the warm air. Car horns blare, little open-sided streetcars clatter, and radios blast tropical rhythms into the streets.

But most striking of all is the brilliant light, the glare of the tropical sun. Rain, salt air, and the relentless sun make new walls look old so they blend with ancient walls, adding an atmospheric unity to the city's architecture.

The importance of Veracruz as the main port of entry on Mexico's east coast is evident today in the omnipresent references to the ocean and ships throughout town: the Chapel of Christ of the Safe

Prickly poppy

Flame vine

Bougainvillea

Voyage, forts, lighthouses, shipyards, and an abundance of delicious seafood. Activity first began in Veracruz when Cortez landed in the harbor and founded the city in 1519, before beginning his westward march to conquer the Aztecs. Almost all mail and commerce went through Veracruz during the colonial era. Its harbor has seen invasions by the United States, France, and Spain.

What to do. In the city, be sure to see the waterfront, fish market, small food markets, and the trim subdivisions. Stroll under the arcades; sit in an outdoor cafe or on a gaily tiled park bench; ride an open-sided streetcar; and visit the marine curio shops near the docks. You may arrange for a boat for tarpon or deep-sea fishing, or a visit to the offshore Isla de Sacrificios. Inquire about boat rentals at your hotel or the customhouse dock. Drive out to the old, lichen-encrusted fortress-prison of San Juan de Ulua. If you haven't seen the El Tajin ruins, hire a car and/or guide for a day's visit.

Where to stay. Veracruz hotels are generally air-conditioned, and most have pools, as well as cocktail lounges and sidewalk cafes. In some you'll find spots for dancing.

From Mexico City to Veracruz

A fast toll road east from Mexico City (Highway 190-D) takes you to Puebla. To continue from Puebla, pick up Highway 150-D, also a toll road. This route from Orizaba passes through rich coffee plantations and flower-garlanded resorts, taking you to the coast and Veracruz.

In the shadow of mighty Orizaba

Beyond the Tehuacan turnoff, Highway 150 climbs to a 7,500-foot summit offering one of the spectacular views of Mexico—the Valley of Acultzingo. The gradual descent of 4,000 feet in a few miles is

Sunlight dapples water *with many tints around sailboat tied down in Veracruz harbor.*

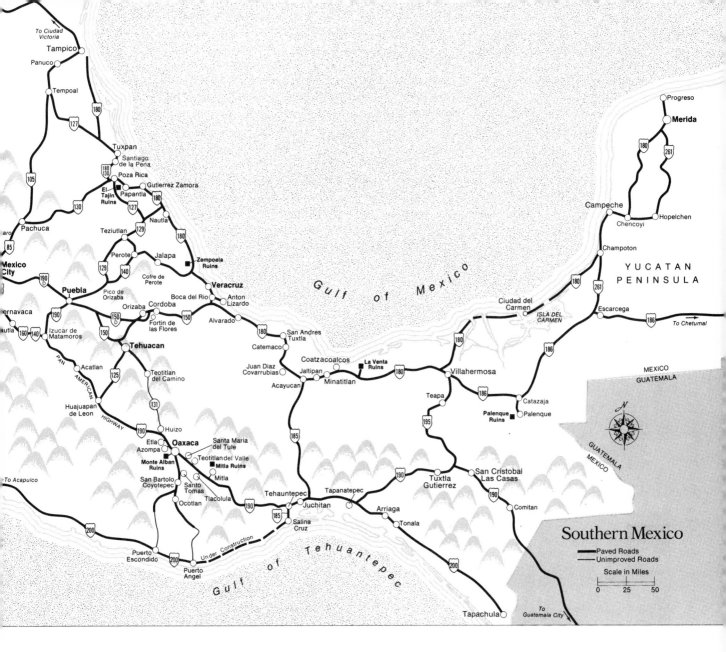

Southern Mexico

Paved Roads
Unimproved Roads

Scale in Miles

0   25   50

Details at a glance

How to get there

Daily flights between Oaxaca, center of Southern Mexico, and Mexico City offer a good view of volcanoes. Flights also originate from other southern cities.

By car it's about 350 miles from Mexico City (about 8 hours) to Oaxaca. If you take the bus you'll spend about 12 hours, passing through scenic countryside in darkness.

Getting around. Best way to view the country-side is by car. Rental cars are available in Oaxaca.

Accommodations. You'll find hotels in the few large cities. From your base in Oaxaca you can journey to surrounding city markets or visit the pyramids of Monte Alban, Mitla, and others. Ruins are also abundant around Veracruz and San Cristobal De Las Casas; hotels are more scarce. In Tehuantepec you can buy a hammock at the local jail.

Climate and dress. Oaxaca has become a popular year-round destination. In San Cristobal you'll need warm outdoor clothing at night or in early morning. November to April is the best time to visit; winter may be crisp and early spring smoky due to burning of the fields. Nobody would ever say Veracruz is cool; late February or early March is pleasant.

Casual attire is appropriate. Come prepared for rain or sun at almost any time of year.

breathtaking even in the rainy season when you peer through breaks in the swirling clouds at the patterns of sun and darkness on the blue, green, and yellow patchwork valley below. If you're squeamish about hairpin turns and abrupt drop-offs, though, take the Puebla-Orizaba toll express-way, which misses the Acultzingo descent.

As you approach the city of Orizaba, you'll see magnificent Pico de Orizaba, also called Citlatepetl (the star mountain). This is Mexico's highest moun-tain—an 18,701-foot peak with perpetual snows on its volcanic cone. The first town of notable size in this warm, lush valley, Orizaba blends industrial claptrap with colonial ambience. Its textile mills are juxtaposed with long rows of tile-roofed dwellings and shops.

Two breweries, coffee and fruit packing com-panies, and cement plants are central to the city's industrial economy. The Municipal Palace (Palacio Municipal), on the plaza northwest of Castillo Park, was purchased by the city from Belgium. Originally, the building was part of the Belgian Pavilion in the Paris Exposition in the 19th century.

Orizaba's orchids and many other exotic flowers provide you with an introduction to an area bedecked with tropical blossoms. All kinds of colors and scents greet your senses and stay with you for weeks after your visit.

Fortin de las Flores—steeped in flowers

Less a town than a flower garden, Fortin de las Flores was a Spanish outpost during the colonial period. Today it is a resort town noted for its exceptionally beautiful gardens (gardenias, camel-lias, orchids). You can visit the plantation that each day supplies the large resort hotel with the truck-load of gardenias that are floated on its swimming pool. The best of the area's flowers can be appre-ciated at the annual flower fair in April.

Cordoba—for peacocks and papaya

Cordoba, a little farther down the highway, is a tropical town dominated by pinks and blues. It is a railroad center for the crops you see beside the road — coffee growing in the shade, tobacco dry-ing on racks or in smoke barns, and vast emerald sugar cane fields surrounding sugar mills.

Its tropical personality is emphasized by the presence of peacocks, mangoes, papayas, and an assortment of other vibrantly plumed creatures and sweet, colorful fruit.

Founded by the Spaniards in 1618, Cordoba has a historically vital heritage. Originally, the Toton-acs inhabited this area. The Aztecs, led by Monte-zuma, conquered them in 1456. The penultimate scene in the War of Independence in the early

1800s took place in Cordoba. The last Spanish viceroy, arriving in Veracruz after the war was over, met Iturbide in Cordoba in July, 1821, and formally acknowledged Mexico's independence.

Down toward the coast are the fields and groves that make eating here a delight. You will see rag-ged banana patches, papayas, spreading mango trees, trees that bear enormous avocados, and fields of pineapple. Beyond, agriculture gives way to rank jungle growth; only a thatched hut in a clearing relieves the monotonous greenery.

You reach the coast at Boca del Rio, a ram-shackle, tropical-looking village with coconut palms, pink or buff thatched huts, a weedy plaza, and a tiny church. Stop to watch the fishermen fishing from their boats.

Jalapa—hillside university town

Returning to Mexico City by way of Jalapa repeats many of the impressions you get on the Cordoba road, but the climb is steadier and you reach pine forests and the plateau sooner. If you become familiar with the history of the Spanish conquest of Mexico, this trip will become much more vivid and significant. The road follows the route of Cortez after he scuttled his ships at Veracruz in 1519 and marched on to the Mexico of Montezuma.

Jalapa is worth more than just a fleeting stop. This quiet state capital has colorful hillside streets and exuberant vegetation, providing the photog-rapher with delightful close-ups as well as panor-amas. Balconies, wide overhanging eaves, shaped rafter ends, carved wooden doors, and grilled windows will captivate you with their intricate detail when you look up the side streets.

Another town known for its floral personality and profusion of blooms, Jalapa offers a wide variety of tropical flowers and fruits. Built on a sloping hillside, the city is the home of the Univer-sity of Veracruz. The university has a museum housing a display of archaeological artifacts, not-ably those of the Totonac and Olmec cultures. The university also has its own symphony and publish-ing facilities. You'll appreciate the resolute courage of the conquistadors when you cross the 8,000-foot pass beyond the town of Jalapa (near the 14,048-foot peak of the volcano, Cofre de Perote) and see the desolate, windswept highland plains. Maguey and aloe hedgerows define a few Indian fields.

Near the town of Perote you'll see grim Fort San Carlos, built 200 years ago by the Spaniards to accommodate troops protecting Mexico City-Vera-cruz stagecoaches from attack by bandits. During World War II it became a prison for aliens; today it is a rehabilitation center where Mexican inmates produce and sell craft items.

Oaxaca

For some of their warmest, richest memories of Mexico, many travelers are indebted to Oaxaca. Three hundred and forty miles southeast of Mexico City by way of Cuautla (a faster route than through Puebla), Oaxaca is a day's drive. If you have time, though, it is worth a stop on any trip continuing farther south in Mexico or en route to Central America. Oaxaca is about 18 hours from Mexico City by overnight train with Pullman accommodations, 12 hours by first-class bus, and 45 minutes by commercial airline.

Oaxaca—for a relaxing vacation

This far south of the border, you're less conscious of being a *turista* and are treated more as one of Mexico's own people. Even the climate of Oaxaca is friendly, without extremes of either heat or cold at the 5,068-foot elevation.

Capital of the state of Oaxaca and set in a broad valley, Oaxaca City is at the center of a constellation of villages. Founded as Antequera in 1522 by a group of Spanish soldiers, the city was named Oaxaca—a corruption of the Indian word *Quauhxyacac* (Place of Trees)—in 1529 by Charles V, who granted the valley to Cortez as his private estate. The many colonial buildings in the city are noteworthy for their massiveness (this is earthquake country) and the lovely pale green color of the local stone used in their construction.

In contrast to Mexico City, Oaxaca's pace is low-key, and its small-town atmosphere unspoiled. Yet with a population of just over 100,000, it is the most important urban center between the capital and the Guatemalan frontier. Descendants of Zapotec and Mixtec builders of Monte Alban comprise two-thirds of the state's population.

Oaxaca is not known for its night life and offers practically none of the tourist amusements available in other parts of Mexico. Instead, the main attractions are its markets, where popular arts and crafts are displayed in a richness and variety unparalleled elsewhere in Mexico, and its colorfully garbed Indian people.

Crafts. You won't have to look for handcrafts—they will come to you. Settle back in the shade of the porticos facing the Zocalo (the park at the center of town). While you sip a cool drink, vendors parade by with striped sarapes, bright rebozos, and lacy golden necklaces. You can bargain right from your table.

It is an easy walk to craft shops, found mostly in a small area north and east of the Zocalo. Here you'll discover the specialties of Oaxaca: pottery, gold and silver jewelry, skirts, blouses, men's shirts, and tablecloths. Oaxaca's knives are famous for the handcarved eagle surmounting the horn

Oaxaca's festive December fiestas

A 3-day fiesta in Oaxaca, beginning December 18, honors the city's patron saint, the Virgin of Solitude. At this time of year her name seems singularly inappropriate for the festivals held in her honor. Carnival-like activities lasting well into the evening center around the Sanctuario de la Soledad, an ornate baroque church a few blocks west of the Zocalo.

As soon as that fiesta is over, the Oaxaquenos begin decorating the town for Christmas. Moss, an essential item for the numerous nativity scenes, is brought from surrounding areas by the Zapotec Indians. Trees and shrubs are adorned with ornaments and gay pinatas, and amusement stands arise overnight around Oaxaca's cathedral at the north side of the Zocalo.

With its elegant bandstand and well-kept park, the Zocalo is the center of all activities. Restaurants under its surrounding arcades provide the best seats for watching the gaiety. It isn't long before the sarape and rebozo vendors are stopping by your table to show their wares.

By December 23 you smell the *bunuelos* frying.

These light, crispy pancakes, sprinkled with pink sugar and syrup, are served from many booths around the plaza. Custom demands that you smash the saucer in which it is served after the bunuelo has been eaten. As the evening advances, you may be deep in shards.

That same evening is the radish judging contest. This yearly competition of imaginative designs created entirely from special elongated, twisted radishes displays some unusual creative skills. The designs typically depict religious scenes, but one year's winner was an Apollo XI display complete with astronauts and spaceships. After the prizes are awarded, the radish figures are sold.

The traditional Christmas Eve parade starts around 9 P.M. Many villages throughout the state participate, each contributing a float and band. People preceding the floats carry colored lanterns and ornaments, little boys shoot firecrackers, and all the bands play simultaneously—but different tunes. It all ends with a spectacular fireworks display and midnight services.

grip and for the fine steel blades often etched with a proverb.

Sights to see. One of the liveliest spots in Oaxaca is the Zocalo, where small boys do a brisk trade in shoeshines for idlers sitting on park benches. The cathedral facing the Zocalo has a clock donated by a Spanish king.

Five blocks north of the Zocalo is the incredibly beautiful Santo Domingo Church, outwardly imposing, with an interior displaying the most gorgeous baroque decoration in all of Mexico. To the left of the atrium is the Regional Museum with treasures of pre-Hispanic native cultures.

Just west of the Zocalo is the market, which explodes with life each Saturday and before important holidays. It is a crowded, fascinating place where you can see Oaxacans and learn about their lives. People from surrounding districts come to barter under billowing canvas sun shades. They may bring flowers, rope, or tin-can mousetraps. There may be a seller who has brought his year's work—a few treasured pink and yellow mythical carved beasts—or a blousemaker from the Pacific whose traditional purple designs are naturally colored from the ink of the sea-dwelling *caracol* (snail). A sanitized, modern new market is ready, but vendors and shoppers are loyal to the old one; when and if they will move is unclear at present.

Monte Alban—hilltop monument to its builders

The ruins of Monte Alban on a hilltop 6 miles southwest of Oaxaca are a monument to the master builders of pre-Hispanic Mexico. The summit was leveled and reshaped, and artificial esplanades and structures were raised in harmonious groupings over a period of 17 centuries (700 B.C.-1000 A.D.) The earliest buildings are those of the inner structure of The Dancers and the arrowhead-shaped observatory.

In its final form, as you see it today, Monte Alban is composed of a huge central plaza limited to the north and south by acropolis-type platforms and enclosed on the east and west by lower buildings. At a lower level behind the northern platform are several tombs open to the public, among them the famous Tomb 7 that held the magnificent jewelry now on display in the Oaxaca Regional Museum. The many tombs indicate the site's special character as a burial area or necropolis. Mixtec invaders occupied Monte Alban around 1200 A.D., rejuvenating it and burying their rulers in the Zapotec funeral chambers.

Villages around Oaxaca

You can drive your car to most of the villages near Oaxaca. You can also get to all of them by local bus (station on Trujano 3 blocks west of the Zocalo) or by taxi (be sure to settle on the price before leaving).

Etla, 12 miles north of Oaxaca, has a Wednesday market; you need not arrive until 11 A.M. or later to see peak activity. The village is noted for making *quesillo,* a cheese boiled into long ribbons and then rolled into a ball.

Azompa produces pottery—pots with a green glaze and small figures of animals playing musical instruments. The road off Highway 190 is not recommended for the family car. The trip by bus takes about an hour; this is the typical second or third-class bus on which the Indians bring chickens and other goods to or from market. English is rarely spoken in the village.

San Bartolo Coyotepec, about 6 miles south of Oaxaca along Highway 175, is easily reached by automobile. (Two Coyotepecs are located one after the other; San Bartolo is the second.) Black, unglazed pottery, made without the use of a potter's wheel, is a trademark of Oaxaca and the surrounding areas. Almost everyone in this village makes pottery including whistles, bells, and animals.

Santo Tomas, beyond Coyotepec, specializes in the weaving of *fajas* (sashes) in the ancient manner using the backstrap loom—one end tied around a tree and the other to a strap around the waist of the weaver.

Ocotlan, 12 miles beyond Coyotepec, has a colorful, bustling Friday market; it is also unusually clean. Occasionally, an Indian girl brings in one of the beautifully embroidered and pleated blouses. Tall stacks of baskets in all sizes and shapes are for sale, and there's a lively market in goats. Be sure to leave the main plaza and walk down the street to see the chicken merchants and sugar cane dealers. During the early morning hours you may see whole families hauling their wares to market on two-wheeled ox carts.

Santa Maria del Tule, 9 miles east on Highway 190, has a famous tree in front of its church. A colossal cypress (ahuehuete) about 130 feet high with a trunk more than 150 feet in circumference, it is believed to be at least 2,000 years old.

Teotitlan del Valle produces the sarapes sold throughout the Oaxaca area. Weavers use upright looms (this village abandoned the backstrap loom at the time of the Spanish Conquest), and card and spin their own wool. The road off the highway to Teotitlan is dusty but passable in dry weather.

Tlacolula, off Highway 190, is about 18 miles from Oaxaca. It has a Sunday market often visited by people en route to Mitla.

Tiny Tarascan girl *weaves bright sashes using a belt loom.*

Colorful dyed fiber *creates vividly chromatic chair seats.*

Ceramic bird *is ornate and sprightly traditional handcraft.*

Mitla's intricate stonework

You drive through Mitla on a paved road to visit the remarkable ruins on the outskirts of town. Mitla is another of the Zapotec-Mixtec ceremonial centers. Intricately carved stone fretwork characterizes the facades of Mitla's temples. Arranged in a repetitive pattern, the designs are basically geometric. This was the fabled abode of Mictlante-cuhtli, Lord of the Underworld, and a sacred city for the burial of Indian kings.

After the ruins, you pass the typical Mexican village of humble, nondescript buildings, pedestrians, perhaps a donkey piled high with fagots or wheat, and a public market. But Mitla has another resource—it is renowned for the weaving of fine textiles by primitive handweaving methods seldom seen outside the more remote areas of Latin Amer-

Mitla ruins, *dating from 500 A.D., were once fabled city of gods and Indian burial site.*

Heart of holiday *festivities,*
Oaxaca's brightly-lighted zocalo
draws crowds for music and song.

Tired from dancing, *Chiapas men doze*
under decorated hats at San Cristobal.

Sightless serenity *characterizes stone head in Villahermosa outdoor museum.*

Natives cross *wide field to reach sugarcake cemetery in San Cristobal.*

ica. The "Mitla design," with a stepped-fret motif, comes from the stone patterns you see on the Mitla ruins.

Much of the weaving is done behind the walls of courtyards at the rear of the room in which hand-loomed articles are sold. But one establishment, on the left as you enter town from Highway 190, operates in a courtyard where you can see artisans meticulously weaving the threads of a creatively designed piece of cloth.

To the Guatemala border

The Pan American Highway, Highway 190, continues south from Oaxaca to the Isthmus of Tehuantepec. It follows the south side of the isthmus through flat country covered with scrubby, thorny brush, then climbs through a series of tightly forested mountains and broad, soft, uncultivated river valleys to Tuxtla Gutierrez and San Cristobal Las Casas. Very few settlements can be found along this road. It is wise to fill up with gasoline before leaving Juchitan; though there is a station at La Ventosa Junction, it may not have unleaded gasoline.

At Tapanatepec, you can take an alternate route (Highway 200) to the Guatemala border. This lowland highway, completed in 1964, is now the favored route. It goes through Arriaga and then on to Tapachula.

Both routes from Tapanatepec are paved all the way to the border, but the coast route avoids the dangerous El Tapon stretch of Highway 190 — 23 miles of road running through a winding canyon where landslides and flash floods sometimes create difficulties and delays. You can rejoin the Pan American Highway at Guatemala's capital, Guatemala City, or from a scenic toll road that leaves the coast route near Retalhuleu, Guatemala.

The Pan American Highway extends for 3,000 miles through Mexico and Central America to Panama City. The road is paved all the way except for a few short sections in Costa Rica and Nicaragua.

Tehuantepec—a woman's world

If the day is hot and humid when you arrive on this west side of the Isthmus of Tehuantepec, you may wonder why you've ventured this far south into Mexico. The towns and villages seem lackluster, though civilization is reaching them fast. The countryside is tropical, but not dramatic or luxuriant with plant growth as in other tropical areas.

You soon become accustomed to a lack of comforts and conveniences, and after 2 or 3 days you discover that its main attractions are the Tehuana women and the Pacific beaches.

The women, tall and graceful, are dark-skinned with smooth features. They wear multicolored costumes which are even more resplendent on Sundays and at the many fiestas and dances. You'll notice them especially at Juchitan, a nearby town about the same size as Tehuantepec with adequate tourist accommodations. In Tehuantepec the women run the marketplace and the men stay home and in the fields. In fact, in this matriarchal society, the women are conspicuously the most active members of the community, even in local governmental affairs.

Veracruz to Villahermosa

Just south of Veracruz, a side road leads down the coast to Anton Lizardo, where Mexico's Naval Academy is located.

A few miles beyond the turnoff to Anton Lizardo at Paso del Toro Junction, Highway 150 goes west to Cordoba, where it ties into the toll expressway that knifes across the Continental Divide to Puebla and on to Mexico City.

For 60 miles south of Veracruz, Highway 180 provides glimpses of the gulf—and shifting sand dunes that sometimes cover parts of the highway.

At Alvarado, you cross the wide mouth of the Papaloapan River over a toll bridge.

South of Alvarado, the route goes through rich sugar cane country, then winds along the shore of Lake Catemaco, up into high volcanic hills, and down into the fertile valley of the Hueyapan River. At the small town of Juan Diaz Covarrubias, a sugar refinery, a molasses plant, and an alcohol distillery provide employment for the inhabitants.

At Acayucan, Highway 185 branches south across the Isthmus of Tehuantepec to La Ventosa Junction on the Pacific side.

Eleven miles beyond Acayucan on Highway 180 is the humble sulfur-mining boom town of Jaltipan. From under Jaltipan, believed to be the world's greatest sulfur "dome," millions of tons of this material have already been removed.

Minatitlan, 13 miles farther, is headquarters for the sulfur and oil expeditions into the jungles up the tropical Coatzacoalcos River. Beyond Minatitlan, you drive through about 10 miles of marshy mud flats to the leading town of the area—the oil and sulfur seaport of Coatzacoalcos. The highway by-passes the town and crosses the Coatzacoalcos River on a toll drawbridge that carries both a railroad track and the highway.

The highway winds through oil fields to the Tonala River, crossed by another bridge. Three miles beyond the bridge, a side road to the left leads to the La Venta oil-producing area. It was in the La Venta swamps that archaeologists found giant heads and other stone figures sculptured by the Olmecs, later removed for exhibition elsewhere.

Visit Villahermosa's outdoor museum

An attractive provincial state capital little known by tourists, Villahermosa is worth visiting even if you do not plan to continue into Yucatan. For many years the city had no road to the outside world; most transportation of both goods and people was by water, on the Grijalva River. This water culture has not appreciably diminished. Villahermosa still has a beautiful riverfront along the placid Grijalva, with an impressive boulevard and flowered plazas.

The archaeological museum in town is one of the best in Mexico. Another museum, an outdoor one called Museo de La Venta, is at the fairgrounds near the highway entrance to the city. This spacious museum is unique in its attempt to duplicate the original site of La Venta. The Olmec culture inhabited La Venta (see page 85); the huge basalt heads were transported here from the site near the Tabasco-Veracruz border. Within the museum you follow marked trails to the various archaeological displays.

You'll find plenty of places to stay. A very good hotel opened in October, 1975, and two more chain hotels opened in 1976. Two important routes originate at Villahermosa. Route 195 is a road going south to Tuxtla Gutierrez. Now paved for the entire distance, the road has an abundance of curves and you should allow plenty of time for driving it. Trailers and many cars should use extreme caution. The road passes near Teapa, where you can board trains to Merida.

The other route is inland Highway 186, from which a paved side road goes south to the Mayan archaeological ruins of Palenque. Highway 261 branches off at Escarcega and runs north to Champoton, where it joins coastal route Highway 180 to Campeche. Eighteen miles east of Campeche at Chencoyi, Highway 180 continues north to Merida, while Highway 261 runs east 32 miles to Hopelchen, and then north to Merida. This affords motorists a circle route south of Merida.

Jungle ruins of Palenque

Seventy-five miles east of Villahermosa by way of Highway 186, a paved road turns south for 22 miles to the archaeological site of Palenque in the Chiapas jungles. Rental cars are available in Villahermosa; buses also run from there to the ruins. Modest accommodations are available in the small town of Palenque nearby.

Considered by many to be the most beautiful pre-Hispanic site in Mexico, Palenque was a Maya center inhabited from the 1st century A.D., reaching a cultural peak in 600 A.D. that was prolonged over three centuries. Most of its buildings are gems of light, airy construction. The Temple of Inscriptions contains a Royal Tomb reached by a narrow stairway down into the body of the pyramid, where it opens out into a magnificent burial chamber. Though the central area of the city has been ex-

The colorful Chiapas

Living inconspicuously deep in the jungles of remote Chiapas, the Lacandon Indians have a peaceful, primitive culture. The Lacandons number only around 300, and are being "civilized" at an ever-increasing rate. Paying silent homage to their Maya heritage, they paddle roughly hewn dugout canoes up and down the jungle rivers of Chiapas, perhaps on their way to Yaxchilan, a difficult-to-reach Maya ruin where they worship the ancient Maya gods that are believed to inhabit the site.

The faces of today's Lacandons so closely resemble the Maya faces depicted in the carved reliefs on Maya temples that they are sometimes referred to as "living reliefs."

Some are so completely isolated from modern innovations that they still rely on such primitive tools and implements as wooden knives and bows and arrows. Even the comfort of a warm blanket is a luxury unknown to these people; instead they sleep in hammocks at night, and are kept warm by the dying embers of a fire built close to their beds.

If the Lacandons are the recluses of Chiapas, the Chamulas are the area's most overtly progressive and aggressive Indians. In the mid-19th century they even rose in open warfare against the "white" town of San Cristobal Las Casas. Their aggressiveness now has been turned to hard trading in the marketplace. Chamula men can be distinguished by their black, or sometimes white, tunics. The decorative colors used and the unique woven pattern of the tunic indicate the village from which each man comes. The women wear black huipiles with red tassels.

The Zinacanteco Indians of Chiapas provide local color. Their handwoven straw hats with wide brims are profusely decorated with multifarious, brightly colored ribbons. The Zinacantecos' basic attire consists of white cotton shirts and trousers, tunics, colorful sarapes, and kerchiefs worn around the neck. On their feet are the traditional Mexican huaraches with heelguards reminiscent of ancient Indian footwear.

cavated and restored, there is much yet to be uncovered. You'll find a small museum at the site.

You can swim on a beach inside the breakwater at Salina Cruz, a fast-developing port about 10 miles from Tehuantepec. Swimming and the general atmosphere are even more delightful about 4 miles south at the small fishing village of La Ventosa—reached only by way of a rough dirt road. Taxis from Tehuantepec will take you there for a small charge. Young people are discovering this as yet undeveloped area. Only two establishments serve refreshments and rent hammocks; one place with no facilities will allow campers to park under a small grove of palms.

Juchitan—Tehuana town

Juchitan is 17 miles east of Tehuantepec in open plain country. Juchitan and Tehuantepec have been rivals over the years, a fact that is evident in the tacit challenge that exists for residents to outdress one another in traditional costume regalia. The town is about the same size as Tehuantepec, but more spread out; it has larger squares and the streets are wider and gracefully shaded by trees.

The marketplace overflows out of a high-ceilinged shed into a series of arches or portales on one side of the main square.

Juchitan, like Tehuantepec, has a matriarchal society, and the two towns share a similar fiesta tradition—the *Vela*, literally "vigil," but certainly a much happier affair than the name implies. Velas are usually sponsored by a family, frequently on the same date each year; for example, the Ruiz family will offer its Vela every year on April 20. Held in a temporary shelter near (not in) the home of the host family, Velas may continue for 1, 2, or 3 days and nights. Guests are expected to cooperate with food, drink, or funds; outsiders may be welcomed on the same terms.

Marimba music is favored, and it is here that the famous *sandunga* is danced. In rhythm a waltz (the obligatory turns display the skirted Tehuana costume to swirling advantage), the sandunga is usually minor in tone, slow in tempo, and haunting in effect.

Getting across the Isthmus

At La Ventosa Junction you can drive north across the Isthmus of Tehuantepec on a good road, paved Highway 185. In less than 200 miles, it stretches from the Pacific Ocean to the Gulf of Mexico across land that never rises more than 700 feet above sea level, following the rail route closely most of the way. Near the Gulf, at Acayucan, is the junction with Highway 180, where you can either turn north to Mexico City by way of Veracruz, or southeast to Coatzacoalcos, Villahermosa, and the Yucatan Peninsula.

San Cristobal Las Casas—pure Indian

Five driving hours—160 miles—separate Juchitan from Tuxtla Gutierrez, capital of the state of Chiapas. Tuxtla Gutierrez is a prosperous, modern commercial center that serves the coffee plantations scattered throughout the surrounding hills. It also has a booming frontier-town atmosphere, because construction workers from nearby dam projects flood the town on weekends and holidays.

San Cristobal Las Casas, clean and quiet, is set in a fertile 7,000-foot-high basin ringed with green mountains. You'll find a pristine charm here that many other tourist spots have lost. The charm of San Cristobal lies in its setting and solid colonial architecture, and in the comings and goings of the many Indian groups who live in the region. This is truly a photographer's paradise.

The diocese was not moved from San Cristobal, once the capital of the state, to Tuxtla Gutierrez when the latter became the capital. So, visit the cathedral on the plaza; it hides a magnificent interior behind an ordinary facade. The plaza itself is charming, with a lacy ironwork bandstand surrounded by shrubs and brilliantly flowering plants. The Church of Santo Domingo, a few blocks away, is not only impressive on the inside but has an extremely ornate facade.

Calle Guadalupe is the street of the shops—not the curio shops of tourist centers but *tiendas* (stores) that sell to the Indians. For several blocks north of the plaza, you look through unmarked doorways at endless stacks of sombreros, huge quantities of leather shoulder bags, and dozens of sarapes and rebozos in vivid colors and interesting weaves and designs.

San Cristobal is organized roughly into districts, each occupied by the urbanized descendants of a particular Indian tribe all working at the same trade. Thus in one area you can watch the weavers, in another area the dollmakers, in another the makers of fireworks, and in another the candle-stick makers, hanging their products in colorful clusters.

The market—a new one on the east edge of town —is of interest because, like all Mexican markets, it mirrors the area's economic life.

San Cristobal is now the departure point for several exciting trips, particularly since a half-dozen delightful new inns have been opened in the town. There are caves nearby for speleologists; the beautiful Montebello lakes are a day-long excursion; and pack expeditions can be arranged into the tropical highland forests for a look at half-buried Maya sites and a visit to Lacandon Indian groups.

Yucatan-
Ruins of a Civilization

The Yucatan peninsula—that immense thrust of land dividing the Gulf of Mexico from the Caribbean—is so flat that the landscape takes on a uniformity approaching monotony. But beneath that deceiving cloak of sameness there exists a people exuding warmth and vitality, and a land with an inexhaustible wealth of archaeological treasures. Images that will linger in your mind might be smooth, bronze Maya faces with sparkling eyes and spontaneous, genuine smiles; the charm of Merida; the *huipiles* (a long white overblouse embroidered at neck and hem), sandals, and pleated shirts worn by the Yucatecans; and the gemlike brilliance of the Caribbean.

Three islands—Isla Mujeres, Cancun, and Cozumel—lie close to the mainland just off the northeast tip of the peninsula; all are accessible by boat or air. A causeway now reaches Cancun.

The peninsula is divided into the states of Yucatan, Campeche, and Quintana Roo—all once within the land of the Maya. For years the Maya sites of Chichen Itza, Uxmal, Kabah, Tulum, and others less well-known to the casual traveler have lured archaeologists and adventurers to this remote part of Mexico. The Yucatan would be interesting even without its ruins, but they make the peninsula one of the world's most fascinating tourist areas. As time and restoration funds allow, more ruins are becoming easily accessible to the traveler.

Aside from its Maya ruins, Yucatan is famous for *henequen* (sisal) rope and twine. Until the end of World War II Yucatan supplied most of the world's high-grade sisal, but synthetic fibers have since cut sharply into the henequen market, bringing difficult times to the industry.

Villahermosa to Campeche

Highway 180 has four ferry crossings en route to Campeche. It is advisable to get an early start from Villahermosa so you can catch all four in one day, beginning with the ferry at Frontera.

This first ferry crosses the Grijalva River 45 miles from Villahermosa at a community called San Roman. The town of Frontera is on the other side. The ferry runs from 3 A.M. until 11 P.M., and the crossing takes from 15 to 20 minutes. There is a small toll for cars as well as for trailers. It is unwise, though, for trailers to use the ferries; undercarriages may be damaged. Inland Highway 186 is a better choice for travelers driving these vehicles.

The next ferry is 15 miles farther along Highway 180, across the San Pedro River. The ferry runs throughout the day; the trip takes 10 minutes. A toll is also required here for cars and trailers.

The third ferry crossing takes longer—25 to 30 minutes. It leaves from Zacatal, a mile beyond the lighthouse community of Xicalango, and runs to Ciudad del Carmen on Isla del Carmen, an island separated from the mainland by the Laguna de Terminos.

The town of Carmen is 4 miles long. Beyond it the island stretches for 22 miles to Puerto Real, where you take the fourth (and longest) ferry ride. The crossing from Puerto Real to the mainland takes the better part of an hour, and ferries run more or less continuously throughout the day. If you miss the ferry and are stranded for the night on the island, you'll find fairly good motel and adequate hotel accommodations.

After the fourth ferry, you proceed along palm-lined Highway 180 for 65 miles to the seaside shipbuilding town of Champoton and the junction with Highway 261 (the alternate route to Merida). Highway 186, the inland route from Villahermosa, is more monotonous, lacking the tropical vegetation for a good part of the way; one does not have to depend on ferries, though. Highway 186 turns east at Escarcega to Chetumal on the Caribbean, thus traversing the peninsula at its base. Those who wish to go on to Merida must take Highway 261 north to Champoton.

From Champoton to Campeche it is about 40 miles of alternating straight stretches along beaches and winding stretches through hills.

Campeche—pirates and Panama hats

Campeche is the progressive, increasingly modern capital of the state of Campeche. It was the first

Yucatan's scrub jungle *still hides ruins.*
Twin discoveries stand near a major road.

permanent settlement established by the Spaniards on the peninsula after the Spanish Crown granted the area in 1526 to Francisco de Montejo for its conquest and exploitation. A fascinating old seaport, Campeche has a wall topped by forts, originally built in the 17th century as protection against pirates. Now, with waters untroubled by marauders, the new section of the city has risen along the beach. You'll find a fine seashore drive, a free-form Municipal Palace, and a 6-story air-conditioned bayside hotel.

Campeche is an important shrimp-fishing center. Drive or walk along the waterfront south of town to see shrimp boats being built by craftsmen who make all the fittings by hand. Fine hardwoods from the nearby forests go into their construction. Venture a little farther—about 4 miles from town—to a pier where most of the shrimping activity centers. You can wander along the pier and watch the shrimp being unloaded. North along the waterfront, you'll see thatched huts among the palms that grow to the water's edge. Here fishermen work on their boats or dry and mend nets.

The Campeche area produces some good buys for shoppers including finely woven Panama-type hats *(jipi-japa)*, hammocks, and wood specialties.

You can visit the old wall and ancient forts, either on your own or with an English-speaking guide who will drive you there in a carriage with fringe on top. The Arms Museum and the Archaeology Museum are both worth a visit; artifacts on display create a vivid picture of local history.

On to Maya ruins

Continuing east from Campeche, Highway 180 branches off north from Highway 261 at Chencoyi, 15 miles from Campeche. This is an interesting route to Merida, passing through Maya villages that have changed little over the centuries. At Hecelchakan there is a museum with pieces from the island of Jaina where the pre-Hispanic Maya had a cemetery and left notable funeral offerings.

But to see splendid Maya ruins, proceed east on Highway 261. Nine miles from Chencoyi is the 11-mile paved turnoff to the right leading to the ruins of Edzna, a site remarkable for its 5-story structures, unusual in Maya architecture. Back on Highway 261, it is 24 miles to Hopelchen where the route turns north to Merida. Forty-five miles away is the first major archaeological site—Kabah.

The curled noses of Kabah

The archaeological site of Kabah is located 65 miles south of Merida. The outstanding building is the

Mountains of Panamas *line shelves in small store. Shopping is good around Campeche.*

Details at a glance

Getting there by air

Merida is still an important gateway to the Yucatan, though Cancun's jetport offers nonstop service from the U.S. east coast (less than 1½ hours from Miami). Connecting flights are available to either airport through Mexico City.

Surface transportation. Paved highways make this area easily accessible to motorists, but it's a long, dull drive through Yucatan scrub. Buses and trains make the Mexico City-Merida run with intermediate stops. A ferry service via Veracruz reaches the offshore islands.

Getting around. Package tours from Merida or Cancun stop at major ruins of Chichen Itza, Uxmal, and Tulum, but you won't have much time at any site. It's easier to rent a car (preferably air-conditioned) and poke around by yourself.

Where to stay. Interesting colonial hotels (most with pools) make Merida a good base for Yucatan exploration. A trailer park near the airport offers full facilities. Cancun has many accommodations—hotels, condominiums, and villas—with more sprouting up each year. Cozumel offers a variety of glamorous resorts, some surprisingly inexpensive. You'll also find simple hotels in other cities and some comfortable accommodations at Uxmal and Chichen Itza.

Climate and dress. Usually humid, weather is best from October to March with clear sunny days and cool evenings. Expect brief tropical downpours from June to September.

You'll see both men and women in cool white cotton—a fashion you might want to adopt. Dress for heat, bring your bathing suit for the beautiful water, and wear comfortable clothes and rubber-soled shoes for climbing around ruins.

Codz Poop (Rolled Mat), the facades of which are completely covered by masks of the long-nosed rain god, Chac. Fifteen years ago the upturned noses were all intact; today, many are missing—taken as souvenirs by thoughtless sightseers. A large corbeled arch at Kabah signals the beginning of the *sacbe* (white road) that once carried Maya religious processions to Uxmal, 12 miles away.

Secluded sites—Labna, Xlabpak, Sayil

The services of a jeep and guide may be secured at Kabah to visit the three lesser-known Maya sites of Labna, Xlabpak, and Sayil. The all-day trip takes you over rough road into the towering bush of Yucatan—it certainly cannot be called jungle and is too tangled to be described as a forest—to these remarkable, tantalizing cities that have barely been explored. Unfortunately there simply are not sufficient funds available to restore all of Mexico's archaeological sites. Highlights include the monumental arch of Labna that once connected two groups of buildings now in ruins; the Temple of Chac in Xlabpak, a restrained design treatment of Chac's notable feature—his long nose; and the elegant Palace of Sayil whose three stories show an extraordinary lack of unity and the use (rare in Maya land) on the second level of columns with square capitals.

Uxmal—the sublimity of Maya architecture

One of the most successful architectural achievements of Maya civilization, the ancient city of Uxmal is noted for the symmetry and proportions of its buildings constructed in the Puuc style of veneer masonry. Uxmal reached its peak in the last half of the Classic period (600-900 A.D.). From the 10th century on it was ruled by a family of Mexican origin, and Uxmal suffered the gradual decline that was the fate of all centers of Maya culture under their foreign conquerors.

As you enter the site, the first structure you'll see is the oval pyramid of the Temple of the Magician. A heavy chain stretched along the almost vertical stairway aids height-wary visitors in making the trip to the top.

Just west of the Magician is the Quadrangle of the Nuns, a great patio flanked by long rows of chambers; the facades are richly ornamented at roof level in the typical Puuc stone mosaic style. Among the many elements in the friezes are representations in stone of Maya huts identical to those of present-day Yucatan. Through an arch in the center of the building on the south side, you can see the majestic Palace of the Governor in the distance. The main facade of the 325-foot-long palace is entirely covered on its upper two-thirds with a

stone frieze composed of many thousands of tiny pieces fitted together to form serpents, latticework, thrones, huts, and columns. The palace is similarly, but more frugally, decorated on the other three sides.

On the same great platform that gives added importance to the Palace of the Governor is the elegantly simple, comparatively small, House of the Turtles—in total yet harmonious contrast.

If you wish to spend some time exploring the Uxmal ruins, stay in one of the several hotels nearby. Advance reservations are advisable, especially in the winter season.

Merida to the Caribbean

From Uxmal it is only 50 miles to Merida. You'll pass through Muna, where Highway 184 takes off southeast to Chetumal, capital of Quintana Roo. At Uman, 11 miles south of Merida, Highways 180 and 261 merge to enter the city from the south, passing the airport.

Merida—Yucatan capital with European air

Charming, hospitable Merida is a blend of large old colonial buildings downtown, modern homes on the outskirts, and thatched Indian huts on the

Chichen Itza's *immense ball court, once scene of Maya games, retains side wall hoop.*

Visitors view *Hacienda Yaxcopoil, 200-year-old French henequen farm.*

streets in between. The town has a large, open market, well-kept parks and boulevards, good hotels, and excellent restaurants.

Merida was founded in 1542 on the site of the Maya city of T'Ho, but its Spanish heritage is predominant. The Yucatan was long isolated from the rest of Mexico and, for a few years, even politically independent. During its isolation Merida cultivated European markets and manners instead of Mexican ones. Now the largest city on the peninsula and linked by highway, rail, and air to central Mexico, Merida plays a vital role as the processing and distribution center for local products.

Many visitors remark on the beauty and tranquility of Merida's main plaza with its S-shaped benches. Two buildings that face on the plaza are of particular historic interest: the fortress-type cathedral—the only one in Mexico completed in the 16th century—and the Montejo mansion, built in the mid-16th century by the Spanish conqueror and founder of the city, Francisco de Montejo. Notice the statues of armored soldiers standing on the heads of Indians on the mansion's beautifully carved facade. The facade is lighted at night, and is truly an incredible sight.

The Museum of Archaeology, located on broad, tree-lined Paseo Montejo, has an outstanding collection of Maya artifacts and a school for teaching the Maya language.

Merida's people are friendly and very cordial to foreigners. They consider themselves Yucatecans, distinct and apart from Mexicans. Often you'll see faces that closely resemble those on the stone carvings in Uxmal or Chichen Itza. The dress of many of the women is the huipil; it extends below the knees, and may be worn with or without a lacy petticoat.

Whereas in other parts of Mexico homes are closed and surrounded by high walls, in Merida doors and windows are open to the street. In the evening people sit in chairs on the front stoop and chat with passers-by, friends and strangers alike.

It is easy to find your way around Merida on foot, though it is somewhat tricky to drive within the city. As in most older Mexican towns, streets are very narrow and one-way. All the north-south streets are even-numbered; those running east-west are odd-numbered. You can tour all of Merida for a few pesos in a little horse-drawn cab. On the Paseo Montejo you'll pass buildings of pastel blues, yellows, and pinks—some Victorian or French in style. Many of the large mansions are former town houses of henequen barons, illustrating the long-time importance of the henequen industry.

Don't miss savoring the delicious food of Yucatan. It is a cuisine different from any other in Mexico. *Cochinita pibil (pib* means "barbecue pit" in Maya) is pork baked in banana leaves and flavored with *achiote* (red seeds ground into a paste with a flavor that combines beautifully with meat and fish). Corn tortillas are used in many snack dishes. There is also *queso relleno*—an Edam cheese hollowed out and stuffed with ground meat, raisins, nuts, and spices.

Dzibilchaltun—ancient metropolis

Ten miles north of Merida on the highway to the seaport of Progreso is a 6-mile paved turnoff to the right leading to the ruins of Dzibilchaltun, an ancient ceremonial center. The largest known and longest-lived Maya site, its structures cover almost 20 square miles. Though a major portion of the central area has been cleared, for the most part the ruins are unrestored. Within this cleared area is a *cenote*, a large, deep, natural well into which offerings (including some human victims) were made to the water gods, and from which a great many artifacts have been recovered.

Also in the central section is the site's most interesting structure, the Temple of the Seven Dolls, named for the offering of seven rubber dolls encountered by archaeologists during excavation. At the entrance to the site is a small but well-organized museum that, for orientation's sake, should be the first stop on your tour.

Progreso—Yucatan's progressive port

On the gulf, 22 miles north of Merida is Progreso, Yucatan's most important seaport serving the fishing and henequen industries. Nearby are Yucalpeten, a huge fish-packing plant, and Cordemex, an equally large henequen-processing factory; both are open to visitors. Freighters tie up in deep water at the end of a mile-long concrete pier. You can drive out to the end of the pier which, in addition to the 2-lane roadway, has a railroad track on one side and a pedestrian walkway on the other.

Progreso is also a seaside resort area with both mansions and humble cottages lining the beach for 3 miles to the next resort village of Chicxulub. The area comes alive in July and August when oppressive heat sends Merida residents scurrying to the cool breezes and gentle surf of Progreso's seashore.

Izamal—Maya holy city

Forty-five miles east of Merida, off Highway 180 en route to Puerto Juarez, is Izamal, the ancient holy city of the Mayas. Most of the ruins are overgrown with vegetation and are difficult to see. Part of the ruins were covered over by a Franciscan church-monastery built in the late 1500s, and they are now being excavated.

The town of Izamal is charming, with a tranquil plaza and carriages for transport, both contributing to the restful, unhurried atmosphere.

Chichen Itza—castles, caves, and cenotes

Thirty miles beyond Izamal (75 miles from Merida) on Highway 180, just past the village of Piste, are the ruins of Chichen Itza, the most visited of all Maya cities unearthed to date in Yucatan.

North of the highway is the extensively restored group of structures preferred by sightseers. The most imposing building is called El Castillo (the castle), and is located in the Great Plaza. It is a pyramid some 75 feet high; each side of its square base is approximately 180 feet long. At certain hours (check at the office or in the official guidebook) you can climb steep stairs up and into an inner temple. Inside is a remarkable stone jaguar, painted red with spots and eyes of a green stone, that may have served as a high priest's throne.

Also on the north side of Chichen Itza are the ruins of a huge ball court and many other buildings including the Temple of the Warriors, which also has an inner structure that may be visited during certain hours. Like the one at the castle, this inner structure was the original pyramid-temple and the one you see today was built over it. Chichen Itza has its cenote, too, into which offerings and human beings were thrown to appease the rain god. In 1885 Edward Thompson, then American consul to Yucatan, bought the area for $75 and spent years exploring the depths of the cenote. Another more scientific exploration was made in 1968. Many of the objects that have been found—of jade, bone, shell, copper, and gold—were brought from distant areas, indicating that pilgrims came to Chichen Itza from far-flung Maya communities to make offerings at the sacred cenote.

On the south side of the highway are older ruins, less impressive but equally interesting, spread out over a larger area reached by paths cut through the underbrush. El Caracol (the conch) is perhaps the predominant structure. Cylindrical in shape, it may have served as an observatory. El Caracol, the Nunnery complex, the church, and most of the other buildings are pure Maya in style; the structures on the north side of the highway, though, reflect the influence of the Toltecs who followed on the heels of the Maya Classic period that ended about 900 A.D.

According to archaeologists' theories, construction began in the city about 450 A.D. It was invaded by the Itza early in the 10th century and occupied late in that same century by the Toltecs, who superimposed upon it their architecture and culture.

Several hotels are near the archaeological zone—one of them built around the manor house of the 400-year-old Hacienda Chichen. Reservations are advisable, especially between Christmas and Easter week when you'll be likely to find the best weather. Most hotel restaurants are open to the public.

You should take at least 2 days—preferably even longer—to explore all the ruins in the area thoroughly. You can take in the most significant structures in a day, if necessary. Guides and cars may be secured in Merida; package tours are also available. The archaeological zone is open daily.

Three miles east of Chichen Itza is the Cave of Balancanche, open every day at certain hours. The cave is a labyrinth of passages and chambers containing Maya-Toltec artifacts including ceremonial vases, jars, and grinding stones. A cenote filled with small, blind fish is located at the end of one passageway.

The cave was discovered by chance a decade ago when a Yucatecan tourist guide removed some stones piled one upon another near the entrance. Evidently used as a ceremonial center, the cave contains the largest collection of Maya-Toltec ceramics found to date.

Valladolid—town built around a cenote

About 25 miles east of Chichen Itza on Highway 180 en route to Puerto Juarez is the town of Valladolid, one of Yucatan's larger cities. An attractive park surrounds a large cenote near the center of town, and a good restaurant is located on its rim. At one time the city's water supply was taken from this cenote. It is a couple of blocks to the left of the main highway on a paved street.

An unusual event takes place in Valladolid during the latter part of January. Known as *Las Candelarias*, the festival is unique for its display of regional folk dances and colorful parades.

The green gold of Yucatan

Yucatan's wealth is stored in its green gold—henequen. For as far as the eye can see, the vast expanses of the henequen-producing agave plant *(agave fourcroydes)* produce an illusion of a grey green, prickly carpet. Razor-sharp, sword-like leaves grow from the plant's core, similar in appearance to those of a yucca. The climate of the Yucatan peninsula provides ideal conditions for cultivation: adequate rainfall and porous limestone soil.

Henequen is also known as sisal or hemp. The name "sisal" comes from a port near Merida that was once the leading port of the peninsula, shipping henequen to all parts of the world. The henequen fibers are made into twine, rope, hammocks, table mats, sandals, and a variety of other woven articles.

The henequen industry got its greatest economic boost in the early 1900s. The invention of the self-binding harvester created a need for twine and rope in tying bales of cotton, wheat, or other harvested crops on farms, especially in the United States. Substitutes for henequen were discovered and manufactured by the mid-1900s,

damaging Yucatan's importance as the world's foremost fiber producer. Despite competition and the industry's gradual decline, henequen still reigns as the most important industry on the Yucatan peninsula.

The harvesting and processing of henequen is simple, but meticulously carried out. Large haciendas cultivate thousands of agave plants in rows about 5 feet apart. The plant is left alone to grow for 6 or 7 years before being harvested for its fiber. The old, outer leaves are cut off the plant with machetes and taken to the defibering plant, often transported the traditional way—in a small wooden cart pulled by donkeys along narrow-gauge railroad tracks.

The cut plants continue to produce spiky leaves that are harvested for another 10 to 15 years. The entire field is then cut and burned over.

At the defibering plant *(desfibradora)*, the leaves are crushed and the fiber extracted by a large, noisy machine. The henequen is then dried in the sun and baled for shipment. Or in some plants, henequen is woven into rugs or made into sacks or twine.

If you're driving to Puerto Juarez, be sure to fill up with gas and buy any necessary supplies; Valladolid is the last town before you reach the coast where you can be sure of finding them.

Down the East Coast

On the highway to Puerto Juarez the vegetation changes from thick bush to jungle—not dense, humid jungle, but the South Seas island variety, ending at the gleaming white Caribbean beaches.

Isla Mujeres—island of women

Just north of Puerto Juarez is the embarkation point for the boat trip to Isla Mujeres, 6 miles away. There is air service from Merida and Cozumel daily, direct or on a circuit that may include Chichen Itza. The round trip by boat can be made in 1 day if you get to Puerto Juarez early enough, though a growing number of hotel accommodations on the island allow you to stay overnight and revel in the tranquility and solitude. Thatch-roofed huts, few cars, and the whisper of palms mingle to create a carefree, manana attitude.

Until recently, Isla Mujeres hadn't changed much since its discovery in 1517. The Conquerors named it — not for the women on the island, as legend would have us believe (mujeres is Spanish for women), but rather for the many small terra cotta figurines of women they found among the Maya ruins when they explored the island.

Isla Mujeres is only 7 miles long and less than a mile wide. A popular boating excursion includes a look at a crumbling Maya ruin, a stop for swimming or snorkeling, and a seafood lunch. Sailing, fishing, and water-skiing are other activities you

can indulge in—that is, if you can't tolerate the quietude that's really the island's greatest asset.

Rainbow-hued tropical fish flash in the remarkably clear turquoise water along the jetties on the leeward side of the island. You'll want to swim, fish, or skin dive here. On the windward side, the surf thunders against the shore.

Cancun—newest in luxury resorts

Just south of Puerto Juarez is a road that hugs the coast south to a posh new Mexican resort development called Cancun. There is a highway-causeway to the island, as well as a jet airport. Some 10 luxury hotels operated by major chains have been built and more are under construction, together with condominiums. A golf course, marinas, restaurants, and all the other amenities of a swank resort are in the process of completion. Aside from the luxury hotels, some moderately priced accommodations are also available.

One important facility that won't have to be built is a sparkling white sand beach—it is already there. Cancun offers the best of the east coast's most alluring characteristics: the crystalline turquoise water is ideal for skin diving and snorkeling, and the tropical vegetation is highlighted by such trees as chicle, mangrove, and coconut. Lagoons for privacy, ultrafine sand peppered with pink conch shells, and loads of sunshine all point to Cancun as the eventual Acapulco of the Mexican Caribbean.

Cozumel—diver's delight

Thirty miles south of Cancun and 12 miles from the coast lies the tropical island of Cozumel, a welcome change from the usual Caribbean island experience. The pace is slower and quieter. And on

Turquoise *river at Chetumal divides Mexico and Belize.*

Cozumel you won't find the degree of commercialism common to the islands farther east.

San Miguel, Cozumel's only town, is a pastel counterpart of many small Mexican towns. Some of its stone and plaster buildings are topped with yellow thatch roofs. In San Miguel and north of town on San Juan beach, are a number of modern hotels and older inns.

Snorkelers and scuba divers will appreciate the 200 to 300-foot visibility of the turquoise waters (30 feet is average along California's coast). With just a mask and snorkel you can easily explore the coral reefs and watch the schools of varicolored tropical fish that glide among them, unconcerned at your presence.

For amateur snorkelers, organized boat trips go to San Francisco beach. A guide will show you how to snorkel and point out different types of coral, fish, and other marine life. They will even catch lobsters, fish, and conch (sea snail, a local delicacy) and prepare a barbecue lunch while you swim. These day-long trips may be arranged through most hotels on the island.

Experienced scuba divers can rent tanks and regulators at several dive shops in San Miguel. But for the best scuba diving, you'll need to hire a boat and guide to take you to incredible Palancar Reef.

Air service to Cozumel makes the island easily accessible. Ferry service is available from Playa del Carmen (shown as Mocche on many maps), 42 miles south of Puerto Juarez on Highway 307.

Akumal, Tulum, and Coba—resort and ruins

Continuing south along the Caribbean coast on Highway 307, it is only 25 miles to Akumal. Another sea-and-sand resort, Akumal is more secluded and more rustic, just the place for dedicated hunters

Acres *of henequen bask in sun prior to baling.*

and fishermen. And for archaeology buffs, this is the base for trips to Tulum and Coba.

Tulum, 17 miles from Akumal, is a different type of Maya ruin. Once one of the fortress cities that were strung along the Caribbean coast, Tulum was among the last bulwarks of the Maya culture, constructed and in use from the 11th century until just before the Spanish Conquest. Long stretches of the wall that once enclosed Tulum on its three land sides are still standing. The center itself was laid out on an urban plan closely resembling that of most U. S. cities—straight streets bordered by buildings, rather than the groupings around plazas favored in most Maya cities. In the Temple of the Frescoes there are still traces of mural paintings. The main building, El Castillo, looks out over the cliffs protecting the sea approach.

From the village of Tulum (there is a gas station here), a new paved road goes north 25 miles to the ruins of Coba. This immense site is now being explored jointly by Mexican archaeologists and the U. S. National Geographic Society. Coba, founded around 600 A.D., must have been a very important Maya center because it is at the hub of a network of *sacbes*—those wide, level Maya thoroughfares that carried traders and pilgrims from town to town. From Coba they led west to Chichen Itza, south to Tulum, and north and east to other Maya centers.

Chetumal—jungle capital

South of Tulum the scenery along Highway 307 takes on a new look as the road passes through humid, hardwood jungle, wending its way 120 miles to Chetumal, capital of Quintana Roo. This port town has a large, busy harbor that ships products of the peninsula such as chicle, tobacco, bananas, and precious hardwoods.

Chetumal has only lately become a stop on tourist itineraries. Now accessible by Highway 186 that comes east from Escarcega and by Highway 307 down the Caribbean coast, its free port status makes it a preferred place for picking up duty-free foreign luxuries. Chetumal is also the take-off point for trips to Belize (just across the river) and to Central America.

Though a hurricane target, Chetumal has modern storm warning systems and extrasturdy building construction that allow the city to continue its busy economic life almost unaffected by the weather. Modest accommodations and good restaurants are available.

For those who wish to learn more about the Yucatan, the best travel book ever written about it is still that by John L. Stephens, *Incidents of Travel in Yucatan*, first published in 1841 and recently reissued in paperback.

Know Before You Go

Planning a trip is not only part of the fun, but it is essential for a smooth stay. Fortunately, going to Mexico, North America's nearest "foreign" country, is extremely easy. Because it is close, transportation is frequent and convenient—and you don't need a visa.

The paperwork

The basic document that you should have handy at all times is a tourist card and, if possible, proof of citizenship. If you're planning to take a car, trailer, camper, boat, or any other vehicle into Mexico, you'll have to get the necessary permits, licenses, and insurance before going. Vaccinations and medications, if needed, should be acquired well ahead of time.

Tourist cards

Tourist cards are required by all U.S. citizens visiting Mexico for less than 180 days. If you're staying anywhere north of Maneadero, a few miles south of Ensenada, less than 72 hours, you needn't have any formal travel documentation except for some kind of personal identification and proof of citizenship. A minor traveling alone, or with someone other than a parent, must present written, notarized authorization from parents or guardian.

Tourist cards are available at Mexican consulates, Mexican government tourist offices, some auto clubs and Mexican insurance agencies, and offices of airlines, cruise ships, and bus companies serving Mexico. A travel agent can usually get one for you. The single-entry cards are free of charge and valid for 6 months. When you apply for your tourist card, be sure to have your proof of citizenship with you (such as a birth certificate, passport, notarized affidavit, or voter's registration slip). Canadian citizens are also required to submit a birth certificate, passport, or naturalization papers when applying for a tourist card. Naturalized citizens must carry naturalization papers or a U.S. passport. The multiple-entry permits are also free,

but for these you must provide three passport-type photographs. Multiple-entry permits enable you to enter Mexico more than one time during the card's 6-month validity.

Aliens residing in the United States are subject to special requirements. They should contact their nearest Mexican consulate well in advance of the date they plan to leave for Mexico.

You'll frequently encounter a 15 percent lodging or dining tax. Visitors are exempt, but you'll need to show your tourist card to have it deleted.

Vaccinations

A smallpox vaccination certificate is no longer necessary when entering Mexico from the United States or when reentering the United States from Mexico. You must have evidence of a smallpox vaccination given within the last 3 years if you are entering Mexico from Central America before 14 days have elapsed.

Though not required by either Mexican or United States quarantine officers, antityphoid injections may be a wise precaution, particularly if you plan to spend much time in tropical areas and remote sections of the country. Consult your physician for other immunizations.

Automobile papers

Automobile permits, required for entry into Mexico, are good for 6 months and may be obtained free of charge from the customs office at the border. Permits are not required for visits to Mexican border towns for periods of less than 72 hours (this includes Ensenada in Baja California and Puerto Penasco in Sonora). In Baja California only, you may use your vehicle for the length of time that your tourist card is valid without an automobile permit. You must, however, obtain a permit if you plan to take a ferry to the mainland from Baja. The same regulations that apply to automobiles would also apply to trailers.

To obtain an automobile permit, you'll need proof of ownership such as a license registration, a "pink slip" or legal title, or a notarized bill of sale. If you do not own the car, you'll need a notarized statement from the legal owner giving you authority to drive the car into Mexico. You should carry the ownership papers with you at all times. If the vehicle is rented or leased, you'll be asked to produce the notarized statement from the owner or a copy of the formal rental or lease agreement. The proof of ownership requirement applies to boats, trailers, and other motorized vehicles.

Your valid U. S. driver's license is also valid in Mexico, but your U. S. automobile insurance is not. Mexican insurance company agents at the border issue short-term policies at reasonable daily rates that are standard on either side of the border.

Automobile accidents in Mexico are handled from a criminal rather than a civil standpoint. This means that drivers are liable to jail sentences in cases where fatal injury results, and even in minor accidents drivers may be held pending proof of innocence. Because of this arrangement, it is very important that you take out insurance coverage with a Mexican company.

It is customary

Clothing and other personal items within reason may be taken into Mexico duty free. Each adult tourist may take into Mexico one kilogram of to-bacco (about two cartons of cigarettes or one box of cigars). Up to 500 grams of unopened perfume may be taken into the country; so may perfume that has been opened for use.

When you return to the U.S., your bags will be inspected at the point of entry in compliance with customs regulations. To expedite the inspection and to avoid having anything confiscated by the customs officials, make sure you know the limits and restrictions on objects you can take out of the country.

Basic baggage

Residents of the United States returning from Mexico are permitted to bring back up to $100 worth (retail value; be sure to keep your sales slips) of articles duty free within any 30 days. There is no time restriction for tourists returning through an Arizona, California, New Mexico, or Texas port; however, a 48-hour absence is required at all other ports to obtain the exemption.

Know Before You Go, a booklet published by U.S. Customs, is available at local offices for a slight charge. It lists such prohibited items as most fruits and vegetables, plants, livestock, poultry, meats, uncured hides, Cuban components, gold coins, medals (except special awards), bullion, lottery tickets, and Decca and Columbia records.

If you are at least 21 years old and return to the United States (except California) by private auto-

Signs for good driving

DETOUR — DANGEROUS CURVE — DIP OR FORD — SLOW — RIGHT TURN AT ALL TIMES — HILL — NARROW BRIDGE

KEEP RIGHT — MAXIMUM HORIZONTAL CLEARANCE — DO NOT ENTER — SPEED LIMIT IN KILOMETERS — BUS STOP — INSPECTION — NO PARKING 8 A.M. TO 9 P.M. WEEKDAYS

ONE WAY — ONE WAY, YIELD RIGHT OF WAY — YIELD RIGHT OF WAY

TWO WAY — ONE WAY, RIGHT OF WAY — STOP

mobile, plane, or boat, you may bring in one quart of liquor duty free. If you are returning to California by private automobile, you may not bring in any liquor. For liquor in excess of one quart, you must pay a stiff federal tax plus duty charges.

Since customs regulations and taxes are subject to change, be sure to read up-to-date state regulations. Where state and federal laws conflict, state regulations prevail.

Taking your pet?

Dogs and other pets may be taken into Mexico (very few hotels will allow them, but most motels will) provided you present a veterinarian's certificate stating that they are in good health. Rodent poison is often placed in seaport rooms; check carefully before letting pets roam. You'll also need a certificate, issued by a veterinarian and visaed by a Mexican consul, certifying that the animal has been inoculated for rabies within the last 6 months. If your pet is out of the U.S. for more than 30 days, you'll need inoculation certificates to reenter the U.S. Dogs can be left at kennels in Texas, California, and Arizona.

Guns and fishing tackle

Special restrictions apply to firearms taken into the country. Check with your nearest Mexican consulate regarding gun permits and regulations.

Any reasonable amount of fishing tackle may be brought into Mexico duty free. You may pick up fishing licenses at the border or from local fish and game wardens. A fishing license is good in any state in Mexico.

For the photographer

Each tourist is permitted one still camera and one movie camera (8mm or 16mm) with 12 rolls of film for each. For anything more sophisticated, you must obtain a special permit.

Don't forget to register foreign-made cameras at your point of departure so that you can prove that you didn't buy your camera in Mexico.

Film is available in most cities. Photographic supply stores in Mexico can process black-and-white film, and Eastman Kodak has color processing plants in Mexico City and Guadalajara. It is recommended, though, that you get your film developed in the United States.

When photographing throughout Mexico, remember you are a guest. Respect the Mexicans' privacy; they are a proud and sensitive people.

Gift shipping

If you intend to have purchases sent home for you, choose shops that are well established and enjoy a good reputation among tourists. Factories and shops that sell frequently to tourists are usually very experienced at arranging for shipment of their merchandise and will handle all details for you.

Merchandise shipped from Mexico to your home cannot be included as part of the $100 exemption. Any article that you have shipped will be taxed on its appraised value at the applicable rate of duty.

You may send gifts valued at less than $10 to friends in the United States without including them on your declaration, providing the addressee does not receive in a single day packages totaling more than the $10 limit. The word "Gift" and the retail value of the contents must be written clearly on the outside of the package. Perfumes, alcoholic beverages, and tobacco may not be sent as gifts.

Prepare yourself for...

To assure yourself an enjoyable experience in Mexico, you should learn something about the conditions, attitudes, and culture of the Mexicans —often a sharp contrast to the conditions you've been used to in North America.

Couple inspects *figurine decorated in bright watercolor.*

A new climate

The climate throughout Mexico varies more according to altitude than according to season. Coastal areas and low sections of the interior are usually very warm, though there are occasional cool days in coastal areas during the winter months. The climate is temperate at altitudes of 3,000 to 6,000 feet. The cool zone extends upward from 7,000 feet.

The rainy season in Mexico is generally from May to October. Rains usually occur late in the afternoon and do not greatly inconvenience the tourist. Though the rainy season may not be the most popular tourist season, the countryside is at its greenest during that time, and many people prefer it to the dry winter months.

A new language

Though a knowledge of Spanish is not essential, it does make a visit to Mexico more enjoyable. You'll naturally learn a great deal more about the country if you are able to converse with the people who live in it. You can get along surprisingly well with sign language, though, and it is almost always possible to find someone who speaks a little English. Most personnel involved in serving tourists speak good English, particularly in larger cities. There are a number of inexpensive, pocket-size phrase books on the market that will give you the phonetic pronunciation of frequently used words.

Different health conditions

There are no serious health hazards involved in traveling in Mexico, but certain precautions are advisable.

Most hotels throughout Mexico provide bottles of purified water in the rooms. If you're ever in doubt about the water, ask for *agua mineral* or *agua purificada*, or buy water purification tablets at a drugstore before you leave home and use them according to the directions on the container.

Though the air in Mexico City may be invigorating, take it easy until you become accustomed to the high altitude. If you feel lazy, give in to the temptation to take a siesta, especially if you plan to go out at night.

Using or buying drugs illegally is a criminal offense punishable by imprisonment. If medical attention is necessary, competent physicians and surgeons are in all the large cities and towns in Mexico. In case of serious illness or other emergencies, contact the American Embassy in Mexico City or the American Consulate in any of the following Mexican cities: Ciudad Juarez, Guadalajara, Guaymas, Matamoros, Mazatlan, Merida, Mexicali, Monterrey, Hermosillo, Nuevo Laredo, Chihuahua, San Luis Potosi, and Tijuana.

Pesos, centavos, and dollars

United States traveler's checks and currency in any denomination may be taken into Mexico. Trav-

Driving *in Mexico allows for flexible scheduling, requires some prior planning.*

eler's checks can be cashed in most cities, and it is advisable to carry the bulk of your money this way. Purchase most of your traveler's checks in small denominations ($10 and $20) because Mexican establishments may not be able to cash checks for large amounts. Personal checks drawn on United States banks are virtually impossible to cash.

After 22 years of stable currency, the Mexican peso is currently fluctuating. Best exchange rates are from local banks.

A word about lodgings

Since it is not possible to keep a book absolutely up-to-date in regard to hotels, we have not attempted to list them in this publication. However, hotel lists may be obtained from several sources:
• The AAA booklet, *Mexico and Central America*, free to AAA members, contains a very good list of Mexican hotels, motels, restaurants, and trailer parks, with prices and brief descriptions. The AAA will make reservations for club members.
• Sanborn's Mexican Insurance Service, with headquarters in McAllen, Texas, provides hotel, motel, trailer park, restaurant, and other travel information free to its insurance clients.
• Major airlines flying into Mexico have lists of hotels in the cities they serve and will make reservations for people taking their flights.
• Travel agents will make suggestions and reservations for accommodations when planning a trip.

In resort cities it may be difficult to obtain desirable hotel and motel accommodations without advance reservations. This is very likely especially during the peak tourist months of January, February, March, and April, and again during July and August. Christmas, New Year's, and Holy Week are also busy times in resort areas because many Mexicans take vacations at these times.

Reservations are always advisable, and probably essential, in Mexico City if you want to be sure of getting a room within a certain price range or in a particular section of the city.

How to get there-and back

Whether you enjoy flying, driving, sailing, or taking a train, choosing a means of transportation for your trip to Mexico can be the most crucial decision in the planning of your trip. Some important factors to keep in mind when deciding are length of stay, distance to be covered, budget allowance for transportation, number of people in your party, and goals or purpose of your trip. All of these considerations should be carefully weighed so that you can get the most out of where you are rather than worrying about how you're going to get to your next destination.

Each chapter contains a special feature on ways to get to that specific area—by car, plane, or other means of transportation.

Driving in Mexico

In general, the main highways are good and well marked. Some driving precautions, though, should be observed.

Highways often are not fenced, and animals are apt to wander onto the road. For this reason, driving at night is not recommended. As one popular Mexico guidebook says: "Burros don't wear taillights." In the daytime, you should avoid excessive speeds and take special care when rounding curves or when the view is otherwise obstructed.

Road signs throughout Mexico are in Spanish. If you don't understand a sign, slow your car and be prepared for whatever you may find ahead.

Only one brand of gasoline is sold in Mexico—Pemex, which gets its name from the words "Petroleos Mexicanos," the government-owned oil company. There are two grades of this gasoline: Pemex Extra and Pemex Nova. Pemex Nova (in blue pumps) has the lower octane rating. Pemex Extra (in the silver pumps) is lead free, has a higher octane rating, and is recommended for high-compression engines. The red tanks contain diesel fuel. Service stations sell Pemex oils, lubricants, and additives. U.S. brands of oil are sometimes obtainable in independent repair shops and stores. (Your U.S. oil company credit card will not be good in Mexico, so be prepared to pay in pesos.)

Gasoline is sold in liters (*litros*). One liter equals about one quart. Consequently, if you order *diez*, you will get about ten quarts instead of the ten gallons you would get in the United States. Forty liters equals about 10 gallons.

You can avoid some routine inconveniences if you carry some basic repair equipment with you.

Camping and trailering—for the adventurous

Attitudes about camping in Mexico are sharply divided. Some travelers recommend camping as the only way to get away from the tourist crowds, to mingle with the people of Mexico, and to explore some out-of-the-way places. Others, though experienced campers north of the border, wouldn't attempt to camp in Mexico.

One group of tourists—avid campers—are usually adaptable souls willing to adjust their normal camping routines to meet the special health problems of food and water in Mexico and the restrictive nature of available camping facilities.

Another—the doubters and disclaimers—sometimes tend to think of Mexico as a land of roadside bandits. But more often, they are simply people who decide that camping loses its appeal when they must cope with the health precautions and campground improvisations necessary in Mexico.

Beaches can serve as primitive campsites if you can find a suitable access road; all beaches in Mexico are public. Camping or RV facilities are extremely primitive at the dams (*presas*) and lakes (*lagos*), but you can use them for overnight campsites. Fishing and water sports are available at both the dams and the lakes.

The American Automobile Association lists recommended trailer parks in its guidebook to Mexico (available free to members). Another excellent source of information on Mexican highways, accommodations, and trailer parks is the series of bulletins and road logs published by Sanborn's Mexican Insurance Service, McAllen, Texas 78501. Sunset's *Western Campsites* has a section containing brief descriptions of campsites and trailer parks in Baja and western Mexico. The Mexican Trailer Park Association also publishes a directory. Send $3 to ANAPARM, A.C., Zacatecas 229-411, Mexico 7, D.F. The directory also offers information on renting and servicing RVs.

Check with your insurance broker to find out just how well protected your trailer is by your U.S. automobile policy. Some companies include trailer protection with the policy for the automobile, at least to the extent of physical damage to the trailer itself. Some companies require a separate policy for the trailer. When you take out Mexican insurance for your automobile, you should find out what coverage is provided for your trailer.

When pulling a trailer, stay on the main highways. Unusually high centers, sharp curves, and narrow bridges are sometimes encountered on secondary roads. If you plan to make a side trip to a small town that interests you, check first with local gas station attendants or other tourists with trailers to find out if the road is suitable for travel with a trailer and if a trailer can be pulled into the town. Many small towns in Mexico have steep, narrow streets through which it would be difficult—and often impossible—to pull a trailer.

Bus touring—an insight to the offbeat

Traveling throughout Mexico by bus can be a great way to see the Mexican countryside and offbeat villages, as well as the big population centers and favorite tourist destinations.

Mexico City can be reached inexpensively and comfortably by bus from border cities such as Tijuana, Nogales, El Paso, Eagle Pass, Laredo, and Brownsville. The best of the bus lines between these points and the capital compare favorably in equipment, safety, and speed with bus lines operating north of the border. Fares are low, and you won't need to pay extra government taxes. Reserved seats are of the reclining type and well upholstered.

Package tours, which include all arrangements, are offered by Greyhound and Continental Trailways, as well as by some excellent smaller operators. Tours will take you anywhere from the dry deserts of Chihuahua (where you can visit Pancho Villa's home) to the high mountains in the interior to the colorful resorts down the west coast. Most tours return via the west coast, inland through Sonora, on to the border.

Drawbacks to bus travel in Mexico are the too infrequent rest stops and the inadequate rest room facilities and lunch counters at many of the smaller stops. One must be prepared to travel 4 (and sometimes more) hours without a stop on some routes. The bus traveler will always do well to take along a box lunch, a common Mexican practice.

To get there fast, fly

Travel by air is the fastest and easiest way to reach your destination in Mexico. Airlines fly into Mexico from all parts of the world. Even if you're going to some out-of-the-way spot, you can usually fly to an airport not too far from it and take local transportation from there, saving yourself tedious and sometimes rugged driving.

Airlines offering service to Mexico from points within the United States include Aeromexico, Air France, C P Air, Hughes Airwest, American, Braniff, Eastern, Mexicana, Pan American, Texas International, and Western. These lines serve principal cities along the tourist routes. Other smaller Mexican airlines reach spots off the tourist track. A travel agent can help you to work out the air routing that is best for you.

The two leading Mexican airlines (Aeromexico and Mexicana) also operate flights from Mexican border towns such as Tijuana, Mexicali, Juarez, Nuevo Laredo, Reynosa, and Matamoros—usually to Mexico City. These flights are less expensive than those from U.S. cities.

If you enter Mexico by private plane you will, like any other traveler, need a tourist card and you'll be required to pass through customs and immigration inspection at the airport of entry. Take with you proof of ownership and registration of the airplane, even though you may not be asked to show them on either side of the border.

Your first landing in Mexico must be at a Mexican port of entry. Airports that are ports of entry are shown on U.S. Air Force World Aeronautical Charts and in the International Flights Information Manual (CAA).

Gasoline costs slightly less than it does in the United States. You may not always be able to get the kind of oil you want, so if possible take along enough to last the length of your stay.

One important caution: Remember that all of central Mexico, including Mexico City, is at a high altitude; you must have a plane that will perform adequately at altitudes of from 7,000 to 13,000 feet. Another caution: Runways are sometimes unpaved, especially in Baja California, so make sure you are capable of such landings.

When you return to the United States, you must land at a U.S. port of entry for customs and immigration inspection. Notify the field of your expected time of arrival in advance. You can do this by telephoning the field from the Mexican side of the border or by calling a United States CAA communications station by radio.

Railroading in Mexico

Being gently rocked to sleep aboard a Mexican train can be a pleasurable experience, and the cost is minimal. Main lines operate with diesel engines, and offer Pullman cars on overnight runs plus dining and club cars. Even though food is not gourmet quality, it is tasty and inexpensive.

Three main rail routes connect U.S. border points of entry with major interior cities. They roughly parallel the Pan American, Central, and West Coast highways to Mexico City.

• **West coast route** from Nogales to Guadalajara includes stops at Hermosillo, Empalme (for Guaymas), Ciudad Obregon, Navojoa, Culiacan, Mazatlan, and Tepic with connections at Benjamin Hill for the Sonora-Baja California Railway from Mexicali. From Guadalajara, *El Tapatio* (fast overnight train) runs to Mexico City.

• **Central route** from Ciudad Juarez to Mexico stops at Chihuahua, Jimenez, Torreon, Zacatecas, Aguascalientes, Leon, Irapuato, Celaya, and Queretaro.

• **Eastern route** from Nuevo Laredo to Mexico City, with through service on the *Aguila Azteca* (Aztec Eagle), stops at Monterrey, Saltillo, Vanegas, and San Luis Potosi.

There is also a fast overnight Pullman, *El Regiomontano*, between Monterrey and Mexico City.

Private yachts and public liners

More and more people are becoming intrigued with the possibilities of sailing their own craft down to Mexico. As yet, information regarding procedures and problems isn't readily available. But, by getting in touch with people who have sailed to Mexico, you probably can gather the most reliable and up-to-date information. Another source of information is the Mexican Consulate; ask for information on sailing into Mexican waters.

Only experienced sailors should attempt a sailing voyage to Mexico. Be sure to take the necessary charts, navigational information, and, above all, a sensible attitude along on your voyage. Better take spare equipment and parts because parts are expensive, if not impossible to obtain, in Mexico. Necessary documents will include your personal identification and tourist card, cruising papers, and temporary import papers. You must clear in and out of each port you visit. Crew lists should be made up in advance to give to the port officials. Fees vary from port to port and may or may not be required.

Several steamship lines offer cruises to Mexico from U.S. ports. Since space is limited, you'd be wise to make reservations well in advance. For details on any of the sailings, see your travel agent.

Sleek cruise ships *ply West Coast, making shore stops at major resorts.*

Index

Abasolo, 60
Acapulco, 27, 43–45, 94
Accommodations, 140
  Baja, 12
  condominiums, 44
  Guadalajara, 51, 52
  Mexico City, 69
  Northeastern, 101
  Southern, 115
  West Coast, 27
  Yucatan, 129
Acolman, 89, 91
Aduana, 32
Aguascalientes, 102–103
Ajijic, 53, 54
Akumal, 135
Alameda Park, 75–76
Alamos, 30–33
Aldama, 109
Antiguo Morelos, 106, 108
Anton Lizardo, 123
Apizaco, 96
Archaeological sites
  Chichen Itza, 126, 129,
    132–133
  Coba, 135
  Dzibilchaltun, 132
  Edzna, 128
  El Tajin, 110, 112, 113
  Izamal, 132
  Kabah, 128, 130
  Labna, 130
  La Quemada, 102
  La Venta, 85, 110, 124
  Mitla, 110, 120–123
  Monte Alban, 110, 118
  Palenque, 110, 120–125
  Sayil, 130
  Teotihuacan, 89–91
  Tulum, 126, 129, 135
  Uxmal, 126, 129, 130
  Xlabpak, 130
  Zempoala, 113
Atotonilco, 59
Aztec Indians, 61, 70, 89, 92

Bacochibampo Bay, 29
Baggage, 137
Bahia de los Angeles, 14, 16
Bahia Gonzaga, 14
Baja California, 10–21, 27
Ballet Folklorico, 75
Barra de Navidad, 40, 43
Barranca de Oblatos, 52
Boca del Rio, 116
Boquilla Dam, 100
Borda Gardens, 94

Caborca, 28
Cabo San Lucas, 12, 19, 21,
  27
Cacahuamilpa Caves, 93, 95
Caduano, 21
Campeche, 126–128
Camping, 140–141
Cancun, 44, 45, 126, 129, 134

Cantamar, 13
Carapan, 65
Carmen, 126
Castanos, 104
Catavina, 17
Celaya, 61, 62
Cerro Pinacate, 24
Champoton, 126
Chamula Indians, 110
Chapultepec Park, 77–80
Charreria, 83
Chencoyi, 128
Chetumal, 126, 130, 135
Chichen Itza, 126, 129, 132–
  133
Chichimeca Indians, 104
Chiconcuac, 91
Chicxulub, 132
Chihuahua, 28, 99–100
Chihuahua-Pacific Railway,
  28, 100
China, 108
Cholula, 97
Choya Bay, 24–25
Chupicuaro, 64
Ciudad Acuna, 104
Ciudad Camargo, 100
Ciudad Constitucion, 19
Ciudad Madero, 109
Ciudad Mante, 108, 109
Ciudad Obregon, 30
Ciudad Valles, 108–109
Ciudad Victoria, 108, 109
Climate, 13, 27, 51, 69, 101,
  115, 129, 139
Coba, 135
Cofre de Perote, 96
Colima, 43
Comanjilla, 57
Concepcio del Oro, 105
Concepcion Bay, 18
Concordia, 36, 101
Condominiums, 44
Copala, 36
Copper Canyon, 28
Cordoba, 96, 116, 123
Cortez Palace, 95
Coyoacan, 84
Cozumel, 126, 129, 134–135
Cuchujachi River, 33
Cuencame, 102
Cuernavaca, 93, 94–95
Culiacan, 30, 34
Customs, 137–138
Cuyutlan, 43

Days of the Dead, 77
Desert of Lions, 93
Dolores Hidalgo, 59, 107
Driving, 20, 136–137, 140
Durango, 36, 99, 100–101,
  102
Dzibilchaltun, 132

Edzna, 128
El Catorce, 105
El Golfo de Santa Clara, 24
El Limon, 108
El Progreso, 16
El Rosario, 16, 17
El Salto Falls, 108

El Tajin, 110, 112, 113, 114
El Triunfo, 20–21
Ensenada, 13–14, 15
Erongaricuaro, 64
Estero Beach, 13

Ferries, 12, 18, 19, 20, 27
Fishing, 138
Flying, 141–142
Fortin de las Flores, 116
Fresnillo, 99, 100, 101, 102
Frontera, 126

Garcia Caves, 107
Gomez Palacio, 99, 100, 101,
  102
Gran Desierto, 22, 24
Guadalajara, 46–54, 102, 105
  accommodations, 52
  sights, 48–51
  shopping, 51–53
Guadalupe, 102
  Virgin of, 59, 62, 91–93
Guanajuato, 57–59, 99
Guaymas, 22, 29–30
Guerrero Negro, 15, 17
Gutierrez Zamora, 112

Hacienda de la Concepcion,
  109
Halfway House, 13
Health, 139
Hecelchakan, 128
Hermosillo, 28
Hidalgo del Parral, 100
Hidalgo, Father Miguel, 59,
  60, 70, 99
Hopelchen, 128
Horsetail Falls, 107
Huasteca Indians, 109
Huejotzingo, 97
Huizache Junction, 106, 108
Hunting, 138

Iguala, 94
Irapuato, 59–60, 62
Isla Mujeres, 126, 134
Ixmiquilpan, 109
Ixtapa, 27, 45
Ixtapan de la Sal, 94
Izamal, 132
Iztaccihuatl, 67, 96, 97

Jacala, 109
Jaina, 128
Jalapa, 96, 112, 116
Janitzio, 64
Jiminez, 99, 101
Jocotepec, 53, 54
Juanacatlan Falls, 52
Juarez, 99
Juchitan, 125
Juventino Rosas, 61–62

Kabah, 126, 128–130
Kino Bay, 28–29
Kino, Father Eusebio, 25–26

La Barca, 54
Labna, 130
Lacandon Indians, 110, 124
Lake Camecuaro, 65
Lake Chapala, 53, 54
Lake Cuitzeo, 62
Lake Patzcuaro, 62, 64
Lake Tequesquitengo, 95
Lake Texcoco, 91
La Paz, 11, 12, 19–20, 34
La Quemada, 102
Las Hadas, 41
La Ubalama, 32
La Venta, 85, 110, 124
Leon, 56, 57, 100
Lerdo, 102
Linares, 108
Loreto, 12, 17–19
Los Barriles, 21
Los Mochis, 27, 28, 30,
  33–34, 100

Mag Bay, 19
Magdalena, 25, 28
Malinche, 96, 97
Maneadero, 15
Manuel, 109
Manzanillo, 27, 35, 40, 41–43
Maps
  Around Mexico City, 92
  Baja California, 12
  Chihuahua-Pacific
    Railway, 28
  Colonial Circle, 51
  Craft Towns Around
    Guadalajara, 53
  Guadalajara, 52

Maps (cont'd.)
  Mexico, 4–5
  Mexico City, 68, 76
  North and East to the
    Gulf, 101
  Southern Mexico, 115
  West Coast, 27, 36
  Yucatan, 129
Matamoros, 109
Matehuala, 105
Maya Indians, 110, 126, 128,
  130–133, 135
Mazatlan, 12, 27, 30, 35–37,
  44, 101, 104
Melaque, 43
Merida, 126, 128, 129, 130–
  132, 133
Mexicali, 11, 14, 22, 27
Mexico City, 6, 56, 66–88, 94
  buildings, 70, 73, 75, 84, 85
  churches, 70, 75, 81
  dining, 88–89
  entertainment, 78, 80, 83, 86
  museums, 75, 76, 78, 81, 84
  parks, 75, 77, 83
  plazas, 70–72, 81, 91
  shopping, 77, 83, 84
  transportation, 69
  university, 84–85
Minatitlan, 123
Miraflores, 21
Mismaloya, 38
Mitla, 110, 120–123
Mocche, 135
Mocoyahui, 33
Mocuzari Dam, 33
Monclova, 104
Money, 139–140
Monte Alban, 110, 118
Montemorelos, 107–108
Monterrey, 107
Morelia, 46, 54, 62
Mulege, 17, 18

National Museum of
  Anthropology, 78
National Museum of
  Colonial Arts/and
  Handicrafts, 93
Nautla, 112, 113
Navojoa, 30
Nevado de Toluca, 93
Nogales, 22, 27
Nombre de Dios, 102
Nopolo, 19
Notri, 19

Ocotlan, 54
Ojinaga, 28

Olmec Indians, 85, 110
Oquitoa, 28
Orizaba, 96, 114, 116
Otomi Indians, 61

Pachuca, 109, 110
Palace of Fine Arts, 85
Palenque, 110, 124–125
Palmilla, 21
Panuco, 110
Papantla, 110, 112
Paracho, 65
Paracutin, 65
Parras de la Fuente, 105
Patzcuaro, 46, 62, 64, 65
Perote, 96, 112, 116
Pets, 138
Photography, 138
Picacho del Diablo, 15
Pichilingue, 20
Pico de Orizaba, 96, 116
Piedras Negras, 104
Piste, 132
Pitiquito, 28
Playa Blanca, 40
Playa del Carmen, 135
Popocatepetl, 67, 96, 97
Poza Rica, 62, 110, 112
Progreso, 132
Puebla, 96, 97
Puertecitos, 14
Puerto Escondido, 19
Puerto Juarez, 132, 134
Puerto Penasco, 24–25
Puerto Real, 126
Puerto Vallarta, 12, 21, 27,
  35, 38, 40, 44
Punta Prieta, 17

Queretaro, 46, 61, 93
Quiroga, 65

Rancho Corralejo, 60
Rancho La Puerta, 14
Rancho Santa Ines, 17
Rancho Santa Veronica, 14
Rancho Santo Domingo,
  106–107
Reynosa, 108, 109
Rincon de Guayabitos, 38
Rio Frio, 97
Rioverde, 109
Rosarito Beach, 13

Salamanca, 62
Saltillo, 102, 104–105, 108
San Angel, 84, 85–86
San Antonio, 20–21

San Blas, 27, 37–38
San Carlos Bay, 29
San Cristobal Las Casas,
  123, 125–126
Sandy Beach, 24–25
San Felipe, 14, 15
San Fernando, 109
San Ignacio, 17–18
San Javier, 19
San Jose del Cabo, 21
San Jose Purua, 94
San Luis Potosi, 105, 106,
  108, 109
San Luis Rio Colorado, 22,
  24
San Martin Texmelucan, 97
San Miguel, 135
San Miguel de Allende, 46,
  60–61
San Pedrito, 21
San Quintin, 16
San Roman, 126
Santa Ana, 22
Santa Ana Chiautempan, 97
Santa Clara del Cobre, 64
Santa Ines, 17
Santa Maria del Rio, 106
Santa Rosalia, 12, 18, 27, 29
San Telmo, 15
Santiago de la Pena, 110
Sayil, 130
Scammon's Lagoon, 17
Seri Indians, 28–29
Serra, Father Junipero, 16,
  19
Shopping, 138
Sierra San Pedro Martir, 14,
  15
Silao, 56, 57
Sonoita, 22, 24–25
Soto la Marina, 109

Taboada, 59
Tamazunchale, 109
Tampico, 108, 109
Taninul, 109
Tarahumara Indians, 28
Tarascan Indians, 54, 64
Taxco, 93, 94, 95–96
Tecate, 14
Tehuacan, 97
Tehuantepec, 123, 125
Tempoal, 110
Teotihuacan, 89–91
Tepic, 27, 37, 38
Tepotzotlan, 93
Tequila, 37
Texcoco, 91, 96
Tiburon Island, 29

Tijuana, 11, 13, 22, 27
Tlaquepaque, 48, 52, 53
Tlatelolco, 91–92
Tlaxcala, 97
Toltec Indians, 133
Toluca, 54, 93–94
Tonala, 52, 53
Topolobampo, 12, 19, 27,
  33–34
Torreon, 101, 102, 104, 105
Totonac Indians, 112–113
Tourist cards, 136
Trailers, 140–141
Transportation, 140–142
Tubutama, 28
Tulum, 126, 129, 135
Tuxpan, 110
Tuxtla Gutierrez, 123, 125
Tzintzuntzan, 65

Uman, 130
University City, 84–85
Uruapan, 46, 54, 65
Uxmal, 126, 129, 130, 132

Vaccinations, 136
Valladolid, 133–134
Vallecillo, 107
Valle de Bravo, 94
Veracruz, 96, 110, 112–114,
  123, 125, 129
Villa Escalante, 64
Villahermosa, 85, 124, 125,
  126
Villa Insurgentes, 19
Villa, Pancho, 99–100, 107
Vizcaino Desert, 11

Xicalango, 126
Xlabpak, 130
Xochicalco, 95
Xochimilco, 83

Yelapa, 38
Yucatan Peninsula, 126–135
Yuriria, 62

Zacatal, 126
Zacatecas, 102, 105
Zamora, 54, 65
Zapopan, 54
Zapotec Indians, 110
Zempoala, 113
Zihuatanejo, 27, 43, 45
Zimapan, 109
Zinacanteco Indians, 110
Zitacuaro, 54

Photographers